MEDITATIONS
of an ADEPT

GILDA M. SCHAUT

TRUE DIRECTIONS
AN AFFILIATE OF TARCHER PERIGEE

iUniverse®

MEDITATIONS OF AN ADEPT

iUniverse books may be ordered through booksellers or by contacting:

iUniverse
1663 Liberty Drive
Bloomington, IN 47403
www.iuniverse.com
1-800-Authors (1-800-288-4677)

ISBN: 978-1-4917-8313-9 (sc)
ISBN: 978-1-4917-8314-6 (hc)
ISBN: 978-1-4917-8315-3 (e)

Library of Congress Control Number: 2015919127

Print information available on the last page.

iUniverse rev. date: 11/23/2015

CONTENTS

INTRODUCTION

The book "Meditations of an Adept" has been inspired by the communications of many souls, some still living on this planet, and others who have continued their lives in other dimensions. Advances in scientific knowledge and the current acceptance of metaphysics have made the printing of this book possible.

I am deeply grateful to my teachers who have inspired me and encouraged me with spiritual assistance. Thank you to my friends Cindy and Lance Davison, who have dedicated so much time in making this book a reality. They participated in the editing, typing and the time consuming task of categorizing all of the messages. I also want to deeply thank my family who believed in me and the depth of my commitment to this work. I thank them for their unrelenting efforts to help me achieve my goals. The process of mediumship was assigned to my husband and me before we came to this planet. Each important decision or change in our lives was directed to accomplish the reception of the spiritual teachings and messages in this book, and my two previous books. May God bless you on your own journey. My life has been a process of learning through books, personal experiences, meditation, and questions and answers asked of my spiritual guide Saint Augustine and my teacher Tumargeo. I also have been blessed to have been able to speak to many different souls who have crossed to the other side, and then moved on to other numerous dimensions. This information has given me a deeper understanding of all life in our universe, our purpose here on earth at this time, as well as, a deep faith in God as our source for everything.

My prayer is that these writings may inspire all who read them to continue to learn and share their knowledge with each other; that we may all grow together and realize we truly are, One with All of Creation.

GILDA'S MISSION

Gilda, I am your teacher Tumargeo, today we will talk about the purpose of your mission. Your mission is to teach others that the mind of God is the continuous media for communication all over the Cosmos! The different vibratory state of each planet, and its inhabitants, is the only difference in evolutionary progress and understanding.

Your solar system is one of the solar systems whose vibrational frequencies you have more knowledge of, and are able to respond to the vibrations of your teachers and angels. The progression of souls through the universe is infinite. On your planet, there are souls in several different stages of evolution. The ones who are less advanced are not aware of these teachings, and they are the ones, who will have to learn these lessons and adjust their thinking. The human mind is a tool that allows the soul to select positive action to advance or negative action and keep on trying. The roll of the soul is accomplished through the higher self. This sublime entity is the projection of the soul on different planes of existence. The roll of the higher self is to demonstrate the perfection achieved by that soul, according to his degree of evolution. Because many souls are used as teachers and guides, some of these souls are more aware of their abilities and are capable of demonstrations that they are not able to explain to themselves or others.

Question: Why can't we remember previous lives and knowledge that we had learned before?

Answer: When a soul enters this planet, a new agenda is their purpose, they need to retain only those aspects of their soul that will allow the manifestation of the proper stage, and the ones with which they must demonstrate their karma. During the life of a person, sometimes there are glimpses of memories, that come to you like a flash of intuition. These are the awakening calls of your higher self, telling you that you should be aware of your actions from that moment forward. Memories are sometimes too painful and dangerous. Revenge is one of the most powerful emotions.

The guidance and teachings of loved ones during childhood are so important. They mold your character and teach you to discipline your emotions. The love that a soul receives from their parents stays with that soul as a demonstration in their own life.

Ishmael, Angel of the Most High

I am the spirit of Ishmael, and angel of the Lord. The time has come to tell the truth, and to announce the New Millennium. This new era will be one of joy and dedication to the principal of love and sharing. The day of reckoning is near. The souls of many, will receive their assignments, and will do as planned. Your participation in this matter has been to write a book. Others will assist those who will be in need. The beginning of a new era is at hand. Hallelujah! I am Ishmael, Angel of the Most High.

DEFINITION OF AN ADEPT

What is an Adept?

The title of Adept is given to students of Truth all over the universe. Their progress is evaluated by Ascended Masters and the accomplishments are not only spiritual, but also physical, emotional and mental. During several incarnations, the Adept is required to express the light, love and knowledge of the Divine Law. The results of the progress acquired during all these incarnations, are manifested as Light is expressed through that individual. Gilda, the assignment in this life was to raise a family, to be born in Chile then become an American citizen. The use of your mental capacity of concentration has allowed you to fulfill your mission as a medium, and as a member of Sologa. You are an Adept. I am your teacher Saint Augustine, who blesses you.

CHAPTER 1

Evolution of The Species

The lesson for today will be about the development of the sense of self. The difference of expression between humans and animals is the conscious idea of their own selves. This process of the mind is one that has evolved for millions of years.

The preparation for this awareness came to the apes when they first encountered some species of apes that were different from themselves. They realized that a sense of group or community was what kept them together. They also realized that these new apes, acted differently than themselves, in regard to aggressiveness, and the idea of territorial authority. The idea of self-preservation made them flee, and accept that there were other apes that were different than them. This discovery was one of the "Ah Ha" moments in the development of self. They were still as a group consciousness.

The evolution of the species took millions of years on your planet. The more evolved brain is the one that can discern differences and similarities. To reach that point of awareness apes began to compare their actions to some of the other members in their group. They realized that the ones, who wanted to preserve their physical being, and be with others, were not necessarily the more aggressive individuals. A sense of caution in special females began to take place. This was the beginning of the sense of oneself.

The diversity of apes and location on different parts of the planet is only one criterion to learn how and why, that homosapiens were the selected group of apes to develop into the human race. Planet earth was a planet that became the habitat for different species of mammals, and other animals, birds, fishes and flora. The surface of the planet, was changing, due to re-adjustments of the tectonic plates, and changes in weather patterns. The geographical structure of the continents was completely different at that time. Monkeys were able to survive only in climates that provide food, shelter, and proper terrain to multiply and search for food.

Planet earth is an experimental planet. The study of the species was conducted as a research project by other societies of more advanced humanoids. These are what you call today: Extraterrestrials. Their participation in the development of the first Homo-sapiens was through DNA intervention, to upgrade the development of the ape's brains. This brought a new awakening of the apes understanding of not only self, but the preservation of family in their group of equals. Males began to take more responsibility in their role as providers, and to appreciate the female role as provider of the continuation of life. This was great progress. Before, the act of procreation was only instinct, and life did not have the value that they understood, after their genetic changes.

The next step in genetic manipulation happened when Homo sapiens was provided with the perception of creativity. This new development of the brain increased the desire to find ways to make life easier. They lived mostly in caves or shelters, and they observed the process of other animals or birds, to build their habitats. That was the beginning of the concept of family groups, and the desire to shelter and protect the individuals of a group. Life at that time was precarious, because they did not have a way to fight big predators. Ingenuity and purpose was their only recourse.

The third genetic development was the beginning of the development of communication, through vocal cord manipulation. The part of the brain that is capable of coordinating sound and ideas was one of the most important developments in the evolution of mankind. The repetition of sound in regards to an object or action was the perfect solution, not only to identify things, but to explain their ideas and feelings to others.

This period of awareness took millions of years and several generations before the concept of language per se, could be manifested. These genetic manipulations took place in different parts of this planet, almost at the same time.

EXTRATERRESTRIALS AND THE EVOLUTION OF MANKIND

The Evolution of the people, who live on your planet, has gone through many different stages of civilization, and adaptations according to the place they have lived, or the renovation of a society after severe cataclysms. Earthians are a race evolved from the apes. DNA from different extraterrestrials, who have been on your planet through different stages of evolution, have helped to evolve certain characteristics and add through time, qualities that facilitate the evolution of man. Because the extraterrestrials that came to humanize this planet were from different planets in other solar systems, their DNA produced different affects in the color of the skin, eyes and eyelids. The hair is a transmutation that is not based on these causes.

Extraterrestrials have been coming periodically to check on the progress of Earthians and to investigate their state of evolution. At the time of the French Revolution they were here and mentally influenced the writing of the decree of liberty. This was a big step in your society and the understanding of who, you are. The second big event was when they came to your aid, during the struggle for independence of the U.S.A. The group of individuals who wrote the Proclamation of Independence were guided and inspired by extraterrestrials. Most of them were men of advanced stages of soul evolution, and ready to listen and write the best degree for independence. During the time that people of this country have observed those principles the country has demonstrated its greatness.

Now the time has come to renew the teachings, and the beginning of a new era of worldwide acceptance, that we are not the only intelligent beings in the universe. This concept will become clear after the cataclysm. The renaissance of the planet to a new vibratory rate, and the formation of new continents, will give the extraterrestrials the opportunity to demonstrate their existence, ability to help and give guidance. They will be welcomed. They will represent the salvation of millions and the reassurance that, you will survive. The understanding that they come in "Peace" and only for the purpose of helping, will be accepted and respected and will open the door to learn new concepts and ideas. The time is near and these communications need to be heard.

DNA AND EVOLUTION

Question: Why is knowledge ingrained in the DNA of some birds and animals that they are self-sufficient after they are born, but humans are so unprepared to cope with life?

Answer: The question you asked is why the humans of your planet, after they are born, can't live without human assistance. Several mammals are in the same category. The structure of the human form is a progressive modification of the DNA of an ape and a humanoid from another planet. This process has taken millions of years to develop. Through DNA manipulation, and restoration of some new diversified methods of cross species breeding; the human of today is the expression of a study in evolution. The physical body is only the outer part or visual subject. The soul, who is the monitor of the other bodies that complete the total "I Am," is the one who gives life to the body. The difference of expression and adaptation to the environment of a neonatal human and a neonatal animal is the soul who is in charge. The human soul brings to the body that incarnates the data of previous incarnations and part of the subconscious experiences. During the process of reincarnation the soul also brings an agenda that will be completed only if that soul is diligent and wants to evolve. The degree of evolution of the soul is the motivator to study and that is expressed as an increase in possibilities of a better life, health and human relationships. These are not all the reasons why humans are so different than other mammals.

The emotional body is one that connects the mind and the soul, in relation to human associations. The same is in primates, cats, and dogs, in their relationships with their peers. The difference is that humans are conditioned by society to act according to principles or tradition. The influence of religious ideologies is responsible for a great measure of protocol regarding the expression of emotion. Humans of your planet are subject to the media, and to the new methods of communications. This new and perfected medium of information is in part, the cause of an awakening of desire to participate, in the new discoveries and better way of living you experience in this country. The development of a society is based on the sum of the degree of evolved souls that live in a country. That is why you have such disparity of people and diversity in different continents. Soul attraction, according to vibratory patterns is a reality. Alpha and Omega.

DNA

Question: In humans there are two strands of DNA, are there other beings that are able to experience more than that?

Answer: The basic strand of DNA is two strands. The result of evolutionary progress, has allowed DNA to move to three sets or four sets of strands or more. The result of these changes is a more adaptable being, more able to cope with the environment. Is this in humans and animals? Yes, this happens in everything that is created.

Question: How many mutations of DNA have we experienced here on planet earth?

Answer: The word mutation is not the right word. The change in DNA happens in humans and animals and requires the assistance of beings of Light. The light that comes to your chakras is the motivation for this change. The forces that compel evolutionary shifts in humans are the different obstacles in their lives. The ability to solve problems and to face challenges is part of the intelligence that the DNA provides.

The soul who is able to sustain a pace of interest and knowledge attracts these beams of light that helps that soul to accomplish the task that they need to do in order to progress.

During your growing years, you too went through a period of intense distress because your desire to learn metaphysics. The environment you were in was not conducive to learning metaphysics. The help of outside entities was necessary and you were guided to move to a country in which the liberty of thought and action allowed you to re-awaken your inner knowledge.

The DNA is a code not only of physical traits but also of past experiences. The soul who wants to develop those experiences needs the desire, and the help of new opportunities to express his or her self.

Question: What about those with twelve strands of DNA?

Answer: The number of DNA is not necessarily a mark of intelligence. Different organs of the human body are built with different kinds of cells. These cells are different according to the function they need to perform. The complexity of function determines the amount of strands needed, and the complexity of function allows the light to manifest in higher quantities. For example, the cells of your brain are built from a base of more strands of DNA than other parts of the body.

LANGUAGE DEVELOPMENT

The lesson of today will be about the development of language and its use in the future of this planet. The evolution of man on this planet began with the ape-sapiens whose DNA was modified. After this modification, they were able to feel there was a difference between one another. The second great achievement of that DNA manipulation was the improvement in communications. They were able to use their vocal cords, but only in making guttural sounds. After several new interventions, they were able to manipulate sounds to indicate places, objects or self. This was the beginning of mutual understanding, and the beginning of basic language.

The perfection of this basic language took several generations. Several ice ages, and geographical changes later, some of these groups met with other clans on their same continent, and realized that those people had different sounds to indicate a thing or group. After this sign language was the media used to communicate. People on different continents, were different, and spoke other languages. Behind every word, regardless where on your planet it is spoken, is an idea. The point is that in the future of the evolution of man, the development of a telepathic language will take place.

The discovery of new ways of communicating, like the computer and I-phone will contribute to a new concept of communication, not audio mechanical but mental. This process will take several generations, and will bring great changes in the emotional and mental bodies of most individuals.

CELLS OF THE HUMAN BODY

Many of the discoveries about the function of the genes, are at this moment, like the first steps of a young child. The subject is complicated and the instruments to investigate the data are not very accurate. The discovery of a new way to recount the multiple functions of each cell, will not only improve these studies, but clarify the meaning of the function in each cell, according to the message that is brought to the cell. The speed of thought is such, that the capacity to grasp these communications is almost impossible. The importance of these studies is to realize that thoughts are capable of influencing the function of our cells and because of that, to alter our blood pressure, immune system or give us the stamina to sustain a healthy body.

The state of complete health is almost impossible. The human body is not perfect. Many minor developments or dysfunctions are always present. To have a perfect physical body, a soul needs to ascend to the realm of soul perfection. This achievement only happens when the soul is in complete accord with the higher self.

Question: Have any souls on this planet ever achieved such perfection?

Answer: Yes, Jesus was one. He came to demonstrate that the physical self is the product of your positive thinking.

The structural physical part of all humans is almost the same. The soul of all humans is not the same. Some souls are more advanced and because of that, are able to think and act in ways that are beneficial for the physical body.

Question: Why do the bodies of dead Saints not decompose?

Answer: The bodies of the Saints are in a suspended state of life. This knowledge is given to privileged souls because they were able to demonstrate their mission with faith and sacrifice. Life is the vital force that maintains the movement of the atoms in every cell. This movement is perceived by us, as light. The light and frequency of vibratory rate of the cell of a Saint, is such that they remain in that vibratory pattern for eternity.

THE MIND

The book that you are reading was written for the purpose of enlightenment and clarification for the students of metaphysics. The purpose is to make clear the concepts of how the mind works because this is one of the questions that preoccupy many of our students. The complexity and incomplete knowledge of that process is because the connection of the physical and the ethereal body are not taken in consideration.

The soul who embodies the physical part is the one who generates the ideas, basic knowledge of time, color, dimensions, etc. The explanation is: each soul brings with him/her self a set of experiences that produce a perception of the environment. This perception changes daily and gradually because the person expressing them has to correlate them with the world around them. This adjustment is what the cells of each individual manifests and what people call "memories."

The new or revised memories are only partially a new product or experience of that being. In the case of a musician or painter, the gradual expression of his art, is not the product of learning during the present incarnation. The studies that scientists and psychologists have made are in reference to the "now." The progress that has been achieved in medical terms is great and the discoveries of the process of learning and remembering are helping some people to recuperate senses they have lost.

HEALTH AND THE HUMAN MIND

The human mind represents the many thoughts accumulated during the present incarnation and the connection with the higher self. This connection is "clear" depending on the response of the soul and the dedication of the person. By dedication we mean, the effort that the person puts forth into accomplishing a certain task. This task can be of a positive or negative nature, as mankind has free will. The result is the same. The mind accumulates this data and according to that data, reacts to the environment. The perception of the environment is so unique to each individual, that only through generalizations can we agree on certain points.

The influence that positive thoughts have on the brain, bring forth a positive charge that helps to enhance the result of a healing or a good quality of health. The negative thought or negative charges that the brain receives produce a chain of negative reactions that affect the immune system.

Most human of today's generation, believe in a system that helps them to "get well through drugs." This system was developed based on the concept that our cells react to chemicals, and these chemicals have the power to lower fevers, relieve pain, and help the immune system to regain control of the body. The development of disease depends on the environment and the way in which each person reacts with the environment. The cause if disease could be psychosomatic, attacking microbes, or allergens. This concept is in part true, and the persons who apply this concept seldom suffer from allergies or minor emotional upsets. The reality is that this is only part of the truth in regards to health. When the soul reincarnates, it takes into consideration the best state of health both physically and mentally and according to the petition of that person, the first changes in the development of the body take place. The basics of this information are the genes that program race, color of skin, eyes, hair, and the type of blood. After that, the mind is in charge of that body, selects thoughts and actions, according to parents, environment, and information acquired through the life.

Faith is the link between the mind and the soul, and that faith can cure anyone according to what they believe, will provide that cure for them. The majority of people on your planet are depending on substances that repress or produce the disease in their bodies. To ignore the cause of the disease is not a sin, but a choice, based on the gratification of the senses. Other diseases caused by the environment, such as accidents, poisonous plants, animals, or microbes and virus, these last take charge of the opportunity that the body offers to them. The immune system of any individual suffers when an imbalance of needed nourishment is lacking, or when depressing and negative thoughts influence the correct assimilation of the right nutrients.

CHAPTER 2

Evolution of The Soul

ALPHA AND OMEGA

The evolution of the souls on your planet need a renovation of their purpose in life, a cleansing of the negative souls, and introduction to the knowledge that there are other humans on other planets. The difficult task to restore the minimum necessities for the remaining survivors will present the opportunity to demonstrate the best qualities in every human remaining alive. This new atmosphere of help will create a new vibration that will be emitted by the remaining souls, which will uplift the consciousness of our planet earth. The new position in the scale of evolution will be the beginning of a new Era, which will bring peace and understanding between the inhabitants of this planet, in relation to other planets in your solar system and the Cosmos. The beings coming to help are explorers of the universe. Their task is to prevent certain catastrophe and to help enhance the abilities of certain humans that are in key positions on your planet.

I am your teacher and I bless you

THE HIGHER SELF

When we meditate and ask God for guidance, it is our Higher Self who enlightens and clears our minds of all erroneous concepts and guides us to choose just actions that are charitable. Our point of view is limited as if we were on a vast plain, and the view of the higher self is as though observing from the top of a mountain. The understanding of the higher self encompasses not only motivation and purpose in this life, but also the outcome of my reaction and the actions of other people. This voice belongs to my spiritual teacher and the only thing the higher self desires is my perfection. The higher self is like a dedicated teacher who helps their student to develop the best of his personality and intellect.

The higher self is not feminine or masculine; it is that part of the "I Am" that experiences of both sexes can express through the soul. Not all past experiences are positive, but in the long run you learn," Do unto others as you would have them do unto you." Because this is an accumulative process, we reach the eventual conclusion that we are part of the "All" that is evolving together. Understanding and empathy are qualities of the soul that you learn through these positive and negative experiences. We advance spiritually through different spiritual spheres, which are places of different vibration, according to our understanding of whom God is, our relationship with God, and how we comply with God's divine laws.

Every human being has a higher self. Human conscience is a voice that tells you, what you are doing, or already did, is not in accord with the Divine Voice. The voice of your higher self is what you call intuition. Divine voice is received by the higher self, who is one with God. The recognition of the "Will of God" is one of the qualities that must be developed, for the one who wishes to walk with God. God's son, Jesus, attempted to explain this lesson through his actions. The purpose of life and the success of the mission require that you trust your inner voice.

The realization that you are able to listen to your higher self creates in you a responsibility, because you know that you are guided. The major responsibility will be to give to others, what you know, and to practice your gift. The purpose of writing these teachings is to spread the ideas of the process of soul evolution in the human race and in all the planets. The process to receive and retain the teachings is related to the evolution of the soul.

In the case of Mother Theresa, her mission in life has been to help the poorest people, and the voice of her higher self has always guided her to express her mission.

Question: Do the people who inhabit the more evolved planets have a better chance of avoiding making as many mistakes as we do?

Answer: In consideration of the state of evolution, the answer is yes, that is truth.

The search for truth or the desire of humans to manifest Divine Perfection induces them to choose. At the moment you make a choice, that act becomes part of your evolution. In Sidereal progress, it is the sum of the actions which produce advancement through the Cosmos. The vibrations of a soul are nothing but the manifestation of the progress and degree of understanding about God. I am Uriel, the angel of light. Divine light surrounds you. Blessed be the Lord. Divine voice will guide you.

Question: Why are we not capable of leaving our physical bodies at will when we die? Also when we decide that we don't have a reason or purpose to continue our life on this planet, as in suicide?

Answer: I am your higher self. The realization and the awareness that your physical body is the vehicle of other bodies, gives you an advantage and a different perspective from your peers. The idea of dying of a disease or accident is in your mind at the moment. The idea is prevalent in most humans because it is the most common way of passing to the next dimension.

Question: Why is it so difficult to leave the physical body?

Answer: The internal organs are a vortex of light and between them is a system of vibratory lines that serve as a balance between them. In order to release the spirit, all these systems need to be disconnected.

Question: How can this be done in a person that is healthy?

Answer: The reason why humans are not yet capable of doing what you ask, is because their emotional bodies have not completed their development. Most humans are a slave to their emotions. Reason is not in charge and the conclusions of their minds, most of the time are unreal!

Question: Do we have a preset time for living and dying?

Answer: The answer is no. The desire to accomplish the goals chosen by ourselves before we come to this planet is what determines the length of your existence.

MIND BODY CONNECTION

Humanity today is learning that positive actions and thoughts promote health and happiness. New studies of the function of nerves and their connections are needed and this information will help to make clear the enigma of health.

The human body is a form composed of billions of cells and these are made of atoms. Each cell functions in synchronicity to a direct order of the brain. The brain is a computer where thoughts are like the words you press into the computer keyboard. The thoughts are products of your mind or your subconscious mind. Because thoughts are monitored by our conscious mind, they influence our body only when we desire. Through experience when we are growing up, we know how to avoid hot or dangerous materials. We learn to refrain from negative comments that can hurt others. All of this knowledge helps us to maintain health and a place in society. Ideas trigger the response in the brain that will carry the message through nerves, to the part of the body that needs to move or react. This can be the movement of your eyes, heart or the coordinated movement of your hands and brain to write a message. All of this action requires energy and energy in the human body is electricity. Electricity is the source of energy we need to maintain life. The system for carrying electricity through the body is the nervous system. When a nerve is cut, the messages from the brain can't reach the limb or part of the body where the thought is being sent. The latest research in science is rebuilding nerves this decade. Medicine is advancing at a great pace and you will see the progress and be amazed at the results.

Because thoughts are the triggers that act on the nerve to send a message, it is of utmost importance to be aware of our process of our process of thinking. Positive thinking and actions are the best way to maintain a healthy body. The more educated societies of today are exposed to too much information in regards to medicine. Sometimes this is a detriment to their health. The person who medicates himself or herself without a doctors approval could make a grave mistake.

The essence of energy is movement. The electric impulse that connects each atom forms a sequence of energy that promotes movement. This could be in the form of thoughts, actions, or subconscious maintenance of our body. The study of the process of communication of the atoms and the link to the nervous system is the solution to many of the unsolved medical problems of humanity today.

During the years that mankind has tried to solve these problems, the interference of religious zealots or ideologies have suppressed many new discoveries. The process of discovery is subject to ethics, and sometimes those codes are written by very conservative minds.

The cataclysm will interrupt the advances in medicine on some continents. In other places the new society of people will be eager to renew and discover new methods of healing. During the new millennium the revision of ethics and the renewed desire to solve the mysteries of the function of the brain, will bring many innovations in surgery, treatment and the idea of disease.

Negative Thinking

The lesson of today will be about the idea of indiscretion and the disposition of the mind to think negative thoughts and create negative patterns. The thoughts that are emitted from a mind that is constantly criticizing are dangerous things that attract negative emotions. This pattern of thinking is prevalent in people who are insecure or who self-analyze their circumstances. To overcome such a negative pattern it is necessary to acknowledge the trespassing of your thoughts, and the importance of trying to be understanding to the person in question. The power over your mind is basically what you need to master.

When the mind wanders and starts visualizing negative outcomes, the sequence of those thoughts forms a change in the immune system and the blood pressure rises. This mechanism is a form of prevention, because humans have been in difficult situations many times during their lives. The person who has advanced discipline of the mind knows this fact and can change this pattern of behavior. "I am in charge of my mind and my body." This is the sentence that you should mention to yourself every time negative thoughts cross your mind.

Learning to discipline the mind is a constant rectification of old habits, and the redirection of positive reinforcement. With time this positive way of thinking will become a habit. This cleansing or removing the negative habits of our mind allows us to see a clear picture of our surroundings and also will liberate our consciousness of the burden of guilt. The respect and understanding of the actions of others is basically what Jesus said, "Do unto others as you would have them do unto you."

Prayer, Alleluia

"Alleluia, The resurrection of the soul and the blessings of the Most High." The thoughts you were just sending into the atmosphere were positive and full of hope. The desire to transform the world into a more beautiful and prosperous society is the goal of many masters. The progress that some countries have achieved is because, some of the leaders have been chosen to guide and pass laws that benefit the people. The process of developing a good government is in part the result of the will of the people. The process of redirecting the conscience of the masses is in part, a process of learning through trial and error. We need people who are conscious of the importance of thinking of a positive outcome for the future of the planet. Visualization is a tool that only works if the circumstances are favorable. The sum of all the positive thoughts, have to be greater than the total of the negative thoughts to bring visualization to reality.

Question: How can we help?

Answer: Keep positive thought and prayers and project them into the Universe.

THE MEANING OF I BLESS YOU

My presence inspired you. Gilda, I am your Guardian Angel, Gabriel.

What is the meaning of "I bless you?"

Spiritual blessings are part of a ritual. The purpose of any meditation is to develop the spiritual being. The aura is the expression of the different vibrations of your bodies, and for your inner soul to be able to receive or emit the questions or answers required for that development, it is necessary to align the rays of light and process these charges, like electric ones. The Teacher, Angel or Archangel has the power to see and accomplish this task. This is what is called, I bless you. It is the acknowledgement of a Teacher.

EXPLANATION ABOUT MEDITATION

I am your Teacher, Tumargeo. I came to bless you and to tell you that every time that you are in meditation you are helping several of your brothers. The act of meditation happens in different levels. On the Earth plane, when your physical body is healthy and at peace, your astral body radiates peace.

In your mental body, you project your thoughts and attract other beings that want to know what you are trying to know.

In your spiritual body, you attract those beings of light that guide and protect you. You should understand that all your brothers or other living beings are on different levels of evolution.

Gilda M. Schaut

Do I need to commit myself to a series of consecutive lessons?

The beginning of a meditation is the link to a new vibration. In your case, the preliminaries are gratitude and single-mindedness of purpose. I am your Teacher, San Augustine.

MEDITATION

The lesson of today will be about the necessity to meditate every day. The process of meditation opens your mind to positive thoughts and knowledge. This state of consciousness is a temporary enlargement of the understanding and a receptive place to communicate with your higher self. Because your higher self is the receptacle of all the knowledge accumulated by your soul in previous incarnations, you are at that moment ready and desire to learn. When you skip meditation and think it is not necessary, the media and environment around you start to impress your mind, and you start to believe in concepts, which are not true. The same way that you eat to maintain the energy level of your body, meditation is for your mind, the source of light and life that maintains a ratio of vibrations necessary for your health, knowledge and peace of mind.

The Light of the world is the knowledge that God is One and we are one with God. The teachings of Jesus were based on that premise and because of that, He chose to be born to the Jewish people. He was scorned and badly treated by his own people because they did not understand the purpose of his teachings. Even today, half of the Christians in this world believe in the salvation of their souls, if they only believe in Jesus. Jesus left many lessons to be learned, not only about the salvation of the soul, but that we should have positive deeds and a demonstration of good actions to repay for bad karma. Jesus reassured us that health and life is based on the idea that God is the Light in each of our atoms and because of that, we are one with God.

APPARITION OF FATIMA

Gilda, in your mind I see that you are wondering about the apparition of Fatima. That took place because it was necessary to prophesize the future of a cataclysm, at the beginning of this millennium. The wording and recollection of the children of Fatima, was very accurate. They envisioned these future events, and they were terrified by the vast devastation. The version or revision of their account is what is being revealed to the public. Many versions have appeared, according to the different sources of information. The Catholic Church knew of this prophesy, but did not want to divulge the news, that the reign of the Popes will end during these first years of this new era.

Question: Will an atomic bomb explode before the cataclysms?

Answer: The question is: Is the explosion of an atomic bomb the cause of the cataclysm? This question is based on the revelation of Fatima. The Truth is that there are several countries in the world, ready to use such destructive devices. The reason why this was mentioned is because the children of Fatima saw explosions that looked like the impact of bombs.

What they saw was the explosion of some nuclear reactors that exploded because the expansions of the plates near their vicinity. This will be a consequence of the cataclysm, not the cause.

The testimony of these children was altered to appeal to the media of that time, and to satisfy the teaching of the church. I am your teacher Tumargeo, who bless you.

ABUNDANCE

The prayers you just said are like rays of light that go directly into space and influence the atmosphere of the planet. The visual perspective is like the projection of missiles of light into space. These light rays are guided by the system of winds on your planet, to the place where they will help restore peace.

During the first part of your prayers, you were emotionally involved in the thought of war in the Middle East. This problem will not be resolved during your lifetime. The degree of evolution of many people who live in those countries will make it impossible to achieve peace. The second part of your prayer was for Africa. The problem of power is in the minds of many. We have to understand that to them, the idea of a country is not yet a form of government that they are used to. The tribes and leaders of the people want to be in charge. The concept of one leader is foreign to them and they are not aware of the dimensions of cities or countries. Education and evolution are the two main factors that need to be addressed in Africa. The millennium will bring peace and help to those living in the Middle East and Africa.

QUANTUM MECHANICAL BODY

Question: What is the "Quantum" mechanical body?

Answer: The mental body is the one that provides ideas to the brain. It is composed of millions of particles, almost invisible, which gyrate around atoms. These particles create a magnetic camp and it is that, which induces the energy.

The ethereal body is one that evaluates and determines individual perception.

The knowledge acquired during several incarnations stays engraved in these bodies and they serve as guidance or reference points to define new concepts.

The mental body only acts as an advocate of knowledge and gives the current or energy necessary for its realization.

Question: How does it reach the brain?

Answer: Do you remember the explanation of your Teacher? The human body is like alpha and omega: the distances in-between atoms are enormous … The mental body or total group of particles in each individual gyrates around the human being and forms what you perceive as density. The physical nature of the human body allows the reception of thoughts through this body and through the osseous structure also.

In cases of factures, osteo malformations or rehabilitation of the human skeleton, the mind participates in the process of healing. The patient must understand why and how the healing includes the mental process.

In the case of a bone that needs soldering, the production of calcium and other substances necessary for that purpose, obey an immune system, which generates the matter necessary for regeneration. This process obeys an internal intelligence and to a degree, factors such as age, degree of rupture or dislocation, physical capacity in calcium units, etc.

The process is long and complicated and in spite of the illness, the person seems to be unconscious of his mental participation in all of this. Nevertheless, his mind is an intricate part of his healing.

Question: What does faith have to do with all of this?

Answer: Faith is the idea of something immaterial. It is also the idea of a realization not yet perceived.

When we apply this concept to a person who broke his or her arm, the healing could be much faster and complete.

During the period of healing, the mind searches for a way to regain its original wellness.

The human body, as a vehicle of the soul, desires to be complete. When this is possible, then every positive thought helps manifest that image.

Question: Is it the same with other aspects of life?

Answer: Gilda, I see that you want to establish a parable between healing and the process of changing the outcome of future events in your life.

The use of imagination as a tool is a wonderful thing but it will not work, if in that process you are part of a group of people or part of a karmic situation.

The single concentration of mind is the reason for the success in healing. The consequences of one's acts are not the total story in some cases. Faith and the desire to accomplish our own will sometimes helps us to reach the right results.

DEATH OF THE HUMAN BODY

What is the process of disintegration of the human body during death?

The disintegration of the body is first the absence of emotional connection. The human body is connected to the other etheric bodies such as the mental and emotional through a silver cord and this connection is severed at the time of death. The chakras are part of the system of distribution of energies for the emotional and mental bodies. The chakras are disconnected at the time of death. The soul leaves the physical body and begins a new period of development in a new dimension, which it is drawn to according to its vibratory rate.

Question: Is there such a thing as an "innocent victim or bystander" and is every soul's death preplanned?

Answer: That is a very interesting question. The concept of a planned exit to a new dimension would be a logical way to think, that we have the power to decide how and when death occurs. The truth is that no matter which way a soul passes into another dimension, that soul is accountable for their death. When a disease is the cause of death, the soul will be aware of why and when they began damaging the physical body. When the soul passes because of an accident, the soul will not be responsible for this, but will recognize during past life review that a debt has occurred, which will bring karma to the soul responsible for such an accident. In the case of violence, no one can have a doubt that such action will be carried on in future lives.

Question: If we preplan our destiny, what good does health prevention research do? Won't that interfere with the karmic destiny of someone who planned to die of cancer or Aids?

Answer: The idea of a preplanned death is wrong. The soul plans different goals that will allow that soul to achieve a better degree of understanding and evolution.

Question: Is suicide justified when a person is terminally ill?

Answer: The human body is the wrap or covering of the soul. The health state of each individual is only the reflection of his or her emotional state or a product of an unbalanced emotional morale. The soul knows that it can leave the body. The soul knows that there is a cause for these states of being. The absence of sidereal knowledge and little faith do not allow humans the understanding of why they become sick. The state of evolution of each being is not manifested only in their soul; it is manifested in his mental, emotional, and etheric body and it is for that reason why mental discipline is so important to keep a person well. The individual may progressively deteriorate their physical being because of negative thinking habits, lack of hygiene or incorrect eating habits, etc. The body, which in the majority of cases was born healthy, has to demonstrate the mental or emotional action that these thoughts produce upon all the cells and internal organs; even if that person wanted to dispose of his or her physical being, the soul will carry on these negative charges into the next incarnation. In the case of illness or a misunderstanding with another human being, then this person will have to re-evaluate their ideas or they will be faced with a similar problem. Suicide does not erase problems; it only defers them until the next incarnation.

Question: Is suicide against moral or religious principals?

Answer: Divine mercy is infinite. The reason for your question is the religious influence on your planet that allows the formation of patterns of guilt with respect to this act. Suicide is not good or bad, it is an interruption of a human life that is not capable of coping with his or her problems.

Question: If a soul commits suicide, will they have to stay in an undesirable place for some time, after crossing over to the other side?

Answer: The soul, who decides to take their life, awakens to see their past life. Their mentors help them to choose a new residence that resonates according to their mental, emotional and soul's progress.

CLAIRVOYANCE

Question: Why in a altered state of mind can we see or hear from the fourth dimension? People who can see in their mind, such as John Edwards, do they go through a similar process in the brain?

Answer: The experience called clairvoyance is the gift of seeing in the fourth dimension. The pictorial view that the seer experiences, comes to them through the mind which is the receiver. The image that the clairvoyant sees in his mind is being projected to him by a master or teacher. These images are projections from the Akashic records of the people the medium is addressing. Depending on the experience of the medium, the pictures and information can be clear or not so clear. The fact that the mind of an individual is used doesn't mean that they have to retain the images in their memory bank. For an example, the computer has a certain amount of data storage capacity, but you can still receive new data and send it out without storing it.

SEIZURES

Question: Why do people who experience seizures say that it is like a religious experience?

Answer: The person who has a seizure, experiences an altered state of mind. When that happens part of his astral body is detached from his physical body and the aura becomes enlarged and susceptible to outside influences. The nature of the experience can be different according to the soul development of the individual having the experience. The soul of an evolved person will attract evolved souls who will try to ease the shock with heavenly images. The person who is in a lower soul development will attract lower souls who will scare the person and make this experience full of fear and difficult to cope with.

Religious Experience

Question: Are there specific genes in the strands of DNA that serve as receptor sites for a religious experience?

Answer: The process of evolution in humans is the same as it is in all different expressions of humanoids on your planet all over the cosmos. The development of new genes that are the receptacles of mystical awareness is part of the evolution in human nature. This awareness is different in different races and according to their awareness of God and the planet on which the humans reside. On your planet the mystical awareness or idea of a relationship with a Creator, is different for people of different races, countries, or cultures. This diversity is due to the difference in soul evolvement of the individuals, and to their capacity to remember previous religious experiences. The genes that are the basis for religious experiences are located in the inner part of the medulla oblongata and they are the door to our growth as human beings and our commitment of brotherhood.

Divine Voice

In the beginning, the "I Am" was the Divine Voice. Divine Voice was and will be the manifestation of all creation. The capacity of perception of humans is limited, because of that the human being can't understand the projection of what is called Divine Voice. You can perceive this discrepancy when different people who have the gift of "seeing the future," express different versions.

Question: Why is that so?

Answer: The clarity or precision of a fact that will take place in the future is due to the vibration of the medium and his or her receptivity. Education is not a big concern. The mental capacity is only to provide words or approximate dates. The evolutionary scale of humans allows them to preconceive future events. The Indians were able to do this, as were other races on this planet. To the measure that a human recognizes their mediumistic powers, they have a responsibility to share the gift. The reaction that different people offer to a medium is in accord with their preconceived ideas. On different occasions you have been able to write of things that will take place in one year or so. The occasion to decide on trivialities is only an instant of every human life.

The important decisions are the ones that change a life.

THE FOURTH DIMENSION

Question: There is a place called the fourth dimension. How should I describe this fourth dimension, as a state of mind? Is the mind the media that allows us to go from one dimension to another?

Answer: The fourth dimension is a state of vibratory reality. The use of the faculties of the mind is only part of that reality. There are other aspects of expressions such as, physical, emotional, and spiritual. The progressive learning of a soul finds expression in the fourth dimension, just as you found expression in the third dimension. One of the different aspects of being in the fourth dimension is that you are aware that you have a soul, and the use of a comprehensive mind, that has accumulated knowledge during thousands of incarnations.

The process of birth, child, teenager, adult, is a slow process of learning through the accumulation of experiences. This challenge is needed in the third dimension as a test, to repay debts to other souls (karma), or to receive benefits of our good actions from previous lives. This process that you call life, from birth to death in the third dimension, is ruled by fears and worries because humans are not aware of the source of enlightenment that can set them free from ignorance.

The more advanced souls on your planet have achieved a degree of self discipline and purpose, and they are the ones who can demonstrate intelligence and help others. But even these teachers and researchers are limited in their achievements.

The reason why humanity is not able to achieve a better knowledge is because the source of knowledge comes through the use of compassionate beams of light, who are in charge and they must instruct wisely, only those who can demonstrate the good or fair use of that knowledge. Knowledge is a tool that in the hands of people, who are ignorant of the Laws of God, could cause much damage to humanity.

Question: When we are in the fourth dimension do we skip the steps of growing up and find ourselves as young adults when we pass over?

Answer: When a person passes from one dimension to the next, what you call death, it is nothing but stepping into another vibratory reality. When this happens, the soul finds his or her way according to how he has conducted himself in this life and according to his beliefs. The awakening of the soul in the fourth dimension is a parallel of when a soul of a child awakens in this world. The process in this third dimension is very slow and takes years for that soul to figure out his place in family, society and the world where he lives. In the awakening of a soul in the fourth dimension, the process of learning about your real self and why you are in this environment, comes to you faster or slower according to your soul evolution. Souls of different evolution go to different places and are attracted according to the vibration of, sense of love, peace, and desire to express brotherhood.

As soon as the process of recollection of past actions take place, the soul shapes the image or idea of how he or she should look to the eyes of others, and becomes the reality which every soul is, a vibrational beam of light. The structure that represents that image disintegrates as quickly as the realization that your soul is immortal, that the mind you used during the mortal incarnation was limited, and that you are an entity capable of learning in other dimensions and able to live a fuller and better life than before.

Question: How long are we allowed to stay in the fourth dimension?

Answer: The souls who reside in the fourth dimension have privileges and assignments, just as you have here on earth. The goals and achievements, which a soul masters during his development in the fourth dimension, are recorded in the Book of Life. The Book of Life is also known as the Akashic Records, which are the ever-expanding journeys of the soul. Promptly the soul will be asked for the opportunity to demonstrate these new aspects of their abilities. These abilities or achievements can be intellectual, physical or spiritual. The concept of time is not a factor. The soul of every human being looks for perfection and that perfection is only found through the effort and perseverance of the soul.

Question: Why do we have to incarnate again?

Answer: The soul who is in the fourth dimension is already aware of the source of his "divinity." He remains in that state of consciousness until the Lords of Karma agree that the soul should return to experience an incarnation in order to develop another aspect of his being. In each incarnation a soul has the opportunity to give and receive. This interchange could be intellectual, emotional or from the soul. Because a soul is in a physical expression, it is not limited in the aspect, to communicate their state of evolution. There are many souls in very different states of evolution on this planet. When a soul comes to this planet, they bring with them the necessary tools to help accomplish their goals. Examples of the selection of tools are: good ability to listen (medium), ability to play musical instruments and understand music, good analytical mind and mathematical abilities (teaching or building), good spiritual evolution (Spiritual Counselor, Psychiatry). The use of these tools and the purpose of that life, help that soul to demonstrate his desire to share and to advance on the road to perfection. The desire to express God is the ultimate goal of our souls.

I am your teacher Tumargeo, who bless you.

CHAPTER 3

Planet Earth and Her Mysteries

WEATHER PATTERNS/GLOBAL WARMING

Gilda, The article that you read today is about the melting of the ice at the North Pole due to pollution of your air. It is just the beginning of a sequence of facts that are happening on your planet right now. Disturbing news about global warming will remain a major concern, and the changes in weather patterns, will bring to mind, that new studies and actions must be taken in order to prevent further damages. Additional cycles of events will bring many sorrows. The desolation and extinctions of different species will be a fact. Many of the rivers that exist, due to the melting of the ice will cease to exist and with that changes in agriculture and water supplies.

In other parts of the Globe, the increase in barometric pressure will bring about great weather changes, to include a lot of snow, sleet and rain. The consequences of these changes will trigger floods and the reshaping of many rivers not only in this country, but also in Europe.

The Southern hemisphere will also be expected to see almost the same effects but to a lesser degree. The melting of the ice at the Southern Pole will change parts of the coastal configuration of the land in Antarctica. The severity of the storms will inflict great damages to the future of that habitat.

The damage to the Archipelagos, of South America and the increase of sea level will affect many of those territories.

The desire to prevent further damages will change the minds of many people, who until today, do not believe that this is happening. Additional laws must be made and enforced to prevent the further pollution of the planet. This is a problem that must be resolved and not ignored.

CLEANSING OF MOTHER EARTH

Science and esoteric thought are reaching a point of finding the many similarities between them, and may prove expression of God in His creative power. The recognition that God is light, love, life and law is the knowledge that Jesus told us more than two thousand years ago. His words were simple, to be understood by the people of that time. The meanings of those parables are still being interpreted according to the soul evolution of the people today. Like Jesus, many other masters have come to this planet to teach about God and His creative powers. People of different races are guided, according to their understanding and evolution. The time has come to be prepared for a change in vibration and way of life for the people on this planet. This is not the first time that this has happened. The reshaping of the continents, seas and weather will offer new beginnings for the survivors of this planet. This cycle of twenty six thousand years is ready to end and a new beginning will take place, as I described in my previous book, "Millennium." This cleansing experience for the planet will allow her to enter into a more evolved sphere of understanding about the creative power of God.

CATACLYSM & HELPING OTHERS

The explanation why is, on a same planet, there are different souls in a different grade of evolution; is because the more advanced souls are in a position to teach, guide or give instructions to those who need to go into their next experiences.

During the process of one individual life, God will put in front of that person the opportunity to express compassion, empathy, and the desire to not only understand why they are in different circumstances of life, but to try to help those persons in need. These acts of kindness are part of the shared evolutionary path that advances civilizations.

The Cataclysm is one of the opportunities presented to people of other civilizations that are more advanced than yours. These souls who will come from other planets to help, know this is the process of evolution of the soul. They are completely aware of the needs of your people, and how to be of assistance. They are coming in Peace, and ready to distribute food, medicine and guidance to the millions of survivors.

During the first tremors, many people will try to flee, producing greater panic and confusion. They will not be paying attention to evacuation routes or the civilized way to keep order. Panic will turn people into their worst enemies. The uncertainty of finding the best shelter or the safest place will increase the desire to move to higher places or to places away from fire and its devastation.

The wise, will be guided by their inner voice. Many evolved souls, will be guided to places where they will be of assistance to others, after the peace returns to your planet. This may happen within two years after the cataclysm. The countries that form the international help assistance plan, for underdeveloped countries on earth, will reach an agreement for the distribution and dispensation of goods and medical assistance. This may happen in one more year. This agreement will involve the study of different societies, and why they are in their current predicament.

They will not be able to interfere in their government systems, but they will be able to explain to them, the changes needed to uplift their standard of living will be based on cooperation, abolition of negative beliefs and acts against human nature. They will need to come to the understanding, that peace and abundance is only obtained through work and the production of goods.

There will be no time to develop the many ideas this group of people need to have, or how to convey these ideas.

The Cataclysm will come, and the complete change of the hemispheres, seas and flows of rivers, will take care of the renewal of the civilization of this planet. I am Tumargeo, who bless you.

KARMA ~ LAWS OF REINCARNATION

Question: Are there souls who are children that want to return to this Planet?

Answer: Many of these souls, are ready to return because they want to experience a full life. Others need to come back, because their soul needs to evolve, and experience new tests.

Question: Do souls who are ready to reincarnate know if they have to pay a determinate Karma

Answer: The question you ask, is Karma a payment of restitution or a difficult assignment to learn to understand self-discipline and poise? Karma is a system of restitution, and a tool to understand, that as a soul who inhabits a physical form, we can choose the best way to cope with a problem. The majority of mortals today are not aware of the laws of Karma. They assume that the troubles that affect their lives are part of their own making. In a way, they are right, but they don't understand that this is the opportunity, to make the best of the inconvenient situation. There is positive Karma. The souls, who are blessed with this Karma, usually are not aware either way why they are so "lucky," as you said. They have earned their happiness, in previous incarnations. I am Tumargeo and I bless you.

EXPLANATION OF THE OCEANS

Question: Where did the water of all of the oceans and rivers in the world come from?

Answer: Your question should be: In which way was the planet provided with this enormous quantity of water?

Answer: The formation of your solar and planetary system was the consequence of a big Nova explosion. The circular rotation around the sun is due to the centrifugal force, and the magnetic pull of the sun. The orbit of each planet is like a road maintained by the gravitational force, and the magnetic pull of the sun. The different positions, sizes, and ellipticals of each planet, influence their form and make up. The distance of your planet earth from the sun is one of the more beneficial factors in the evolution of your planet. Through millions of years your planet has been bombarded with different asteroids and meteorites. During one of the early stages of evolution, a cataclysm due to the refractory pulls of passing asteroid, caused a change in the structure of the earths crust. At that time, the constitution of the crust was boiling magna, small areas of water and incandescent minerals. The combination of this material, and the earth's movement produced a chemical reaction, and the evaporation of this boiling lava and materials, produced a great weather storm that lasted for several years.

During that period, the influence of the sun and the rotation of your planet, polarized the masses of the earth crust, and the formation of continents began. The polarization of water began when the temperatures began to decrease and the formation of salty masses of water became the oceans of today. The configuration of the first continents where completely different from the ones of today. During the evolution of your planet there have been several cataclysms, and the reformation of masses of earth has taken place. Men of today are only aware of some of these periods in the story of your planet. Through archaeology and astronomy, there is an idea of the evolutionary progress that this planet has been through. The real knowledge will be studied during the second and third generation after the new cataclysm. Data will be preserved and restored, and due to the events that will happen, new ideas and inventions will reveal many of the facts that until today have been evasive. I am Tumargeo who bless you.

EFFECTS OF EL NINO & LA NINA

Gilda, the law of expansion and contraction acts as the motivator for this phenomenon that produces intense changes in climate. This in turn affects the masses of earth plateaus on this planet. The studies of your scientists show the effect of the El Nino & La Nina weather patterns, and the effect that this has produced on your planet. The vast impact has been in places like Africa, India and the territories of the lower United States. This pattern of weather will intensify during the next few years, and the desolation and urgency to cope with the tragedies, is today inspiring many to find solutions to these problems. The magnitude of these problems are difficult to solve, because changes on the planets are slow, and depend sometimes more on the politics of the countries involved rather than humanitarian resources or help. During the year two thousand and ten, many of the resources for fuel, and heating, will be under a new and progressive initiative that will try using new sources of energy that will be cleaner, healthier, and less expensive. The production of new products and the use of these products will help save the destruction of forests and will provide jobs and a cleaner atmosphere.

The evolution of the system of communications and their visual expansion with products that can be available at better prices, throughout the world, will be a form of progress and awareness that will unite consciousness of all humans. Because of that, research and innovations of old products, will occur all over the planet. The process of material progress will increase greatly. The methods used by diverse countries to achieve this progress, is a problem that will have to be solved through mediation and diplomatic means. This will change the trade system, and the balance of power. The unrest and ambition of many will be felt in every society. The difference in ideologies in government and countries, will be a difficult problem to solve.

The idea of a united world leadership is very far away in time. Humans are not ready to let go of their ideas of nationality, race or patriotic sentiments. This is the lesson for today, God bless you.

PLANET WEATHER & EXPANSION OF UNIVERSE

Gilda, the assignment for today, will be to write about the development of a force that is expanding and is producing a pattern change of weather in your solar system. The center of gravity for your solar system is the pressure maintained by the atoms that form the system, and when this pressure changes the outer expression of weather patterns are affected.

Question: Where is this force coming from?

Answer: The explanation to your question requires the knowledge of logarithms that you are not able to understand at this moment.

This information we are giving you today is one way of explaining to you, that the changes of weather patterns on your planet are not all man made. During the first three months of next year, the violence of the weather in some of the northern states of the USA, Northern Europe and Asia, will be felt as a threat to their communities. Resolution will be taken to help people in distress, and provide for their necessities. During this time, several changes will occur on the battlefront of Afghanistan. That country has one of the most mountainous territories. The conditions of life, and the influence of the drastic weather, will help them realize that this war has to end and only then will conditions improve. There will not be a surrender of the mind or beliefs. Their beliefs are ingrained in their minds. Peace agreements will be a political move that will restore a time of reconciliation and reorganization of their resources. The recognition that the teachings of Osama bin Laden didn't work, is one of the main achievements of this war. The Muslim communities are interested in continuing with their faith, and demonstrating to the rest of the world that it is not in their intentions to destroy innocent people.

WAR & ATMOSPHERIC CHANGES

Gilda, today's meditation was about the soldiers who were trying to restore order in Iraq and Pakistan. In a war there're no winners or losers. The progress of the methods of religious education and form of government is

35

what is being revised. Each country or nation goes through a similar process and the extreme chaos is the result of violence. Because of the new methods of communication, discovery of television, several countries that are behind in their state of education, desire change. Because every change has the opposition of the ones who have acquired power or posts in government or religion, the task ahead is not easy. This awakening and desire for material things and civic liberties is the cause of dissatisfaction in all of the inhabitants of your planet. This war is one of many. The solution to these problems is far from being resolved. Meanwhile, the scientific advance and sense of charity and goodwill of some countries and individuals will start to produce effects.

The second concern is the realization that the change in weather on the entire planet is affecting the fauna and the flora. Because of the elliptical path of your planet around the sun and around a bigger center that is your galaxy, your planet is experiencing these visible atmospheric changes. The scientific knowledge you have today on your planet is not enough to prevent or oppose future disasters. The capacity to coordinate equipment, medicine, means of transportation and food are the best help at this moment. The instinct of self-preservation will do the rest. I am Tumargeo who bless you.

DISCRIMINATION OF RACES

Gilda, the lesson for today will be about the discrimination of races, and why we will have to reconsider the position of the government, in respect to the minorities that are part of the communities of every country on this planet. The adoption or assimilation of people of a different race, to the customs of a new country, takes time, and also the opportunity to reshape their lives and beliefs. Because it is an instinct of human nature, to preserve traditions and customs, these changes and adaptations are difficult to accomplish. One of the most rigid ideas is religious observance. The cause of the majority of the unrest in the world today, is because foreigners bring with them their ideas of God, that are not necessarily the ones of the country where they reside. This problem is a common denominator for many countries in the world. The nations that are more lenient in their ways of thinking, for example: the Netherlands and USA etc. are at the point of reconsidering their hospitality. The reason is the zealots of this world, are taking advantage of the media, communications, and new rapid systems of recruiting people who are dissatisfied with their way of life. Their indoctrination is fast and effective. This is like a contagious disease that is spreading quickly. The resolution of powerful countries to combat these ideas with force, is not effective, because these people are not ready to understand a new way of life. They don't want to change. The reason people don't want to see a solution to this problem is because there are few countries ready to try a new way of solving these problems.

Question: Which way?

Answer: The answer is to apply the teachings of the Masters who have come to earth to teach people peace and brotherhood.

ADAPTATION OF THE SPECIES

Question: Why are the Bees disappearing? Is it because of infection, insecticides or some other reason?

Answer: The bees on many parts of the planet are disappearing because they use an inner guidance that allows them to know their location and to find their way back to the hive. This subconscious guidance is part of the DNA of these insects. The reason they are disoriented is because planet earth is changing the velocity of its rotation and that decreases their awareness of where their flight path will take them. It is as if you are driving your car, and all of a sudden the road is not there, because the road has been moved to one side, and you are not able to see it. This phenomenon is one caused by the expansion of the Universe. Every 26,000 years, the rotation of the planets around the sun, expand their orbit. The causes an acceleration of the rotation of the planets to maintain their course.

Question: Is there something we can do to help the Bees?

Answer: I am amazed at the ideas that you think about, to update the DNA of the bees! The work to bring that idea into reality, will take many years. The natural adaptation of a species to the environment happens when the majority of the species is ready to succumb to the changes that afflict that particular species. In the case of the bees, some of them will figure out a way to counter balance the direction deficit, and they will pass this knowledge on to others. These re-adjustments are ones that have taken place on your planet for millions of years. The acceptance of changes, and adaptation to the environment happens to animals, insects, plants, trees, fishes and humans. Your concern is commendable however; this is the natural order of progress.

Nuclear Power

From Tumargeo your teacher: In the near future, the most interesting question will be asked of you.

Question: What do you think about nuclear power?

Answer from Gilda: I think that if God has given us the opportunity to discover this, it is because; as the earth moves forward we are going to need a more reliable source of energy. Along with God's gift we must ensure that we use it for good and in a positive way.

Tumargeo: Your answer is based on the knowledge of your soul. We asked this question, because we wanted you to realize that there are many scientific inventions, which will use nuclear power in the future of mankind. Nuclear energy can provide the earth with all of the electricity that it will ever need. It is also capable of providing you with a source of power for travel throughout the universe. The inventions of today are only basic ones, and they will stay that way until the end of this era.

The formation of a new generation of souls who will be able to discover new applications for nuclear power, are already being trained. These souls will develop such devices during the third generation, after the cataclysm. By then, this planet will have a general idea of the importance of nuclear power, and the resolve that it should only be used for positive purposes. The Intergalactic Federation will enforce rules of conduct, and will acknowledge mankind for their participation and contribution to the sisterhood of planets of this solar system.

ATOMIC WASTE

On our planet we have a problem with atomic waste and how to dispose of it properly. What do other advanced civilizations so with this problem?

Answer- Different planets have found different solutions. One of those solutions is to transport this waste to a planet that is not occupied by living things. These are planets that have been in orbit for millions of years and they are void of live specimens.

Another solution was to transmute such waste into a different kind of chemical product. To accomplish that, they devised special containers, where they add products that eliminate part of the emanations of uranium, and solidify the rest of the contents. Then these are sent to places on that planet, where they are buried at a very great depth. The problem on your planet is the use of such dangerous products, without the advanced knowledge needed to handle it.

RADON GAS

Question: Is Radon gas really dangerous?

Answer: The gas called Radon is the emanation of a gas produced by radium. The causes of the poison that this gas produces is the way it effects such individuals who have the propensity or who are apt to have difficulty breathing i.e. asthma, cardiovascular and lymphatic disorders and pulmonary malfunctions.

When the gases, which the magna produces under the Earth's crust, are compressed, they look for a way to escape and they find different places more porous than others. The terrain is a combination of different layers of soils and according to their density; they are more or less appropriate to allow these gases to pass through. The study of appropriate sites for building houses should be one of the priorities in the minds of contractors or builders. The study of this and other important factors in the safety of a building site will be of major importance in future generations.

ECONOMIC SITUATION

Gilda, I see how you want to understand the economic situation of your country. The reason for this depression is the result of greediness. The idea that the value of money is not the most important thing, but the desire to acquire everything that you think you need, but in reality you don't, is what is happening to this country. This is the reason that this country is in such a bad economic shape. The illusion provided by credit cards has altered the good judgment and sense of security that people need to live peaceful lives. There are no shortcuts to solving this problem. The people, who really want to live a safe economic life, are the ones who don't spend more than they can afford.

Question: What are the consequences for my children and grandchildren?

Answer: The economy of the USA not only depends on the way consumers spend their money. The international commerce and trade is what really will bring this country to a very hard awareness of it's position in the trading place of the world. This will take years, and not all of the countries are ready to negotiate in favor of others.

NASA & MARS

The Mars program and NASA's progress in the launching of the rocket and development of equipment necessary to explore and investigate, was part of a greater and more complex study of the planet. The group of people working in that project are guided and protected. Their mission is to discover water and certain minerals, which will indicate that life, as you know it on your planet, existed before on Mars. In years to come, new technology will enable physicists and other scientific people to probe into the core of that planet and find evidence of a society of beings that used to live underground.

The messages you have written came from the Akashic record of the people who lived on that planet centuries ago. The change in the composition of their atmosphere eliminated the possibility of life.

Question: What happened to all of the souls that lived there?

Answer: Life is eternal. The souls who left the planet Mars, were attracted to different spheres, according to their degree of evolution. Some are reincarnated in your planet, some are in the process of recollection and assimilation of truth, and others went to planets that will provide them with the opportunity of learning or teaching; The soul is a vortex of light, and as such, assumes the form of humanoid according to the parents who are willing to procreate. The placement is done according to their degree of soul evolution and purpose of their Karma.

Question: This is the same for all the souls in the Universe?

Answer: Yes, it is the same for the souls who need reincarnation as a medium of learning or repayment.

Question: Then there are souls who don't need to reincarnate?

The process of reincarnation is one that allows the soul the opportunity to give or receive the help it needs to restore the equalization necessary to pass from one sphere to the other. When a soul completes a cycle of twelve spheres, then that soul has the privilege of resting or the choice to go where and when it wants to express in human form. These incarnated souls are on different planets, to guide, teach or explain to others the process of the soul. Because there are so many millions of planets in different degrees of evolution, not all of these souls need a physical expression.

UFOS IN SOUTH AMERICA

Gilda's Question: Are there UFOs in South America?

Answer: Yes, there are two different groups of UFOs in Brazil and in Northern Peru. They are studying the resources and the cultural impact that will affect the millions of people, after the cataclysm. They know already of the changes that will take place, and they want to be ready to assist as many survivors as they can. The UFO's are in constant communication with their mother ships, and the planet that they came from. The expansive amount of lands that they are able to supervise is enormous. Some of these UFOs are able to travel millions of miles, before they touch base with their mother ships.

Gilda's Question: What about the country of Chile?

Answer: This is a very mountainous country. Several of the volcanoes will erupt, and parts of the country will suffer great damage due to the earthquakes that will erupt and reach high levels on the Richter scale. Several changes will occur on the coastline, especially in the south. The configuration of those thousands of islands, will suffer great devastation. Most of them will be submerged underwater and the tip of South America will be much smaller in size. Different rivers will change courses and many lakes will increase in size. The climate will change also, with their winters becoming milder, and their summers more tropical.

Gilda's Question: Will the northern part of Chile be different?

Answer: Yes. A great change will be seen. The dessert will be opened to the formation of a higher plateau, and two big rivers will also traverse it. These will be part of a transformation, and the beginning of a new generation of people who will adapt themselves to their new surroundings and climate. The abundance of minerals rich with sulfates and other components in the soil will promote the growth of trees and vegetables for food and will help transform this part of Chile into one of the most prosperous and fertile places of that country.

God bless you, I am Tumargeo

UFO PROPULSION

Gilda's Question: I do know that the magnetic force is a major component of the power that propels UFOs. What is the source of energy of the magnetic force that produces such power to move the UFOs at such a velocity?

Answer: Gilda, the reason for your question is because you remembered your knowledge of past times. Yes, you knew that the reason why you could concentrate electrical energy is through magnets and other methods. The propulsion of the UFOs is based on magnetism. The source of energy is the sun, which produces Hydrogen Atoms, which are necessary for the dynamism (atomic energy).

The purpose of the UFOs who came to your planet was to analyze the atmosphere, the state of evolution and degree of civilization of the people of your planet.

GOD, OUR PLANET AND NEGATIVE ENERGY

The lesson of today will be about the presence of God. You already know that the life and love of God is expressed on your planet, as a physical form, and the love of God, as kindness to others, understanding, and the emotions that go with these sentiments. The sensation of gratefulness you feel, when one of your prayers is answered, or the joy to see the progress of expression of a soul, who is demonstrating the love of God; is what helps you to advance in your studies, discipline your mind, and always reconsider your actions and words.

The relationship of members of a family is one that allows us to perfect the spirit and pay karmic debts. In your case, you have experienced the problems of understanding people within a family. This test of the soul helps us to see that other souls, see the world different, and they are in a different understanding of how their thoughts and actions affect other people. The sum of all these every day emotional experiences, positive or negative, is part of the evolutionary expression of a planet.

When a planet accumulates too much negative karma, the aura of the planet is exposed to the negative weather and the influence of those ET's, which want to use the resources of your planet for their own benefit. I am telling you this because; you need to know why some humanoids of other solar systems are taking advantage of your planet. There is a degree of evolution of the soul in every different solar system; the more evolved humanoids that are experts in teaching, engineering, medicine and geology are the ones who will come to aid planet earth after the cataclysm. An example of this are the experts in your country, who go on mission trips to less developed countries to help teach the people, new ways to live better lives through clean water, food production, and communities working together to help each other move forward.

Question: In a book I read, Great Eagle said that during the evolution of our planet many extraterrestrials have come to help with the evolution of mankind and some are actually here now.

Answer: During the creation of your planetary system a group of advanced souls came to earth, along with chosen planetary souls of your solar system, to supervise Divine Creation. These are the Elohim or planetary teachers. They came to supervise the evolution of the human species. In order to do that it was necessary to first create the basic nutrients and shelters. God's idea was to create an Eden. The souls who came to live on this planet first, had to go through different phases of education and testing.

The first tribes basically were animals, and it was their instinct that allowed them to survive. Next there were nomadic tribes that moved from one place to another in search of water, food and shelter. Eventually they found other humans like them. The interchange of genes produced new humans that little by little formed groups called clans. The discovery of fire and its use, made these humans begin to think of ways to improve their standards of living. The discovery of metals and tools gave them the superiority over others who had not achieved their degree of evolution. The negative aspect of this new development during that phase of evolution was to use their power over others. The free will that God gave to people of this planet was the cause of millions of wars and unnecessary deaths. The creation of a government with representatives was an attempt to provide better standards of life and make humans more conscious of their actions. The souls of many humans were and are being guided and perfected by the Elohim, in an effort to advance civilization. These are the forerunners or illuminati. During all the history of this planet, beings of light have come to help. These beings were creative and innovative in religion, science, education, medicine and nutrition.

Question: What is the role of the space people?

Answer: Space beings have intervened in several places on this planet. The genes of humans mixed with beings of other planets are the basis of the different races on earth. This happened millions of years ago. There are no written records of this, because when this happened, humans were not able to write. Later on humans started to record their thoughts and those are part of the explanation of the Bible. These explanations are not very clear because the descriptions are in the form of parables of what they were seeing. There also are the hieroglyphics and pyramids in Egypt and Central America. Now each country of this world is capable of maintaining a degree of international communication, and this facilitates the capacity to be conscious of what is happening in the world. Nations who form the European block are at this moment in peril of a reform, due to the changing of their money and its effects on their unity. The political power is being balanced with the productive and economic power of different continents. The social and economic advances of China and South America are evening up the scale of these powers. All of these changes happen over millions of years and the Lords of Karma know that the evolutionary force will eventually help humanity to resolve these problems.

Question: Why haven't the ET's visited us for a long time?

Answer: The ET's now come, only as observers. Their intervention is only in case of extreme necessity. They must respect Divine Law, and be responsible for their actions. For example a mother doesn't give a knife to her son until he can use it safely and responsibly. The same applies to our space brothers, they know that they can't teach us their knowledge, because we are not evolved enough to use it responsibly.

THE PYRAMIDS

The lesson of today will be about the reason why the pyramids were erected, and why the narrow internal tunnels were built. The building of the pyramids was a project to reveal to mankind, the power of the Pharaohs and the advanced knowledge that Egypt was aware of. The calculations and

45

supervision of their buildings was inspirational. During several generations, people of those regions worked on those constructions. The direction of the sun's rays was in part, one of the corner stones of that project. According to the direction of the suns rays, a sketch was produced that was to be built according to Divine guidance. The process was long and painful, and the security of many people was in peril.

The necessary stones were brought from a quarry south of the Nile, and this was only possible during certain months of the year. These enormous slabs of stone were floated on the river in balsam rafts that were made with strong trees that grew south of the Nile. The suspension and setting in place, was done in part by humans and in part by priests that had the knowledge of levitation. They helped to set these stones according to plans and sealed the blocks with a mixture of sand, egg white and a rare soil that was extracted at the shores of the Nile.

The pyramids were tombs for the Pharaohs and all others who were part of his court.

The tunnels were part of a system of air passages that not only maintained a degree of oxygenation but an access to the different chambers inside.

Question: Is anything under the pyramids?

Answer: The pyramids' are built on solid ground and there is nothing under them. The sole purpose of their construction was to establish that the Egyptians were an advanced society that understood astronomy and were capable of building these masterpieces for posterity.

THE MAYANS

Question: How were the Mayan people able to calculate time and astronomical distances?

Answer: The evolution of mankind is based on the substitution of one culture by another. The Mayans were people who were instructed by the

Nephilim, the space brothers who came to develop their race and they were the ones who informed them of the mathematical equations. The knowledge of the cosmos and the basic assistance of how to plan their cities was one of the legacies that the Maya received from the Nephilim.

THE HOPI KACHINA

The Hopi people were in a region of the United States of America where primitive people used to live. The memories of their ancestors were the recollections of their shamans. The word Kachina is the name for the beings, who came to them from a different place, and they said they were from the "stars." The reality is, these people from another civilization were the Atlanteans. The Atlanteans that survived the Cataclysm wandered through the area inhabited by the Hopi. The Hopi realized this new race was more advanced in knowledge and healing, and they were willing to share this knowledge with them.

THE EMERALD TABLETS

During the reign of the Egyptian Pharaoh, Tutmoses the III, the teachings of a God called Thoth, began to attract the attention of many scholars in Egypt. This teacher was a reincarnation of one of the most advanced teachers of the sciences. During that life in Egypt, he developed several new concepts about light, sound and medicine. His knowledge of the Cosmos, allowed him to teach about the solar system and the positions of the planets in relation to the earth. He was a real teacher, who became immortalized as a God by the people.

Question: Why is he portrayed with the face of a bird?

Answer: He is portrayed with a face of a Ibis, because to the Egyptian people, the Ibis is an intelligent bird, able to survive on the Nile, where there are so many predators like crocodiles, snakes and other birds of prey.

Question: Was Thoth the God of Wisdom? Was Hermes Trimegistus a reincarnation of Seth?

Answer: I am in your aura. I am the soul, of the one you call Hermes Trimegistus. I was a representative of the Pharaoh and had studied in the best schools of esoteric teachings. I was born in Greece and at the age of twenty one years, I left my country to travel. I went to Byzantium, Ethiopia, and Egypt. I was impressed by the degree of knowledge and civic awareness of the Egyptian people. After three years of learning their language and customs, I was presented to the Pharaoh. The court was the most important and magnificent place I had ever been. The Pharaoh wanted to know about my credentials and studies. He decided that I should stay and teach at the palace. I was assigned a name, teacher Hermes. I was rewarded with plenty of money and liberty to instruct new concepts in mathematics, medicine and astronomy. The work of my previous teacher, Thoth, was the base for the new discoveries in those fields, which I had learned in Greece.

The Emerald Tablets were considered the ultimate sum of knowledge, at that time. I read them and I knew that I should develop a new system of teaching, what today we call astrology. In the field of Medicine, I was able to try a new method using medicinal plants. The extracts of plants, barks, and the fluid of plants, that had healing properties was applied to my patients in minimal doses as an experiment, to see effect and find the antidote, to produce the cure. This method is called Homeopathy. The work of many years and the realization that man is part of nature, gave me that idea. I was not the reincarnation of Thoth. I lived a long and prosperous life. I am Hermes Trimegistus, your brother in Christ.

CHAPTER 4

Faith and Healing

ARCHANGEL MICHAEL'S PRAYER

Gilda, I am in your aura and I came to bless you. I am the angel of the Lord Michael. I see that you want to help the ones that are in distress. Your soul is of light and your prayers will be answered.

Let us pray: Divine Light strengthen my soul, help me to send thoughts of love and comfort to those in pain. The love of God is all around us and His healing powers are rays of Light that cleanse, heal, and restore the peace and the process of healing in the physical world. Gilda, your healing heart is in the right place. God Bless You.

FAITH AND HEALING

The lesson of today is about the meaning of faith. Faith is the firm belief in the presence of God in us. That is a universal statement. The universal laws apply not only to people of your planet, but also to all creation. To achieve this universal knowledge the soul needs the evolution required and the experiences that only reincarnation can give. The process called reincarnation is a recycle of the soul in different bodies and many different experiences. The experiences and lessons learned during the many incarnations create an awareness of a power that is beyond our comprehension. This power is the Light of God that assists us in deciding and acting in a positive way. That small voice within is the inner guide that we need to listen to.

In the process of healing, the light that is blocked in our auras is overcome by a direct order that comes from the soul. The Chinese have studied this process for thousands of years. Modern medicine achieves good results due to drugs and drastic operations. The inner result of those methods doesn't cure the basic cause of the disease. The etheric body is a copy of our physical body. The process of healing affects this body, the same way that you rectify the design of a dress pattern that does not fit. Some diseases are congenital and only through the process of reincarnation can you get rid of it; others are caused by the environment, bad habits, or contagious microbes that attack the immune system. The soul who has developed a firm belief in his relationship with God is guided to prevent the attack of these agents. After attaining a certain development, the soul is allowed to function as a vortex of light, and to be able to travel to different parts of the universe. I am your teacher and I bless you.

NECESSITY OF PRAYER

The lesson of today will be about the necessity of prayer. The reason we pray is to concentrate the mind and spirit in the idea that God is All. This phrase is the clue to the renovation of the circumstances that maintain a definite situation. Because we are spiritual beings, the all-encompassing light that pervades the earth, is the common denominator that we all share. This source of light is in a continuous changing movement. During the act of praying, the light that is part of the person, who we are praying for, is activated and without that person knowing, that light begins to vibrate faster and faster. This change in vibration attracts the right thoughts or the right attitude, and the beginning of a new set of circumstances develops. In cases of advanced disease or malfunction of organs that have cancer or genetic diseases, these prayers can reach the inner connectors that can reverse the action of those cells. To change the genetic code it is necessary that the development of a device, not yet discovered, be applied to the source of this deviation.

In your society, the input of prayers is directed to the influence of the soul and the ability of the mind to change the prognosis of future events. This is the same for physical, material, and spiritual endeavors. The factor of Karma is one of the reasons so many prayers are not being answered. The diseases that are basically inherited are the ones that are difficult to change. Diseases that manifest because of contamination, or malnutrition, or bad habits, are the ones easily changed. The purpose of prayer should be to maintain in mind an image of the perfect person and visualize them as whole and perfect. Those ideas work in the inner self of the person you are praying for, and without that person knowing they will manifest a new desire of perfection.

The healing of the mind is the most complicated of all. The regeneration of the cells of the brain is one reason why the process of thinking happens. There are many malfunctions of the brain, and multiple reasons they can occur. There are genetic diseases of the brain, and there are the ones due to an imbalance in nutrients of the brain cells. Drug and hallucinogens are other causes. Then there is trauma, as in accidents or the shocking effect of terror or great danger. These outside influences affect the brain in the same manner that hallucinogens do.

The study and development of a new scientific advance in medicine will develop a new understanding of the process of the connectors of electric inputs that allow humans to express their ideas and emotions. This will happen in the new millennium.

PRAYER AND HEALING

The lesson of today will be about the power of prayers. To pray is to send thoughts of a positive nature to a person or group of people, animals or plants. All of these respond to the vibrations of prayer. There is a communication between God's creation that includes all creatures. This media is the mind of God! God's mind is a powerful media and the person who is capable of connecting with it is in charge of changing the molecular structure of the individual to which these thoughts are directed. The result of positive prayers also depends on the consistency and the love, by which they are sent.

Question: Why can healers do this better than a regular person?

Answer: The healer is a soul who is experienced in the art of healing through many incarnations. This soul accumulates this knowledge, then when they pray, the thoughts are charged with such positive attitude that the healing can have immediate results.

I see that you understand the process of no interference, or not to change the person's karma. In those cases the healer senses a rejection from the soul who they are being asked to heal, and they understand that this is a special case that is beyond their reach.

HEALING WITH PRAYER

Gilda, I am a person who was watching you when you were praying for healing. It was amazing to see the change of color in your aura. The presence of beams of light were with you. They reached and mixed their powerful rays with yours and this doubled the power of healing. I was able to see the effect of those rays, when you were in a state of trance, a voice was guiding you to remember each person and visualize them. It was then that these beams of light of peace and healing connected to the aura of these people. Their vibrations changed according to the force of the healing. Yes, there are several degrees of healings. The response to this vibration will be manifested according to each individual's karma. I am giving you this explanation to set your mind at peace and let time demonstrate the effects of these healings. I am a soul on the twenty third sphere and like you; I was always ready to serve God. May God bless you.

I am your teacher Tumargeo and I came to teach you that, in the prayers for healing you must lift up your hand or hands so that the Light of God can flow to the person you are praying for. In case you are not able to do this, ask for guidance.

HEALING & PRAYER

I am one who was watching you pray for others. I was in your aura and came to tell you that this has helped me to understand the process of healing from the perspective of what is happening, from the other side.

The person needs healing because their mental or emotional body is not expressing itself properly. To see this happening is amazing. During the healing, angels come to your aura, and project their light, and the process of healing begins. The principle that we are all one, allowed for this healing to reach the soul you are praying for, and influence the correct pattern required for proper function. All minds are connected. Yes: Faith has made you free of disease, means that in your case your faith, as a medium, allows you to send this divine healing light to the aura of the person in need.

The person, who you are healing, could be of any denomination, race or understanding. The love of God is for all his creation. Thank you Gilda for allowing me to tell you what you need to understand. I am Joakin, your brother in Christ.

PRAYERS FOR MIDDLE EAST AND AFRICA

The prayers you just said are like rays of light that go directly into space and influence the atmosphere of the planet. The visual perspective is like the projection of missiles of light into space. These light rays are guided by the system of winds on your planet, to the place where they will help restore peace.

During the first part of your prayers, you were emotionally involved in the thought of war in the Middle East. This problem will not be resolved during your lifetime. The degree of evolution of many people who live in those countries will make it impossible to achieve peace. The second parts of your prayers were for Africa. The problem of power is in the minds of many. We have to understand that to them, the idea of a country is not yet a form of government that they are used to. The tribes and leaders of the people want to be in charge. The concept of one leader is foreign to them and they are not aware of the dimensions of cities or countries. Education and evolution are the two main factors that need to be addressed in Africa. The millennium will bring peace and help to those living in the Middle East and Africa.

HEALING

The discoveries of new methods of healing and the use of different plants and flora are part of the knowledge God has provided man. In the jungle, intuition is developed as a means to survive, and the use of inner guidance is another useful part of their way of existence. Every society explores and uses their surroundings according to their intelligence and degree of evolution.

In your actual "civilization" the use of synthetics is part of the mass marketing way of solving basic problems of supply and demand. The basic use of resources and the production of future resources, have to do, not only with demand, but also with land fertility, composition of the land, weather, and thermal control. The temperature of the land and proper nourishment of the seeds are basic for the development of a plant. In tropical environments this condition provided the best resources for germination and the vast and diverse flora is exuberant. In climates where the temperature is low or too hot, none of this takes place.

In the evolution of mankind the progress and selectivity of food, shelter and climate has been a factor in changes that has affected not only the physical body but the emotional and mental ones as well.

BECOMING A HEALER

Question: What is needed to become a healer?

Answer: Your question is difficult to answer. I am in your aura and bless you. I am your teacher San Augustine. You want to know about holistic healing.

The medical doctor that graduates from a university is a person who studies and learns intellectually. The holistic healer is the one who wants to heal his fellowman through divine powers. A holistic healer does not have the advantage of knowing how or why the healing takes place, but offers his body as an intermediary for the beams of light to direct and project the rays of light, and promote healing. The purpose in allowing this type of healing is because humans know that they have a soul and that several of these diseases are emotional.

The graduate doctor has in this or another incarnation, a time he dedicated himself to the art of healing. His career is based on preserving knowledge already experienced in another incarnation.

Different healers have different gifts.

HEALING WITH COPPER

Questions: What is the significance of copper in regards to health? Are there any medicinal qualities to cooper? Did the Inca's use a lot of copper?

Answer: The use of copper in the healing of human body dates back as far as people can remember. The medicinal powers of copper are in relation to the balance and quantity of this mineral in the human body. The absence of such produces a minimal but dangerous effect. The brain and neurotransmitters of the nervous system do not function as they should and because of that mental diseases are manifested. In the case of a surplus amount of this mineral, the positive charge of some electrons will result in the manifestation of basic schizophrenic patterns of thinking.

The influence as a conductor of electricity and restorer of good health in the case of arthritis is milder. This is because it is only an external inducer and not a participant in the blood stream. In cases of advanced arthritis, the use of copper bracelets or jewelry is recommended. The Incas used this knowledge and the jewelry was assigned by the Shaman to those that needed it. In the case of mild arthritis, the use of outer copper will not make much difference.

INSTANT HEALING AND MIRACLES

Question: Why is their instant healing miracles and others take so long to heal?

Answer: First the patient has to know about their disease and has to be willing to be cured. At that moment, Divine Light starts spinning and this vortex of light irradiates positive charges. If the patient is conscious and willing to recover his health, the healing process is faster. If the patient is conscious of his disease but does not care and does not make the least effort to improve, then the light is withdrawn and the molecular decomposition process begins.

Question: What are the requirements for healing?

Answer: The desire to be healed. Asking Divine Intelligence for help. Thinking positive, eating nutritiously, exercising, getting proper rest and getting rid of the negative habits that are dangerous to the human body. I am Ismael, Angel of Light of the eighth spatial Sphere.

ANGELS AND HEALTH ANGELS

Question: Do angels appear as human beings when they come to help people?

Answer: I am your teacher, San Augustine. Angels are beings of light and as such they cannot materialize. The visions people see are transparent in nature. In the case of a "solid" person who appears to help in a time of distress, it is a Master who disguises himself that way to help. The person who prays for help and has their wish granted has a duty to restore their faith to worship GOD.

Question: Are there health Angels? How are they able to help?

Answer: I am Ishmael, the Angel who came to instruct you. You want to know how we are able to help. During your meditation you were aware when the Divine Light penetrated through your sacred chakra. In the center of this chakra is a vortex of light that develops and purifies positive charges that are distributed in each patient according to their needs. In the human body, there are various centers of light and if one of these does not function properly, an imbalance is produced which is manifested as disease. These are the centers, which we are able to use to help according to the faith and karma of one's soul.

EMOTIONAL BODY AND DISEASE

The causes of many diseases are the imbalance of the emotional body. This imbalance produces the symptoms and the malfunction of different hormones.

You understand that your Father in Heaven, God, has already forgiven that person you have karma with. God is love. God knows that through our mistakes, we evolve. It is as humans, that we may hold grudges against those who have trespassed against us. The process of forgiveness is composed of two parts, to forgive your enemy, and to forgive yourself. In this process, faith is the key factor. If you understand why, then you are able to transform your negative thinking, and put on a new face in life that will be positive and constructive.

When a person is physically diseased the negative emotions act as a suppressor of their immune system. The process of forgiveness opens an understanding that will trigger a renewal of the process of healing. That is what you were reading in Mark 2, and all of a sudden there was a light in your understanding. Jesus said to us, that we have the power of healing ourselves, as God has already done in heaven.

WHY CHILDREN GET SICK

Question: You want to know why children get sick?

Answer: Universal mind is one. The relationship with each human being is through his mental and emotional body. The direction of actions and emotions in a child depends on the mother or person in charge of him or her. Human beings perceive or comprehend their spiritual surroundings and they are always conscious of the mental vibrations, which they are related to. In the child it is manifested as the guidance of his or her well being, which is perceived as an approval or disapproval of their acts.

The sudden change in temperature, schedules, cleanliness, place of living, and the people around them, all influence the immune system. Immunity is the propensity for protecting the physical body against disease.

In a child, when soul does not yet know how to express his discontent, they may produce a pattern of disease even as an infant. The mind works subconsciously even in an infant. The desire to please the parents sometimes produces changes of improvement. The doctors know that by attacking bacteria, as an example, analyzing it, taking the temperature, blood analysis, etc. he or she will get their conclusions. According to this data they proceed to prescribe the medicine or other methods adequate to the findings. The internal cause has not been resolved. In other cases, there are congenital diseases and in those cases the cause should be found.

ADDICTIONS

Question: Why are some people addicted to drugs? Is it because they have inherited a gene that makes them indulge in their habits? What about the influence of negative souls in their surroundings?

Answer: The reason that people get addicted to a substance is because they enjoy the sensation the drug produces in them. This could be for two reasons. The person could be addicted because it is in his genes and that person has a programmed tendency, and cannot reverse that urge.

The souls who are being influenced by other negative souls have a choice. These individuals know that these drugs are destructive to their physical selves, but their will has surrendered to these powerful entities.

Question: What can be done to help the souls mentioned above? The question should be: Why do these people want to kill themselves? The choice is free will. The person, who is addicted to drugs and enjoys its feelings, is solely responsible for his or her actions. Before someone can help them, they need to know if this person wants to end their addiction and secondly if he or she wants help. Only then, can they be helped.

Each case is different according to the degree of the addiction and the desire to get well. Some may require the expertise of a medical doctor, or an intervention with rehabilitation, guided by their family and friends, or the assistance of a well-balanced soul who is willing to guide and help them with prayers, for a positive outcome.

MULTIPLE PERSONALITIES

Question: Are people with multiple personalities people who let several discarnate spirits take turns in the possession of their bodies?

Answer: The reason that the phenomenon happens is because of the disassociation of several bodies that compose the human being. The aura of a human being is the projection of his or hers vibrations. In the case of these people, due to a terrible accident or casualty, which happens in their life, an opening in the aura is created which permits other entities to enter the aura and take possession of their physical body. The aura is a projection of vibrations of a person and that attracts other beings that are anxious to reincarnate.

Question: Can they be cured or completely healed?

Answer: The person who projects those rays of light does not know if he or she has a wound in their aura. The reason modern medicine cannot heal these people is because the remembrance of what produced that rupture is very painful. This human does not want to remember.

Question: It is necessary that he or she remember?

Answer: The doctor who wants to heal a patient has to find out the cause of his or her disease. In these patients the individual forgets the physical and emotional damage that induced the disease. The soul escapes from his or hers physical form and finds itself in an etheric world, where they see themselves surrounded by other etheric souls. Then when he or she decides to return to their physical body, they realize that another soul has taken their place. The person can see them and knows that they are in their body. This act of lending the physical body to other souls is called possession.

Question: Can it be cured?

Answer: The physical body heals but the emotional body remains damaged.

To restore the love and emotional balance, which this soul needs, it is necessary to apply drastic measures of healing.

Gilda, Jesus chased the demons from some possessed people!

Yes, that is the truth. The power and knowledge of Jesus allowed him to do the healing. I do know that you believe that faith is all-powerful.

Gilda, you will have to understand that faith is also relative. The healing of these people not only implies the understanding of the problem, but the absolute power of the astral forces. On the astral plane, a being of light or a being with a high grade of initiation can act.

Question: What happens to the person responsible for damaging another souls' aura?

Answer: The entity or person who commits such an atrocious act, has to face the consequences. After his or her etheric after life, he or she will be feeling the pain, humiliation, and fear that he did to that soul. He or she will have to receive in their aura, multiple entities of his or her same vibration and feel the wickedness in their own aura. The idea of "paying" our debts in that sense is a very real episode for each being. I know that you wanted to ask if there was a method for holistic healing for these ill souls but their pain and shame does not permit these people to utter the truth.

AUTISM

Questions: Why does the autistic child refuse to acknowledge the world around him or her? Is this an inherited problem? Are they conscious of their surroundings but do not want to accept that fact? Are they intelligent and capable of learning? What does not allow them to function normally?

Answer: Autism is a dysfunction of a physical connection and it is due to a factor in DNA, which allows humans to respond to one another. That DNA is a very important factor because without it the soul that occupies a body cannot bring out or express his "I" or what he or she thinks, to the exterior world. Intelligence and the ability to learn are not what are missing.

Question: Will there be a method or operation to help autistic people in the future?

Answer: The capacities to understand and to act are two different things. Human beings are not ready to understand these functions. The untruthful idea that people act by instinct is not correct. Thoughts of preservation, cleanliness, eating, sleeping, etc. are almost automatic.

Abstract thoughts require not only intelligence and reasoning but also the *consent* of the soul from the individual. That is the point which human beings of your planet neglect to investigate. The explanations of great clinical psychologists do not explain the why and they do not know why. In cases of Karma, the soul can express his or her bitterness or resentment and choose a body that will be a burden for that family. The Law of Karma knows that the duty of the offender is to pay with dedication and love. Every case is different and the Karma has to be paid according to the offense.

When the degree of receptivity and understanding of the inhabitants of this planet reach a complete understanding and acknowledgement of the soul, only then will that problem stop existing.

Question: Are people with Autism conscious of their surroundings?

Answer: When an autistic being begins to recognize that his physical expression is part of what is around him, only then can he learn the most minimal acts of self-sufficiency and be aware of what his surroundings are.

Question: Do people with Autism consciously decide to refuse acknowledgement of the world around them?

Answer: The consent of the soul is the key to this problem.

BLOODLESS SURGERY

The degree of skill that the people of Atlantis achieved were not only superior to the one your society is aware of, but they were able to suppress the flow of blood during an operation and cauterize wounds with a laser-like light, that not only sutured the wound but helped the tissues in the process of healing. These miraculous tools were given to them because they were ready to acknowledge divine processes that take place during the physical part of any physical operation or surgery.

Question: Are our ET Brothers aware of these proceedings and do they also use techniques?

Answer: The development of surgery and tools is different in every society according to the understanding of their physical, mental and emotional selves. Many societies of your own planet are at this time using Shamanism as a means of elementary spiritual healing. The process of healing is the restoration of balance in the physical, emotional and mental plane. The way that each society approaches the problem and the tools and implements used are only methods to accomplish those goals.

BRAIN TUMORS

Question: Medical doctors state that brain tumors are increasing and it is alarming to them because they do not know the cause. What is the reason?

Answer: The main reason for this growth is the development of scientific investigations that are possible and available in your country. The ratio or number of individuals is different in different parts of the world. In the countries where life is simpler and stress is not as predominant, like in South or Central America, brain tumors are not that common. The reason some individuals develop brain tumors are pathological, stress related, or genetic. The pathological reasons are ones that are understood and treated. Stress related tumors usually are the ones, where the soul is incapable of continuing his or her assignment and wants to quit. The genetic tumor is the one where cells are deformed and are not able to absorb the nutrients to act or perform as healthy ones.

CANCER

Questions: What are the reasons for cancer? Is one of them rancor or hate?

Answer: It is more complicated than that. Cancer is a degenerative disease that manifests when the cells grow in an erratic manner. One of the physical causes is genetics. The other is the propagation of carcinogens that accumulate in the weaker organ and because of that it is more prone to be affected. In the spiritual plane, the person who refuses to comply with his contract of life develops cancer. In the emotional plane, human beings accumulate negative thoughts because during life they have to face and react to negative trials. In the mental plane, negative thoughts.

ALZHEIMER'S DISEASE

Question: Can you shed light on Alzheimer's disease and why it affects the elderly?

Answer: Alzheimer's disease is a progressive decline of mental capacity due to a degeneration of brain tissue. The disease is the effect of a progressive deterioration of cells that have not renewed the outer part of their body. The physical cause is not a virus but a hereditary DNA expression. When the emotional body experiences a state of frustration and an absence of purpose, the brain cells begin to deteriorate. This disease will be a thing of the past, when the process of DNA research reaches the knowledge of how to eradicate the disease through DNA surgery.

Mental Disease

Question: Why do we become mentally diseased?

Answer: The human body is a combination of bodies, astral, emotional, and mental layers. There is a purpose to why these bodies evolved this way. When one of these bodies loses their interior force, it becomes diseased. There are several reasons to lose your mind. It could be a reaction to a medicine, because it produces hormonal imbalances or it could be a disturbance of the physical body. This happens when a human being is confronted with problems so overwhelming that he cannot resolve them and he searches for a way out. The physical expression of fear is to run, the emotional is to cry or to be mad and demonstrate anger, and in the mental plane it is to separate from the aura of the person. That separation manifests as a form of depression, if that being is of a positive charge, and euphoria if they are of a negative charge. The astral body is an immediate template or reflection of your physical body, which brings from past incarnations measurements and impressions of what you have already learned.

CHAPTER 5

Life on Other Planets

DISCOVERY OF NEW PLANETS

Question: What can you tell me about recent planets that have been discovered? One is very brilliant and the other one, is one and one half times larger than the earth and is surrounded by four suns.

Answer: The question you ask will be answered by one of the teachers of the Cosmos. Dear Gilda, I am one of the many teachers of the Cosmos. You are interested in this subject because you already have experienced the teachings of one professor that guided you through the writings of your book.

One of the new planets discovered by the astronomers, was in the Constellation of Andromeda, and it looks like it is made of gems, but in reality it is the reflecting light of the sun that is at a distance, almost as earth is from your sun. The dimensions of both sun and planet are much larger than earth.

The second sighting, of the planet and four suns, is in the Constellation of Pegasus. This planet is inhabited by humanoids of highly evolved souls and they are light years more advanced emotionally, mentally and physically than humans that exist on your planet. The reality is that they belong to a binary solar system. The perception of four suns, from earth astronomers is wrong. A nebula distorts the visual perspective. I am Lundy, the teacher who will help you during this incarnation and others.

INTERGALACTIC FEDERATION

A delegation of the Intergalactic Federation is at this moment planning the rescue mission of your planet. The representatives from different planets in different solar systems have agreed to help restore a degree of basic living conditions, to the millions of survivors on your planet. This operation will take place as soon as weather conditions allow them to do so.

The coordinated effort of these forces is one of the duties of the interstellar group. They are ready to intervene is this process of restoration of discipline, and the protection of the ones in need. Their peaceful contribution will bring a sense of purpose, and a hope needed to survive.

The Federation has appointed three major delegations to patrol and visually map the different relocations of survivors. This massive event will require a preplan of not only transportation, but medicine, food and shelter.

The damages caused by water displacement, wind and snow, will be enormous.

A group of scientists will reach the conclusion that major changes in the weather patterns will affect the countries of the Northern Hemisphere. The continued rains and quantity of snow will influence the river flows, and the balance of humidity in the atmosphere. This imbalance will produce winds of great proportions, especially in the Northern Hemisphere. The opposite effect will be happening in the lower hemisphere. The higher temperatures of the summer will dissolve great quantities of icebergs, and this mild weather will change several landmasses in Antarctica. Enormous territories will emerge from under the ice, and will be mapped and named. The migration of cetacean and penguins will begin, and many of them will perish.

The impending reality of the future of this planet is a renewing of the expression of the soul of this planet. I am your teacher Tumargeo, who blesses you.

ORLIN AN ET

My name is Orlin and I am an extraterrestrial being. I belong to the Intergalactic Federation. I am one of ETs that will land on your planet, after the cataclysm.

The place where we are assigned to land is near the Baltic Sea. Those lands will suffer great geographical changes. We are prepared to communicate with the people and to aid them during this crisis and period of transition. They will be scared, sick, and overwhelmed by our presence. Most of them, will welcome us. Others will think that this is the end of the world, and an invasion of their lands.

Question: How will you control aggressiveness?

Answer: We understand why they feel the need to assert their possessive instincts. We will communicate with them telepathically and try to let them understand that we come in peace and for the purpose of restoring normality. The individuals, who are unable to understand, will be allowed to continue their existence in another dimension. We are a group of twenty mother ships and the amount of land that we can aide is extensive. The restructuring of mountains and hills that are taking place will create a sense of disorientation for the survivors. Rivers will increase their flow and there will be dangerous floods. The re-adjustments and the final settling of these physical changes of the earth will take about four weeks. The terrors of the tremors, and winds and rain, will prevail in the minds of humans, well after this period of time. Not all of their material possessions will suffer damage. The ones, who are able to relocate, will have to start with nothing. These are the ones that we will try to aid the most. They need to understand why this has happened, and that their planet will be a safe place in which to live in the future.

Question: How will you be able to help?

Answer: The first thing we will provide is a sense of Peace. We are here to help you overcome your fears, and help you to initiate a new way of life. Different groups of people will react differently according to their degree of soul evolution and understanding. To us, all are part of the creative process that is God. We will advise them as to how to purify water, how to move to safer places, how to find shelter or provide shelter for them. Most of the resources for food will be completely destroyed by the winds and rains. Some of their stored food will be contaminated or in a state of decomposition. Food and water are the primary necessities that provide the body with energy. Because of that, food in the form of a powder, and water will be provided, until they are able to produce food by themselves. They will be able to see us, and listen to us. We are ETs that come from Pleiades. Our mission is to aid your brothers and sisters in other parts of the world. I am Orlin, and I bless you.

PLANET ITKAR

The planet we will describe today will be the one that is in the Constellation of Ursa Major, and belongs to a solar system with eight planets. This solar system was formed approximately at the time when your solar system was formed. Its name is Itkar. This is the second planet in orbit from its sum. Its volume is twice as much as planet earth. The elliptic around its sun is twice as large and slanted in a way that provides different kinds of climate, than your planet. The atmosphere is composed of air, and the particles of oxygen that help the life of plants and creatures to express a different expression of life, in a different kind of atmosphere. Their skies are luminous and iridescent. Their days are longer and their nights are shorter. They experience the spectacle of the visual Universe and they are aware of life on other planets.

Terrain: The terrain is of similar composition as yours. Parts of their planet are covered by large mountains, and other parts by valleys and vast prairies. There are several large lakes and rivers. Their continents are small and like islands in a vast sea. Because of that, the climate is mild and the vegetation tropical and subtropical. The condition of the weather, allows them to enjoy (most of the year) a life outdoors. The rains and occasional storms are mild in comparison with earth's weather. They have two moons, that are similar to yours, and they maintain a balance of attraction on the waters of the seas, and subsequently are an influence in their mild climate. The flora and fauna is abundant as are the trees like your tropical palms and the most beautiful flowers and fruits. They only have small animals that thrive on the fruits of their planet. There are no poisonous snakes or spiders.

People: The people who live on this planet are humanoids and eight to ten feet tall. Their way of living is similar to yours in the sense that they eat fruit and drink juices. They live in communities of sixty or more individuals that have a common goal. The equality of male and female is a fact. According to their degree of soul evolution, they are aware of their duties and responsibilities. The way they express love and dedication to the group is by doing their part of the work necessary to provide food, shelter and necessities of the group. A network of intelligent masters that provide and distribute the learning materials needed, links these groups. These more advanced minds are accountable for their actions and their only purpose of existence is one of service to the communities.

They procreate at certain ages, and they are able to foresee the gender of their future offspring. The period of gestation is six months. Their babies are beautiful and they are loved and cared for by all the members of the community. The parents provide love, shelter and guidance till the baby is three years old. At that time, he is able to express his or her faculties and be part of the group.

The Ikars are humans eight to ten feet tall and they have a head proportional to their height, and an elongated neck. Their eyes are of different colors and they can see twenty percent more than earthlings. They don't have hair on their bodies. Their nose is composed of two orifices, and the mouth is small, and without teeth. They have ears that are at the side of their skull. They perceive sounds at a better level than you do. They have two arms and hands that end in four fingers. They have two strong legs that end with feet and toes like yours. Their lung capacity is great, because they need to filter part of the oxygen of their atmosphere. Their brains have 20% more gray matter, and they can absorb data faster and in greater quantity than any Earthian.. In medicine, they are more advanced in genetic manipulation and are already able to eradicate diseases that still affect people on your planet. Their state of mind evolution, allows them to belong to the Intergalactic Federation.

Transportation: On the sea, on land and in the air, they have perfected the methods of transportation, because of the needs of their people. Their ships are like your transatlantic ships, but they travel at a much higher rate of speed. On land, they have vehicles that can also travel at great speed. When traveling to a different community, the vehicles are entered into tubes that are like bridges. Most of these communities are all inter-connected by these tubes. To go to other destinations further away, they travel in small air balloons that can carry ten to twenty individuals. They use a larger version of this to travel across lakes, rivers or short distances between islands. They also have mother ships to travel across the Cosmos. These mother ships are shaped like a cigar, and they can carry twenty flying saucers each. They will be the ones to come to the aid of the people of Africa. They are prepared to assist in their best capacity. I am Tumargeo, who blesses you.

PLANET KURDOS

The lesson for today is about the planet Kurdos that is in the Constellation of Riga, and in a solar system with six planets. This planet is the third planet around their sun, and is very similar to your planet. This planet is almost the same size as earth. Their degree of evolution is twice what it is on earth.

Terrain: The proportion of their continents is similar in size as the ones on your planet. The vast oceans are teaming with fish and mammals. The temperature is Mediterranean, and during their winters, the snow and storms are as severe as the ones that happen on your planet. They know in advance of any atmosphere changes, and they are prepared to go to special shelters, that provide the safe protection needed. There are three continents. They are far apart, and they communicate telepathically. Their purpose is to research a way to instruct other societies about the need for information about weather patterns, scientific data, and soul development. Their brain capacity is twice the size of the capacity of people on your planet. They are capable of studying changes in parts of the universe, and the causes of those changes.

Transportation: They travel at enormous speeds, and their interspatial vehicles are made of alloys that can withstand the different temperatures and difficulties of interstellar travel. On their planet, they go from one place to another, in special dynamic vehicles that are safe, rapid and run on solar power. They have perfected the use of solar power to the degree that electricity is a thing of the past. The combination of solar power, and chemical reactions, produce heat and power for their many needs.

Housing: Their buildings are made of materials that are safe for their occupants and pleasant to the sight. They don't require kitchens or recreation rooms. Their system of nutrition is provided by the atmosphere and some liquids are available is disposable packets, and are stored in every home. They dedicate their time to studies, and to service of their community and planet.

Educational Process: The process of learning begins as soon as they are born. They absorb knowledge rapidly, because their brains are more developed than the humans of your planet. At the age of two, they are capable speaking, communicating telepathically and responding to personal instructions. Higher education begins when they are adults. The sense of responsibility and duty to the community and planet is ingrained in each individual. The decision to study a specific subject is based on an aptitude test and the recognition of the soul's evolution. Their system of exchange of professionals that are able to maintain the different plants that provide all of the major necessities for their planet is one of precision and is based on the honor system of service. Because of the different climates that exist in different parts of their continents, they need a variety of devices to build and maintain their structures. These machines are moved by solar power and remote control.

Physical Beings: The Kurdos people are humanoids, five to seven feet tall. They are physically very similar to Earthians. Their head is proportional to their bodies. They have fingers like you have, and they have hair. Their eyes are beautiful and of different colors. There is only one race. Their sense of hearing is amplified, as is their sense of sight. They can hear and see twenty percent more than you are capable of doing. Their brain capacity enables them to absorb information in a variety of subjects and in more amounts, in less time. They are very well informed about your planet and your people. They know of your future cataclysm and they are ready to assist in the best way they can. They will be here after the cataclysm.

I am your teacher, Tumargeo, who bless you.

PLANET BALSAR

The lesson for today is about the planet Balsar that is in the Constellation of Scorpion and in a solar system with six planets. This planet is the second from their sun, and the size is three times bigger than your planet. The time that this planet takes to go around its sun is so long, that each season is like a year to you.

The inhabitants of this planet are a race who has evolved from ape-like creatures, and their humanoid form is very similar to earthlings. Because their time of evolution is more advanced than yours, they already are capable of mentally communicating with each other and use different methods of teaching and distributing their resources. The time of computers and robots is something of the past. Their knowledge of the universe is vast, and they belong to the Intergalactic Federation.

Their society consists of four different races, (Yes, they get along). There are different aspects of their facial features that mark that racial difference, also the form of the eyes, and coloration of the skin. They are all eight to ten feet tall and are well developed physically. The colors of their eyes vary according to their race and continent where they belonged initially. Their nose is similar to that of humans, but smaller. Their mouth is like a slit, because their source of nutrients is in a liquid form. Their heads are proportional to their size. Their skin is porous and adapted to their climate. Their respiratory system is different from that of earthlings, because their atmosphere is more humid and hotter. Several regions that are at higher altitude are places where they go to replenish their stamina (such as your vacations). Their advanced knowledge allows them to use all of the resources of the planet, and build necessary shelters and modes of transportation.

There are vast oceans that are traveled in very large vessels. Atomic power and a combination of gas energy and electromagnetic power propel the vessels.

In the air, their transportation includes the mother ship, space ships and other devices that they use to transport and repair equipment in far away places. They are ready and willing to assist your planet, and at the moment are studying the best methods of distributing of food, water and medical aide. I am Tumargeo who blesses you.

PLANET UBITE

The lesson for today is about the planet Ubite that is in the Constellation of Ursa Minor. This planet is the second in orbit at a distance from its sun that allows humans life. Its mass is similar to planet earth. They experience different weather patterns than that of earth. Their spring, summer, autumn and winter are shorter in length because of the difference in the relationship of their planet to their sun.

The temperatures on this planet are higher, and that is one of the reasons that they live mostly in the upper or lower parts of their hemispheres. There are two big continents and several big islands. Their luminous nights are part of the beauty of this planet. They have two moons. These are almost as big as your moon, and they reflect the light of the sun.

The inhabitants of this planet use this light to cultivate certain plants that they consume as nutrients. The law of gravity or pull of these two moons, acts as an equalizing force that influences the tides of the oceans and all the liquids on the planet. Because of that, their seas and weather patters are much calmer that those on earth.

The mountains on both continents are tall, and covered with snow. The northern continent, is smaller, and because of the position on the equatorial line, provides the better climate for human habitation. The other continent expands from the equator to almost the tip of the bottom of the planet. This is a vast mass of land with several different grades of topography. There are very fertile regions, almost tropical, at the most Northern part of the continent. It changes gradually to different climates and vast pieces of land, with different plants and flora. The most southern part is cold and rich with minerals and special flora like Alaska is on your planet. There are three major islands and two of them are inhabited. Here are big rivers and lakes. The temperature ranges from icy cold to one hundred and twenty five degrees Fahrenheit. Their air is more rarified than yours. The composition is different, and because of that, the Ubite have a respiratory system different than that of your planet.

The Ubites are humanoids that are six to seven feet tall. They are very well proportioned; their head has two eyes which are large and expressive and of different colors. They also can cover their eyes completely, because the membrane or eyelid is of a different thickness than that of earthlings. They have two ears. These are the only orifices at the side of their skull. Their sight and hearing is more acute than Earthlings. Their mouth is like a slit, and they don't have teeth. Their nutrition comes from the liquid extract of plants. They do have a nose. This is small and only for the purpose of breathing. They don't have a good sense of smell. They don't have hair on their bodies. Their skin is an adaptation to their climate. The color is almost gray, and they can sense any change in temperature with it. That is one of the reasons; they live only in certain parts of their planet, because they are very sensitive to changes in temperature. Their arms are strong and their hands only have four fingers. Their legs are long and strong, their feet are similar to Earthlings. Their span of life is from eighty to one hundred fifty years. They are aware of their immortality and they know that their spiritual life is eternal.

They are also aware of the existence of other inhabited planets, and they are capable of seeing and observing their life on their man made screen. These are similar to your TVs, but with more advanced technology. Their civilization is about two thousand years ahead of yours.

One of their major innovations is their transportation system. They have a system of vehicles, which are automatically programmed, and run from one point to another non-stop through special see through tubes at high speeds. These connect buildings with other buildings, or are suspended, and can connect places to places where the terrain is difficult to travel by land. They are completely safe, and provide fantastic views. They have special vehicles to travel on snow and difficult terrains, like jungles or vast savannas. They have ships, propelled by atomic power and smaller boats for recreational purposes. They have mother ships, that can carry twenty spaceships and travel throughout the universe. They are aware of the impending cataclysm and they are ready to come to earth for assistance. They are assigned to land in the Northwest and parts of Canada. I am your teacher Tumargeo, who blesses you.

PLANET OVIDE

The lesson for today is about the planet Ovide that is in the Constellation of Cassiopeia. The planet Ovide is the second largest planet in that solar system. During the formation of this solar system, several of the planets which were orbiting their central sun collided and a ring of debris formed around one of those planets, like that of your Saturn. This planet is surrounded by three rings and is as big as Saturn. Its position is the 3rd planet, from their sun, and this allowed a climate that can sustain humans. Ovide takes two and one half years (of your time), to go around its sun. During the formation of this planet several continents took form, and the oceans were deep and cold. After several eons of time later, the climate changed and the atmosphere settled. The process of evolution of animals and plants was long. During that process, numerous large mammals and marsupials occupied the lands.

The first humanoids appeared when the land was ready to accept these new human beings. They were the creation of different more advanced ETs, who were sent to investigate this planet. Because on this planet there were no apes, their race descended from certain marsupials. These humanoids are twelve feet tall, and there is only one race. They have long arms and legs, and they can run faster than any humans on your planet. Their faces are similar to other humans, with two eyes, a nose and mouth with several teeth. Their ears are at the side of the skull and they have ear lobes like you have. They don't have hair on their bodies. Their skin is soft and receptive to the humidity or dryness of their planet. Their eyes are very human like, and have irises of different colors. The Oviden can produce sound, because they have vocal cords, but they only use them in certain cases. Most of the time they communicate by mental telepathy. They are able to hear several decibels more than the Earthians. They can see very well and they have reached a state of evolution, in which every person can have perfect hearing and sight.

The topography of this large planet has several large continents, which are separated by deep seas. The continents that are at the equator of the planet, are the more prosperous and with a larger population. The continents too close to the poles, are not desolate, but scarcely lived on. These continents are visited frequently to supervise the mining and studies of animals and forests. There are tall mountains, enormous canyons, lakes and abundant rivers. The continents in the central zones have a milder weather, and their seasons are long and more like summer and autumn. They don't have deserts. There are vast areas of land that are without vegetation but they are not covered with sand. There are enormous volcanoes, and some of them are active. Their knowledge of seismology and the movement of the underground plates give them the advantage of preventing seismological disasters.

The temperatures on Ovide are mild and almost tropical. Because of that, flora and fauna are abundant. Rains are copious, and deliver almost all of the drinking water needed. Their rivers are as big as the Amazon and they are a source of communication, because they are used as navigational connections in-between cities, and for transportation of cargo goods. Their source of electricity is atomic. The immense waterfalls are also used as a source of electrical power. They have developed a vast network of communication, and they can contact any place on their planet, and other planets through a vibratory system similar to your computers. So far most advanced technology, is used by any resident, and is free because it belongs to all of the inhabitants. This open media of communication creates a cohesive unity that helps maintain the purpose of life and a desire to learn and share their knowledge.

People born on this planet, are considered in oneness with all the inhabitants of this planet. Their basic teachings as babies come from the couple that has conceived them, to the age, when they are able to take care of their physical bodies. Then they are able to receive instructions through a telepathic system. This is connected to the device that I explained before, and they learn in synchronization with their peers, of the same age, all over their planet. These homogenous teachings result in a society that can understand the problems of their planet and be able to cooperate unanimously to find solutions. There isn't any schooling with classroom instruction on this planet. They live with their parents to a certain age, until they are capable of maintaining a cultural discipline that allows them to live by themselves. If they wish to achieve a higher degree of cultural instructions, they can pursue and choose different teachers, and dedicate themselves to learning. People are selected according to their inclination, attitudes, and desire of service.

Their system of government administration is the result of many past experiences. Because of the vastness of the continents and population, government is divided into different groups of people who belong to each continent. These groups are responsible for the wellbeing of their people and for solving the problems of their continent. There is a sharing of ideas of representatives of these continents, who consider major problems: Example, like an impending catastrophe due to shifting waters of one of the major rivers. In those cases, they have the power to call on the resources necessary to resolve the problem.

Ground transportation on Ovide: Their cities are places where millions of people live. These cities are planned and built with the idea that people need to move and go to different places. The transportation is in the form of tunnels that are built on different levels, and they allow people to choose their destination. The vehicles are like long cylinders, with compartments that can carry about one hundred individuals at a time. These are powered by atomic force, and they cannot collide, because they only run one way.

Air transportation on Ovide has a great variety of vehicles: From the two-person personal air traveler, to the mother ship that can travel through the Cosmos. These different vehicles, are made mostly with strong alloys, that can withstand high temperatures and pressures. Their knowledge of interplanetary voyage is extensive.

Ovide belongs to the Intergalactic Federation and they too, are ready to come to earth to assist, after the cataclysm. They will be assigned to land over the Congo basin and the central part of Africa. I am your teacher Tumargeo, who bless you.

Planet Ilco

The development of a new race is a matter of great concern to the planners of these matters. These masters of Divine Intervention are able to create new specimens that are receptive to change. These new specimens are willing to experience the life that will be their medium to evolve in.

These are the Elohim. These great Souls are appointed by God to manipulate the DNA of certain species, and improve the appearance, knowledge and adaptation of their terrain. In the specific case of the planet Ilco, they developed a species, which was more able to accomplish these requirements. Their basic form was a praying mantis and their evolution was assigned to two Elohim. The particular structure of their arms: Example wings are separate from the body, and they can rotate and execute different tasks, as humans can. The elongated faces are in part the expression of their ancestors; the scalp is covered with plaques that perform a safety role for protection of the brain. Their lower extremities are similar to the humanoids, but they don't excel in running as your species does. Their strength is in the muscles in their thighs, and the purpose is to be able to scale the mountains where they live.

Question: Do they live in family units?

Answer: No, they are a race that lives in groups of twenty or more. Each one of these groups has a leader and they are responsible for the welfare of all.

Question: Do they have shelter or houses?

Answer: Yes, they are perfectionists, and are capable of constructing large shelters. These shelters not only provide a place to live, but also have sections where people study, and sections dedicated to children and a section for recreational pursuits.

Question: What do they do when they are sick or in an accident?

Answer: The healing process is one of regeneration of their energies and of their inner selves. When this happens, they have a special place where they regain their stamina. Such places are constructed separately from their dwelling places. The healing arena (like a hospital concept) is a place of rest and healing. In charge of these places are souls who understand the process of healing. They are light years more advanced, than planet earth, and because of that, their success in healing is remarkable.

Question: Do they feel the effects of gravity, as we do, and the effect of aging? How do they die?

Answer: First question: They are affected by gravity as you are. They do not age, as you do, because they have a different DNA. Their physical beings are preserved with a regenerational process. Second question: They do die? The soul that is ready to exit his body, because he is aware that he has accomplished a required term of learning, finds a special place that he likes, and peacefully asks for direct guidance. His soul is then directed to a special environment that is ready to receive his soul, and prepare for a new reincarnation. Yes, they know about reincarnation. The physical body is disintegrated and returned to the planet.

Question: What about the Fauna and Flora?

Answer: The different species that thrive in those mountains are; a species like rabbits that are able to adapt to the climate. In the valleys, there are several species of birds, with beautiful plumage, and they sing in the most beautiful tones. They have two races of small ponies; they use as recreational members of their group. They enjoy seeing them, and taking care of them, when the weather changes they have special shelters for them. They are not pets, and they are not used as transportation. I am Tumargeo, who blesses you.

THE PLANET NADACIUS

This planet belongs to the constellation of Cassiopeia. There are nine planets in this solar system. This planet is four times bigger that planet earth. Its elliptic around the sun takes a long time, according to your idea of time. It rotates on its axis, and that rotation has a tilt that allows the planet to advance around its sun and experience the different facets of day and night.

This planet belongs to a binary system, and as such, they are able to see two stars that are their fountain of existence. The people who live on this planet, are in the 10th sphere of evolution. Their physical being is humanoid and they resemble your species. Because they have evolved in spiritual, mental, and emotional understanding they don't live the same way you do. To begin with their planet is like a pristine paradise of nature. There are luscious landscapes, lakes, rivers and mountains. There are four continents and two of them are the bigger than the others. The vast seas that are in between these big masses of land are full of different species of fish and some mammals. The temperature on this planet reaches about 120 degrees F and it is a very comfortable temperature due to the thick stratosphere.

The people who live in Nadacius are tall, nine to ten feet, and they do not speak. They communicate through mental telepathy. They have a brilliant intelligence, and are aware of other constellations and planets. They belong to the Intergalactic Brotherhood. Their purpose is to eradicate injustice and maltreatment in other societies that are evolved. They are the forerunners of the programs of balanced nutrition and the innovation of laws to prevent abuse and maltreatment of animals. Their work is done through mental telepathy, broadcasted to those people who are doing this kind of work, on lesser evolved planets.

On their own planet, they have lots of species of animals and they treat them with love and respect. Because they don't consume animal meat for food, they don't have herds of cows and chickens as you do. They only drink special juices and a product from a plant that through a process becomes dry, and is made into a flourlike substance. This meal is fortified with minerals and vitamins that are specifically made for each person according to age, location and mental function. They are physically strong and in good health.

The Nadacius are humanoids, their head is larger in proportion to yours, and they have two eyes, a nose that consists of two orifices, and two other orifices as ears, at the sides of the head. Their eyes are large and slanted. They have a nocturnal vision and a daylight vision. Their pupils are capable of enlarging or constricting at will. They don't have eyelashes, because they don't need them. They have eyelids that retract to the superior part of the eye, when they are awake. Yes, they sleep; it is a form of rest necessary to recharge their energies. Their mouth is a round hole that is used to ingest food or drinks. They don't have teeth because they don't need them. They have two arms, and they have hands that have four fingers. Their legs are tall and strong and their feet long and very similar to your feet. The only difference is that they have only four toes.

Question: We evolved physically from the great apes, from which species did they evolve from?

Answer: They evolved from a different species, one that you don't have on your planet.

Question: What happens if they are sick or injured in an accident?

Answer: The idea of being sick is not one that stays in the minds of the Nadacius. In case of accident they have healing knowledge and advanced technologies that return them to health.

Housing: The concept of shelter is for them, a place to relax and be reunited with other members of their group. They congregate for specific purposes to discuss new projects, or decide on innovations to be manifested on another planet. They prefer to be outdoors and only seek shelter when the weather is too strong with intense winds or solar flares, then they go underground to special shelters, where they have all the nutrients and comforts they need.

Question: Do they live in family units?

Answer: The Nadacius people are a group of beings that are attracted by their mutual ideas, ages, and interests. These groups are as large as sixty to one hundred. Their purpose is to co-operate with the group and to maintain a harmonious relationship. There are males and females and they mature at the time of readiness for conception. There are different groups specifically for younger people and others for older people. Couples are selected from the group, according to their compatibility and desire to have a child. They don't have to be "in love." Their offspring are raised by the community and they are lovingly cared for by specially appointed "nurses" until they are capable of integrating with other groups of adolescents. They are happy to belong to a society where love is provided by every individual of the group.

Weather: The weather patterns of planet Nadacius are due to the rotation around the sun and the rotation on its axis. There are four distinct seasons. Two are like your summer and winter and the other two, like your spring and autumn. During the spring and summer there is the renewing of vegetation and a period of gestation for the animals. Spring brings the melting of ice and the wind patterns change. There are no hurricanes or storms of vast proportions. The temperature starts rising and because of that, patterns of clouds and winds create a resonance that is audible to all the inhabitants of the planet. Summer is the culmination of the maturity of plants, trees and the development of the new animals born during this period. These animals are strong and ready to live through autumn and winter.

The people of Nadacius have different tasks according to each of these patterns of weather. The configuration of the planet consists of three kinds of terrain. Big mountainous chains are part of each continent, and they provide the water necessary to irrigate the valleys.

The mesas are flat and extensive terrains with a climate that is similar to your Mediterranean climate. They sustain several animal species. Some of these animals resemble the bears and equines of your planet. There are also some bird species that are of bright plumage. The valleys are irrigated by rivers and lakes. These are the places where most of the inhabitants of this planet live. The temperature is a constant beautiful hot and humid climate where flowers, ferns, and tropical trees grow.

Question: Does it rain?

Answer: Yes, the rains are the continuous cycles to renew the process of replenishing their source of water.

Communications: Their mental capacity to communicate telepathically, gives them a complete assurance that everybody knows what the other individual is thinking. They do have freedom of choice and because of that, they can state their reasoning and disagree with the thoughts of another individual. They have overcome the negative custom of thinking one thing, and telling the other person something different, in order to appear agreeable to that person's way of thinking. Long distance communications are by telepathy, because they are aware that thoughts travel at enormous speed through the Cosmos, and can be heard by evolved beings all over the universe.

Question: They don't use computers?

Answer: The use of computers was part of their past. In your mind, I see that you think, they must use some kind of communication in their spaceships. No, the panels in their spaceships are part of the system that measure altitude, decompression and other very important data necessary to travel through space. The people who travel in those UFO's don't need other methods of communications.

Question: So until humans of this planet are sufficiently evolved spiritually, mentally, and emotionally, they will not be able to participate in the Intergalactic Brotherhood?

Answer: Yes, those are some of the requirements. The knowledge of interspace and other astronomical data is also very important.

Transportation: The people of this planet understand the knowledge of dematerialization, which is the disintegration of the atoms of a solid figure and the re-integration of those same atoms in another place they want it to be. They are able to do this process just by thinking about it! This ability to displace their bodies at will, gives them great mobility and freedom. They are able to enjoy their lands, flora and fauna, and be part of all the beauty that surrounds them.

Question: Have they visited our planet before?

Answer: Yes, they have been here from the beginning and are aware of your different races. They are interested in the evolution of the people on your planet.

PLANET UPSILON

The lesson for today will be about another planet in the Constellation of Scorpio.

This is a big planet and is the third in orbit around its sun. The name of this planet is Upsilon. This planet is two times larger than your planet. The elliptic around its sun, is twice as long. Their seasons are also twice as long too. Their stage of evolution allows them to participate in Intergalactic travel and be part of the white brotherhood. Their society is formed by groups of people that are living together for one purpose: To help others and learn new concepts that will guide them to be better components of the universe. The use of resources, and the knowledge of the terrain, allows them to solve the many problems they have had to face during the cycles of renovation on their planet. There have been several eras of different formation of their continents and this process has affected the flora and fauna. Because they use more of the gray matter of their brains, they are capable of foreseeing events in the future that will affect their living spaces, and are able to plan ahead to prevent disasters. They have a great knowledge of the universe, and this is a great help to them in planning their voyages through the universe. Their experience will be valuable to help Earthians during the process of adjustment to new surroundings. They will be helping in central China, and in the mountains of Tibet.

Terrain: The surface of this planet is similar to earth, the only difference being a different constitution of the soil. The formation of profound craters and volcanic residue has influenced the atmosphere, and as a consequence, the earth is dry and not very fertile. There are extensive regions, where the soil is in better fertile conditions, and that is where the inhabitants of this planet live. There are six large continents, distributed all over their planet. The two largest continents are the ones where most people live. There is only one race. Their state of evolution is about two thousand years ahead of your civilization.

People: The Upsilon are people ten feet tall or more. They use only telepathy to covey their thoughts. They can hear, and make sounds because they still have vocal cords. They are amazed to see that you use so many languages to express your ideas. They are humanoids and strong and slender. Their sight is superior, because they can see thirty percent better than humans on earth. Their hearing is also more acute, and they have two ears. Their head is proportional to their body and they have two eyes that are large and slanted. They can cover their eyes like you do, and protect them with lashes. They have two powerful arms and legs. Their extremities end in hands that have four fingers and feet similar to yours. Their skin is porous, lighter than yours and color varies according to the place where they live on their planet. They need clothes to protect themselves from their climate. These thermal outfits are custom made and are replaced when they outgrow them. The material responds to the changes in the weather and provides the comfort needed. Fashion competition doesn't exist.

Housing: Their housing includes large spacious buildings that contain separate quarters for families, singles and children. These buildings are made of a mixture of different soil components, and provide shelter and recreational areas.

Nutrition: The Upsilon people eat some vegetables and fruits. They have a digestive system similar to yours. They enjoy cultivating their crops and also processing some of the vegetables and fruits to save them for the winter or for times when they go and visit other parts of their planet, which are arid. They admire the beauty of your planet, and they are aware of the changes that will come in the near future.

Transportation: On the planet of Upsilon, they have numerous forms of transportation. For travel within their cities they have above ground rail lines that are monitored by a central control station. These small capsules seat four individuals and are extremely fast and efficient. For transportation of larger groups, they have an underground system that consists of large tunnel tubes that can transport as many as three hundred people at a time. These vessels, travel at great speed and their safety devices are excellent. For space travel they have flying saucers, and these are made of metals, and alloys they have found on their own and other planets. These are powered by atomic power. Their system of intergalactic vehicles include mother ships that can transport about twenty five flying saucers at one time. These vehicles are made of numerous alloys that are found in abundance on their planet. For this reason they can withstand the extreme temperatures and difficulties of interstellar travel. Their source of propulsion is atomic and electromagnet forces. They have traveled extensively through the near galaxies, and their knowledge of universal space is vast and up to date. For terrain vehicles for use on their planet, they utilize special built carts that resemble your tanks, and they are propelled by a mixture of compressed gases and electromagnetic forces. These strong vehicles are capable of transporting hundreds of people and can go long distances. I am Tumargeo who blesses you.

PLANET USPECIA

Your next assignment will be to write about the inhabitants of the planet Uspecia. This planet belongs to the constellation of the Taurus the Bull. This is a big planet and is a binary planet. The two satellite moons are as big as your planet.

The evolution of the humanoids of this planet began millions of years ago. They are aware of the many inhabited planets in other constellations and they can communicate with them also.

They are the ones that are coming to your planet to assist and reconstruct your new society. Their degree of evolution is far superior to yours. They will provide guidance, first aid and healing. They will land after the cataclysm. Their mother ships are enormous, and they are capable of transporting twenty flying saucers. The era of a new future will begin.

Greetings: I am Ator and one of the ETs that will come to your planet. The aftershock and the anguish of the people will be such that they will welcome us. We come in peace. We are aware of your necessities for food, purified water, and shelter in order to survive. We will provide that and also the assurance that a new pattern of weather and circumstances will bring a better, more peaceful future. The rehabilitation of some buildings and knowledge of electricity and scientific information will be preserved. The process of emotional recovery, will take about half of a year, then people will realize that their only option is to hear our guidance.

Question: For how long will you remain here?

Answer: That depends on the place, the amount of damage and the spirit of adaptation of the people.

Question: Are there different ETs from different planets who will land on different parts of the world?

Answer: Yes. The intergalactic Federation has studied this problem, and they will assign special units to places where they are already acquainted with those ethic groups.

Question: What will happen to those people who at that time will be in a transatlantic vessel or airplane?

Answer: Some of the vessels that will be at sea will have a chance to survive. They will be in very rough waters, and winds, and for a time, unable to keep course. They will realize that the change in direction is due to a new position of the compass. The reestablishing of a new pattern of light weather will be acknowledged. Some of the airplanes, which will be in the air at the time of the cataclysm, will be able to land, after realizing that their idea of the place of landing is completely changed. These are the larger airplanes that are able to fly at high attitude. Smaller aircraft, will succumb to the fierce winds, and rains. I am Ator, your friend in Christ.

The inhabitants of the planet of Uspecia are humanoid, twelve feet tall and they are trained to respond to the call of the less fortunate humans on other plants. Their degree of evolution is such, that they can see the changes in a society on another planet.

They know when a cataclysm will happen, and why it will happen. Their knowledge of the universe is vast and they posses the most up to date equipment (like your telescope) to see and map future events in the cosmos.

Their society is composed of several people from different races, with a common purpose. These different races, as on your planet, developed in different parts of that planet. Today it is only one unified race, and it contains a diversification of expression in human form. The evolution of their mind, emotional being and soul, allows them to live in harmony. There is only one concept of God the Creator. The realization of their participation in the creative aspect of God, allows them to manifest the transmutation of atoms and the unification of atoms. They are able to be in other places physically, only by the process of thinking (teleportation). They only communicate through telepathy. Their span of life is three times as long as you Earthians.

Their planet is very different from yours. The composition of the planet is of different materials. Their earth is formed by chemicals, which allow humidity to filter through this porous ground mass and produce different kinds of flora. The colors of these plants and the flowers are difficult to describe. They are not only beautiful, but they express their degree of evolution, and can transmit their thoughts. There is no fauna. Their seas are enormous and there are sea creatures, like anemones, and other sea plants. There is no coral. The people, who live on this planet, because they are so advanced in civilization, don't need policeman, lawyers, or armies. They know that they are responsible for their own actions. They use certain minerals, to build their spacecraft and to produce energy. They are able to move through the atmosphere at enormous speeds.

PLANET ISARNO

The next assignment will be about another planet named Isarno. This planet is in the constellation of Ursula Major. There are seven planets around its sun. Isarno is the second planet and because of the distance from the sun, and the size of the elliptical pass, this planet has some similarities to yours. This planet is as big as your planet, and rotates on its axis. The phases of day and night are similar to your planet. The only difference is that they don't become completely dark in at night because their two moons reflect the light of the sun and provide a very visible light throughout the night. These two moons, are as big as your moon, and are not inhabited. This planet has great oceans and four continents that are distributed over their globe. Their first inhabitants were animals, birds and fish and a luxurious flora. They never had poisonous snakes or any other kind of snakes. For several millennia this was like a paradise.

A new civilization began with the landing of neighboring advanced beings. With their intervention, the first humans of that planet began to learn how to survive with the nutrient s available, and they adapted to this mild climate. These humans multiplied and formed clans and as on your planet, they went through different stages of evolution. During their stages of evolution, almost parallel to yours, they developed a system of distribution of goods and assignments of responsibility to certain groups of people. They didn't have a system of money exchange. Their society is more advanced, in that sense, and they allocate goods to individuals according to education, effort and dedication to their role in the community.

Physical Bodies: They are humanoids, they are six to seven feet tall and they are able to communicate with sounds. Their "words" are different than yours, due to a different set of vocal cords. Their sense of harmony, like music, is well developed, and they enjoy that aspect in nature and in concerts, that is part of their recreation. Their sense of hearing is acute, and they have two ears at the side of their head. They don't have hair. They do have two big slanted eyes, and they can see fairly well during their "night." Their nose is small and with two orifices, to maintain their air intake, and exhale. Their mouth is almost like Earthians, but they don't have molars. They have two front teeth and they are to help them pull apart some of nutrients they need. Their skin is porous, and they need protection from the environment. They use all kinds of natural products for that purpose. Their females are attractive and agile. They are used to outdoor activities, and they only use shelters during a part of the year, when their climate turns cold. They have several offspring during their lives. They plan their families, and they are loving and industrious mothers. The males are raised and learn from an early age they are responsible for the care, guidance and wellbeing of their families. They live in groups of families. The children are ready to leave the group, when they are able to support themselves, and are ready to take on more responsibility in the community.

Question: Are Isarno human's decedents of the apes, like we are?

Answer: Yes, they are decedents of a species like your orangutans.

Transportation: Their planet has four extended oceans, and because of that, they needed a system of transportation by sea. They built great ships that were similar to your ships of today that were propelled by turbines. Today they have created new methods of transportation. These vessels are like your destroyers, big, flat and powerful, and they are propelled by atomic energy. These are for the transport of goods and people. On Land, they use a system of suspended trains that connect cities and points of interest. Their advanced technology, allowed them to build these suspended "cars" that are very fast and efficient. Their new idea of transportation by air is a elongated dynamic tube that is propelled by jet engines and maintains its course by a motor that functions by gas and compression. These cylinders are capable of transporting about two hundred passengers. They can go from one continent to another. Their speed is double of what your jets are capable of.

Weather: They have two very distinct weather patterns. One is the long spring/summer, and then the fall/winter, which lasts less time, and is milder than what you experience on your planet. During the spring/summer time, the flora is luxurious, and the provision of fruits, vegetables, and flowers are of an immense variety and provide food for all of the inhabitants of the planet. The temperature can reach one hundred and sixty degrees in some places, and at that time, rain comes down is great quantities and lowers their temperature to one hundred and twenty degrees. This is not a excessive temperature, if you realize that they live on a planet that is surrounded by a ring of gaseous substance, that dissipates the rays of the sun. In fall/winter times, the temperature drops to allow a mist like icy rain, to fall continuously for several months. The pattern of the winds that are propelled by the evaporation of the waters during the summer, raise and propel the clouds of gasses and dispels them around the planet.

Question: Do they have tornados and hurricanes like we do?

Answer: No they don't. The reason is because they have two satellites. The pull of these two masses, balances the gravitational pull of the water of the oceans. Their "storms" are milder, and their winters are too.

Question: What about the light of the two moons at night?

Answer: The light of two moons is like the light of your full moon, twice every night. Because of this light, they are able to use part of the night for several events that are not possible, during the day when it is too hot. They can see during the night, and use this time for several projects like: studying, traveling and building housing. They used to live in communities, like your cities, but due to their degree of evolution they prefer to live in special buildings that offer them multiple facilities. They design these buildings according to the necessities of group age, and purpose of life. They are connected by passages that are like your bridges, and they have access to the numerous ways of transportation, when they are needed.

Education: Their education begins when they are ready to ask questions about their surroundings. Their system of education is based on the desire to learn and the capacity of learning in each individual. The evaluation of this is done at an early age, and according to their findings, they are guided to different degrees of teachings and physical training. Physical training is very important part of their life. They enjoy the outdoors and nature. High education is reserved for those who are able to continue to express their mind's ability, and they are scientists and researcher of that planet. They are completely aware of their place in the cosmos, and they can participate in the Intergalactic Brotherhood. They know about your planet earth and they are ready to come to aid the survivors, after the cataclysm. Their space ships have been coming to your planet for a long time. They are prepared to bring food and basic healing to the thousands of survivors that they will help.

Question: How will we communicate with them?

Answer: Ideas are the basics of each language. Because of that, they will communicate through mental telepathy. People will be surprised, to realize that they understand what you are thinking. They will come in peace. They will land in parts of Asia, and in the high plateaus of China. I am Tumargeo who bless you.

Planet Isteo

The lesson of today is the description of a planet that belongs to the Constellation of Cassiopeia. The planet is in the third orbit away from the central sun, and it's elliptic is twice as long as that of earth. This planet has twice the mass of your planet, and was formed around the same period that your planet was born.

The evolution of planet Isteo went through great periods of diversification, affecting topography and climate changes. The appearance of animals and plants gave this planet the opportunity to develop human beings. Their first humans were a genetic manipulation that changed the emotional body of these animals, similar to your apes, but bigger in size. Their aggressiveness and sense of territorial authority was changed for the common goal of uniting their groups against other common enemies. At that time, there existed several prehistoric animals, large in size and extremely dangerous.

The second DNA change was a brain that was able to record more data and retain information. These small changes gave them an advantage over other animals. The third DNA manipulation was the idea of respect and protection for the females that procreate. This was the beginning of an emotional body.

After the first changes of their primary race, a cataclysm redefined the structure of several oceans and lands, and many of the big animals died due to the changes in climate. The human survivors realized that it was easier to provide food and shelter without the danger of the big animals, so the group decided to travel and see if they could find other survivors. This was the beginning of the race we call the Isteo. They are eight feet tall and strongly built. Their mental capacity is great compared with people of Earth. They are aware of the process of DNA manipulation, and they have used the same process to help species in other newly evolved planets.

Question: Have they come to our planet to use that process?

Answer: No

Isteo is a binary planet and the other planet that is in the same orbit is called Farien. This is a smaller planet and doesn't have people living on its surface.

Climate: The temperatures are almost the same as on your planet. The difference is that they don't have as many months of winter. In places where it is too cold, they explore the terrain for minerals when the weather permits, but no-one lives there.

Topography: They have several big continents and large oceans. Only three of these continents are inhabited and provide a climate necessary for their expression of life. The tallest mountains are on the continents that are uninhabited. The existence of volcanic output and tremors make those places unstable. On the continents where they live, there are mountains and valleys. Lakes and rivers cross their land and a rainy season provides most of their drinking water. They don't experience many storms and snow.

Fauna: There are several animals, and they exist as they were created and maintain the ecology of the planet. The Isteos do not use the animals as you do on Earth. There are abundant birds of different sizes and color. They are similar to yours but their size is bigger. There are fish and some crustaceans in the sea, but no big mammals like your whales or seals.

Flora: There is an abundance of tropical and semi-tropical plants and trees. These provide most of the fruits needed as nutrition. There are very tall trees and bushes that they collect for specific purposes.

Question: Do they have medicinal plants.

Answer: Yes, their knowledge of the use of medicinal plants is extensive and comprises the basis of their healing medicine.

Physical description - These humans are tall, slender and physically strong. Their head is proportional to the body, and they have two eyes, similar to yours. Their iris is green. They have two ears, with earlobes. Their nose is small and protrudes over a mouth similar to yours. They have only four teeth and they are used for eating fruits and certain nuts. They don't eat meat. They have hair only on their heads and pubic areas.

Question: Do they use clothes?

Answer: Yes, for protection against the sun and rains. Most of the time they used minimum protection according to the weather. They also have protective outfits to visit other continents and to go into space.

They live in groups of fifty or more, and they are aware that this group is part of the All. They select a place that provides for their needs, and stay in that place for a period of time, studying their surroundings, and providing guidance and care to the animals and plants. The co-ordination of these groups is maintained by more advanced intelligent beings, who coordinate their productivity and distribution of assignments. Each of these groups are dedicated to a specific project that will help the community.

Education: The education of an Isteo begins when he or she is able to understand that the time spent with their parents, as guides and teachers is over. From then on, they learn how to understand telepathic language, and express their needs. Discipline is also part of this stage of life. They learn who the people around them are, and why they must learn to obey and respect others. During that period, they learn about plants and animals and how to consider them parts of their environment. All of these first teachings prepare these souls to be ready for a new degree of teaching by specialized tutors, this prepares them to learn discernment and reason. Visual devices are used to demonstrate some of the mathematical problems, and to demonstrate subjects such as chemistry, physics and astronomy. They are aware that certain individuals are more apt to study specific subjects, and they are encouraged to do so. At a certain age they are separated according to their aptitudes, and regrouped with others that have the same abilities. This system of teaching is upgraded according to the capacity of the individual to pursue higher knowledge. When they are ready to work as professionals, they are assigned to a specific group to demonstrate their abilities.

Transportation: Their cars are made of plastics that can stand different temperatures and weather conditions. These vehicles are programmed with specific speeds, according to the place where they are traveling, and they are of a tubular aerodynamic form, that can transport eight individuals. The cars are propelled by a mixture of chemicals that they extract from certain plants. These vehicles glide over the surface of the planet on solid ground or water like your hydroplanes. They have various models for city travel or rugged terrain. At sea they have great vessels propelled by atomic power and submarines for underwater observation and research. Small recreational vessels are also available for lakes and rivers.

Isteo is a member of the Intergalactic Federation. They have great mother ships for traveling in space and these ships can carry twenty flying saucers. They are aware of the cataclysm that will affect your planet and ready to aide your people after the cataclysm. They will be landing in the northeast of China, as that region will suffer enormous devastation, affecting people, animals and plants.

Planet Samenty

The lesson for today will be to describe the planet that belongs to the constellation of Abdebaran, and is the second largest of the solar system similar to yours. This planet is about double the size of earth, and its climate is very similar to yours. The name of the planet is Samenty and it orbits its sun in about one and a half times the time it takes for your earth to orbit it's sun. They have different seasons, and temperatures in different parts of the planet. There are two big oceans, and the rest is land. These vast continents are similar to your subtropical regions. The climate is mild and humid. There are several periods of intense rain and the rest is calm. The flora are exotic and colorful and there is an abundance of fruits and berries. There are animals and birds. They are similar to some of your species. There are no poisonous animals, insects or plants.

Configuration of the land: There are several mountains, as tall as the Himalayan's. There is also chain of small mountains that separate valleys. On one of the continents is a large plateau that has a climate similar to Australia. In those regions there grows a certain kind of grain that they use as nutrients. There are many large rivers, and lakes. They have trees, large ones, similar to the ones that grow in your North Carolina. The flora is more diversified on the plains.

The People: The Samenty people are humanoids. They are in the eight sphere, and they are evolved enough to know that they belong to a system of Interplanetary Brotherhood. They are six feet tall, and very similar to earth people. They have hair, and their faces are almost like yours. The only difference is the nose. They have little noses, and larger eyes. The eyes are of different color, and they can see about thirty percent better than you can. This is because their eyes are different. Their mouths are proportional to their faces, and they have lips and small teeth. They live from about one hundred and fifty to two hundred years of age of your time. They don't get married. They reproduce when they are adults, and capable of sustaining a family. Their concept of a family is different than that of the earth people. A male and a female agree to raise a family only when they are mentally, physically and emotionally ready. Then they agree on how many offspring they will help to prepare for life. A Samenty child is loved and guided not only by his parents but also by all of the community. They are telepathically aware of the thought of the people who care for them. Their advanced system of education, prepares them to cope with a vast amount of knowledge. When a child is equivalent in age to your teenager, he or she will be tested for vocational studies. Then they will be sent to pursue future studies. There are places of specialized learning, but most of the basic learning is provided with a system similar to you computers, but much more advanced.

Nutrition: They eat mostly fruits, and seeds. They also consume grounded grains. They do not eat animals. They drink water and juices. Their water is the product of rains and the rivers are replenished by evaporation that constantly takes place.

Shelters: Their dwellings are different depending on where they live. The people, who live in the lower lands, live mostly outdoors and their houses are tropical and practically made. Their advanced civilization uses different materials for construction, and they are able to enjoy the beautiful landscapes, and be protected from the humidity and intense rains. Yes they have large cities. These are the cities of the future. People, who live on the higher grounds, have different buildings and systems of protection from the weather.

Industries: They have perfected their use of materials and are capable of illuminating their dwellings with a very innovative method of producing electricity.

Transportation: They have vehicles that are capable of running at great speed. These vehicles have a built in protective devices that foresee any danger, well in advance, and take corrective action to avoid any potential accidents. They also have super air dirigibles that can transport hundreds of people at a time. These are propelled by electromagnetic force and atomic power. They also have flying saucers that are different dimensions, according to their use. Yes, they can travel through space and visit other planets.

I have some questions about the teachings of these messengers from the Pleiades.

Answer: The Pleiades is a cluster of stars in the constellation of Taurus that is the location in the cosmos. The importance of those teachings is that they make people review the reality of their life and why they were created. The concept of beings of light that are more advanced and ready to help us to understand the future is in itself, a leap in progress. The other great help of those teachings are the assurance that the future will be a better more radiant place to live. To awaken our minds to new teachings and to understand that we are not the only ones in the universe, this is a great step that mankind will be able to achieve in the next generation. The changes that are happening right now are in part preparation for a new consciousness. The resolutions that leaders and countries take now will affect the well being of millions of people in the world. These teachings are not the only ones and these messengers of light are blessed in their mission.

CHAPTER 6

Soul Stories

THE POSITIVE AND NEGATIVE EFFECT OF KARMA

Your new assignment will be to write the many letters that people from the other side of the veil want to impress on you. These souls are prepared to tell their stories, because they want to let people know, that life is eternal and the good and bad deeds that they did, were the cause of their place on the other side of the veil.

These are the stories of countless souls who are ready to bear witness to the process reincarnation.

The messages that these people are bringing are related, because they are examples of the work of karma. This law of Karma is a gift that can work two ways. There are positive and negative consequences to our actions. The ideas of love, understanding, and uplifting of others, always bring a positive Karma. The thoughts of power over others or the desire to interfere in others lives bring negative Karma. These souls are ready to tell the stories that made them realize the power of this law and it's consequences.

SOUL OF JOSEPH

Gilda, I am one, who was at the Calvary and saw the crucifixion of Jesus. The splendor of the souls, who surrounded our Lord was so great! The first few hours after the crucifixion were full of sorrow. The development of a storm and earthquake, made everybody run for shelter. The thunder and rain that was pouring down, made a sad vision of the three, who were crucified that day. I will always remember the words of the Lord: Forgive them, because they don't know what they have done. His glorious Soul rose to heaven, and a silence and reverence remained in the heart of the people surrounding Him.

The presence of the Roman soldiers, made it impossible to get close to the cross. Hundreds of believers prayed for his soul. My name is Joseph and I was young and desirous to learn about this glorious Rabbi. God bless you.

PRIEST OF BENARES

Dear Gilda, I am the spirit of a priest who saw Jesus at the temple of Benares. He was peaceful and quiet. He listened to every word of the priests and He spoke with wisdom. The things that are written in the book: "The Aquarian Gospel of JESUS THE CHRIST "by Levi Dowling, is just the condensation of all that he taught us. His influence was great and brought several changes in the way we perceived our lives and our doctrines.

I am a Priest of the Brahmas and I bless you.

SOUL OF MARK THE APOSTLE

I am your brother in Christ, Mark. The difficulties you will go through, after you publish your books, is an experience that we, at the service of the Lord, have been through many times before. I remember the constant insults of my brothers, when I was a follower of Jesus. They did not understand the relationship or the mission, which we were committed to do. I am Mark, yes and I was a young chela at that time. I know how you feel and I can assure you that, you will be able to assume your responsibility, as we did so many thousands of years ago.

God Bless you, I am your friend in Christ, Mark.

SOUL OF CONSUELO OF THE CROSS

I am the soul of a novice. I was born in Spain the year 1283. I did learn to write and read and I dedicated my life to serve God. My parents were proud of me and they approved of my decision. I studied at the Carmelite Order and during my time as a novice, I learned to pray for the poor and meditate. Then I started to see visions and I understood that I was a medium. I was afraid that I will not be able to prevent something bad; that I knew would occur in the future. When I was aware that I could hear the voice of the spirit, my soul gave thanks to God. From then on, I dedicated my meditation to listen to the souls that died in pain and sadness. This desire to help others, urged me to ask for help from my superiors. It was then, that I was not allowed to meditate again. The sadness and disillusion that I felt from that day on, was enormous.

Gilda, What you do, is the same as what I did then. God bless you. Now that I am on the other side of the veil, I know how important it is for some souls to talk about what happened during their life and the lessons they learned or missions they failed to accomplish.

I am Consuelo of the Cross, your friend in Christ.

THE SOUL OF MELINDA

I am in your aura and I came to tell you I am amazed to see, hear, and write my thoughts instantly. I am one of the many souls who came to learn your gift. When I was in my last incarnation, I received messages from beyond, but I always doubted them. I thought it was my imagination. Now I am on this side of the veil, and I know that these communications are real and more common than people want to give credit for. My name is Melinda and I bless you.

THE SOUL OF CARL SAGAN

Question: I would like to know if Carl Sagan has changed some of his points of view in respect to the existence of other humans on other planets?

Answer: The soul you call Carl Sagan is in your aura.

I am Carl Sagan and I am in the eighth sphere. I am impressed by what you have witnessed. You are a person dedicated to the studies of the soul. I was a skeptic and a scientist. During my life, I realized that it was impossible to prove the existence of other humans in the universe. Therefore, I tried to justify my ignorance, with several theses, and explained why I did not believe it in life on other planets. I have been on the other side, for a number of years regarding the evolution of my soul. This is one of the things that I was not ready to acknowledge. The concept of unity in the universe, as expressed in light, love, law and life was what I was trying to avoid during the process of my education. The recollection of past lives and the sincere desire to understand these new surroundings brought me to the conclusion that I needed to investigate the common denominator that allows us to converse with each other. This question stayed my mind for a long time. I suppose that I was not ready to except the guidance of the spiritual teachers.

Question: Did you see your past lives?

Answer: Yes I did. I have reached the conclusion that life is eternal and the purpose of our oneness is to evolve and express the best of our qualities through mind, soul, and physical being.

Question: Are you aware that there are other humans in different degrees of evolution, on other planets?

Answer: Yes. I am not only aware of that, but I was also able to contact some of them. The answers to many of my questions have been explained. I understand now, the importance of their presence, and the reasons why they did not disclose their participation in the creative process of humans, until now.

I am humbled and impressed, to realize that you are capable of not only listening to me, but can also listen to some of these extraterrestrials. Gilda it has been a pleasure to talk to you and I realize that there are souls ready to face the truth and to teach others. I am Carl Sagan and I bless you.

SOUL OF ABISDOTE - EGYPTIAN PRIEST

I am in your aura and I want to tell you that you are a vortex of light. I see the colors that swirl around you and the white light that is in your crown chakra. I am amazed at the volume of light that is generated by your soul. My name is Abisdote. I am one of the souls who lived in Egypt during the reign of Amontepeth the III. During that incarnation I was treated with respect and deference. My master was a man of science and he knew about constellations, planets and the stars. Many of the High Priests were also educated and versed in several languages.

The purpose of this reading is to inform you that a soul retains all of the information that they acquired in previous incarnations. When the time is right, the soul can reincarnate and retrieve that part of the knowledge. The cognitive part of the brain is programmed to not only accept new information, but to look for answers to those questions deep in your soul, because we know part of the answer.

Today I am a place in the eighteenth sphere and waiting for my next assignment. The problems of planet earth are not the only ones in the Galaxy. The Federation of planets appoints certain souls to the teachings and guidance necessary to maintain balance and progress.

My new role will be as a director of one of the launching pads for interplanetary discovery. This assignment is one of many that I have practiced in previous lives.

I am most grateful that you have listened to me. I am one with the spirit of Peace. God bless you.

Pharaoh Akhenaton

Was Pharaoh Akhenaton poisoned and later put in a sarcophagus? Where did they bury him?

The Pharaoh Akhenaton was in power to restore order and peace to the people who lived in Egypt. He accomplished that goal, and restored the confidence of the people by developing their work ethic and their quality of life. The priests that were overseeing the temples of the gods were dismissed and they resented and hated this new system. Akhenaton knew of their plotting and he was forewarned about it. He also knew that his mission was almost complete. He was poisoned and embalmed, but he did not suffer becuase he went into a trance and left his physical body, before they gave him the poison.

Was his wife Nefertiti alive when this happened? Yes, she was ready to commit suicide but was executed by the priests. She was convinced that Akhenaton was alive and someday they would be together again. Their souls were of course reunited in the spiritual plane. Several followers of Akhenaton remained as counselors of the new regime, and helped to stabilize the country during the change of power.

Soul of Rosalie

I am a soul who was doing what you are doing now. The year was 1254. Yes, I was living in a convent in Spain. The Mother Superior was a hard and severe soul. She did not believe in spirits and she mortified me because I did so. My name was Rosalie. I died of influenza when I was 26 years old. During that life I learned to listen to my voice from within. Now I am reincarnated and in a different country. My soul remembered that incarnation and I am applying this knowledge to write and support the spiritual movement of the religious groups of my choice. God bless you for listening to me.

THE SOUL OF ANATHOLY - PART 1

I am a stranger in a land that I don't know. I am aware of many souls who walk near me. I have been in this place for a long time and they don't talk to me. I came here because my lungs were bad. The disease was long and painful. During my life, a mining company employed me. I died when I was 38 years old. Many of my fellow workers had the same disease.

Question: Where did you live?

Answer: I was living in Siberia. Yes, I am Russian. My name is Anatholy. I was a chief of a group of 20 men. My life was short and hard. I want to know how I can get to a new place.

Question: Do you want me to call a guide to take you to a better place?

Answer: Yes I do.

Response: I will continue this conversation later with you, when you are at the new place. You can ask me all the questions you want.

After a short period of time at a new place:

Question: Did somebody come to help you?

Answer: I am Anatholy and I will tell you what happened to me after we talked. I was walking in this vast land with no trees and I could see many people walking to different destinations. Then a man, older and taller came to me and asked me why I wanted to be guided. I said, I feel lonely and lost. He offered to guide me, and we followed a path that leads us to a new and a different landscape. Here I could see several trees and a well and many animals like sheep and horses. This was like a dream come true. We stopped and he showed me a bench. It was a bench against a hut, and he asked me to sit down.

Life is a continuous expression of our minds and soul. That is what this guide told me. I was absorbed in the beauty of the place. A great peace filled my soul and it was like a warm blanket that covered my cold body. My guide asked me why I was here, and I answered him that I knew that I died of consumption but after that, I was lost. He explained to me the process of dying, and how the soul is released from the physical body. The part that I did not know, was that the etheric body, and the mental body, are attached to the soul and they depart together. That is why I was able to see, and think, and hear. Then I realized I was ALIVE! I did ask my guide if I would live at this farm forever. He said no. I asked why. He answered that the reason is because sooner or later, you will realize that these surroundings are a projection of your mind. He left and here I am, happy to listen to the birds, and to realize that I am not sick, and able to explore these beautiful surroundings. I will thank you for your help and if you want I will tell you if I find here the happiness that I never had on earth. I am Anatholy.

Gilda, I am your teacher Tumargeo. Anatholy is a soul that needs to regain the assurance that he is a living soul. The process of the mind is to find the answers to his soul. Sooner or later he will realize that he needs answers to more questions. Then he will come to you again and explain his progress.

THE SOUL OF ANATHOLY - PART 2

I am the man who died from a disease of the lungs. I spoke to you before. I see that you remember. I am in a different place now. When I was in the place where I saw the horses and dogs, I was really happy. Then I began to remember my past life. The thought of incompletion came to mind. Why? I did remember that I was married. My wife was six years younger than me. Her name was Tlianka, and gave me two sons. I was proud to be a father. During the period that I lived with her, I was faithful and a good husband. Then the government called all men under the age of thirty to enlist. I left the mines to accept my duty. She cried and asked me not to forget about her. I was afraid that she would not be able to provide for our sons. We lived in the city where the boys were protected and provided for by the government. The pension assigned to them was some help until they are able to work. Tlianka is a factory worker. She is not an educated person. Then I asked, why had I died, when my children and my wife needed me? My appointed guide came to me, and told me that I had already learned the necessary lessons of the incarnation. The lessons pertaining to my wife and children was for them to overcome their tragic situation. Then he said: Do you understand that every life is like a step upward in understanding? In your past life you learned to love and respect your wife, feel the joy of being a father and feel the sense of responsibility that that implies. Then he asked me if I wanted to see my dear ones. I said yes, and in a blink of an eye, we were in front of a screen on which part of my life was projected. I saw my parents, when they were young and healthy and saw myself growing up. Many things that I did wrong were there too; those made me feel sad. I was starting to understand; this was to teach me that acts of kindness have effects and the negative actions also have effects. The recall of my actions was like a cleansing of my soul. I wanted to tell all of this because I know you will listen and write this down. I want others who are alive to understand how important it is to act honorable and good. I will come to you again; I am Anatholy who blesses you.

THE SOUL OF ADEL

I am a soul who is in your aura. My name is Adele, and yes I was a nun in the region of central Europe and I was assigned to work with poor. During the year 751, I was sent to a town where the plague was rampant, and I decided to live and help the many souls who were pleading to God for help. I know that I was an instrument of the Lord. He allowed me to heal through my hands. The love and light that I let flow through them was like a heat that passed through my body. Many years later, my deacon said that I was making black magic and sent me to a camp for delinquents. In that place, I received the blessings of the Lord, and continued to assist the poor.

After I died, I realize that the healings that I did, were part of the evolution of my soul. I was prepared to do that, before I came into this world.

Gilda, you're a soul of light and your ready to teach let the light and love Lord guide you. I am Adele a soul of the sisterhood of Christ consciousness.

SOUL OF DAPHNE

I am the spirit of Daphne Felicia Jones. Last night you were watching a program about an incident that happened that I was involved in. The attack happened while I was at work. All of a sudden two young males entered the building, came to where I was working and grabbed me by the arms and dragged me outside to a car. I was pushed into the back seat by the taller of the two. He had a knife, and told me not to scream or resist or he would kill me. The other one drove the car. We drove for about 25 minutes and stopped at a convenience store. The one driving went to buy sodas and snacks. When we were back on the road, the guy that was next to me tried to rape me. I fought him off with all of my might, but he was too strong for me and he had a knife. After that we came to a stop at a cabin and they pulled me out of the car and led me into this really dirty house.

Question: What kind of a car was it?

Answer: It was a four door sedan, dark in color, about five years old, and the seats were vinyl.

Question: What happened next?

Answer: They kept me in the house and raped me many times. I tried to escape, but the tall one, called Tom, followed me through the bush and caught me. He slapped me and took me back to the house. Three days went by, and on the fourth day, I tried to escape again. Tom was asleep and the other one was not there. The door to exit the house was old, and it squeaked. When I tried to leave the door made too much noise and he woke up as I was leaving. He caught me again. This time it was much worse. This time they tied me up to a post. The only time that I was untied was when I had to use the toilet. During this time I couldn't take a shower nor could I sleep because I was tied to the post. When Tom announced that we were moving, I thought that this would be an opportunity to leave something personal for the police. The only thing that I could think of was to leave a ring that wasn't expensive, and was a gift from a friend. When we left we drove for about two hours and stopped. This time they tied my ankles so that I couldn't run. They also advised me to be quiet or else. The next stop was at a shack on small dirty road. Then they killed me! I know it seems strange, but I immediately felt relief and joy as my soul exited my body. I am now in a place of peace.

Please tell my mother that I love her and that all of my pain and suffering is behind me. A protective cocoon surrounds me from the love and understanding of the souls who are with me now and I feel safe. Thank you for all of the prayers and this communication. I am Daphne Felicia Jones.

THE SOUL OF A FOUR YEAR OLD CHILD

I am the spirit of a child that came to this planet to learn patience. I am four years old and live in a family with two more children. My older brother is seven, and my little sister is two. My name is Gregory. Yes I know that I have to be patient with my older brother as he is in a wheel chair. I don't know why he is in that chair, but I know that he can't play or do things that I do. Alma, my younger sister is too small to play with me. She cries a lot and needs constant attention. Because of that, I think my Mom doesn't pay too much attention to me. I want to punch my brother and let him know that he should do something about it.

Question: Why is this happening to me?

Answer: Gregory, you are too little to understand why your brother is unable to walk. During the next four years, your brother will go through several operations, and you will realize that it is not easy to be in that wheel chair all that time. Your understanding and love for your brother will increase, and that will bring a healing in a relationship, that was a negative one. The reason for your Karma will be disclosed to you when you end this life, and pass into the new sphere of light. I am Tumargeo and I bless you.

THE SOUL OF A THREE YEAR OLD CHILD

I am the soul of a three-year-old girl, who died of a disease. My guardian angel is with me now, and she is guiding me to this big, big room, where there are many, many people. We are all waiting to be called. My time is not yet come, and I know who will be my parents. They are young and healthy. I choose to be healthy this time. They are nice and educated. They are very happy to have me, and they already have a room ready for me. I can see it. Your name is Gilda, and my angel says to me that you are a dedicated soul. God bless you.

JOHN THE DIVINE

Gilda: May I ask about John's soul and what he thinks about my assignment to write the book: "Messages from the Spiritual Dimension"?

Answer: The book you wrote about the interpretation of the visions of the apocalypse that I saw two thousand years ago is the new version for this time of man. Yes, I am the soul of John the Divine; I am the forerunner of the Light. Jesus our brother told us, his disciples, about the cataclysm. Many times he elaborated over the subject. One day I was praying, when all of a sudden I began to see these visions. They were vivid and terrifying. They made such a deep impression on me that I wrote everything down. There were no words to describe the things I was seeing. These clear images came to me like the movies you see today. I was able to see and hear all the voices and sounds. The reason this prophecy was placed at the end of the New Testament Bible is because people thought this would be the end of the world. The truth is this will be the beginning of a new era of peace and new ideas. The concept of God and our relationship with Him will be completely different. The realization of our place in the solar system and the universe will be completely different. A new degree of soul evolution will restore proper ethics and principles that will transform this planet into the place God created where love, brotherhood and co-operation will be the norm. Dear sister in Christ, we are the forerunners. I bless you and congratulate you for a job well done. I am John the Divine

JOHN THE BAPTIST AND JOHN THE DIVINE

Tumargeo - The duty of a chela is to listen to his master. The duty of the prophet is to listen to the higher souls who are in charge of the evolution of a planet. The Elohim are the archangels, who are in charge of the different stages of evolution of a planet. The Most High appoints them, and they assign different duties to different souls according to the soul's development. The prophets that came to this planet during the life of Jesus were assigned to learn how to prophesy and to write the words of the Master.

John the Baptist was the first, and he was able to warn the people about future events. John the Divine came to the side of the Master, when he was teaching the evolution of the soul. Many of these teachings went unrecorded. These teachings were so great, that John the Divine not only was greatly impressed, but also wanted to write about those concepts. It was then; during one of his meditations he saw the various episodes of the Apocalypse. They were projected in his mind like scenes from a movie. He could not make sense of these visions, but he decided to write them down for posterity.

John the Divine is here: Dear friend in Christ, my mission was accomplished and the guidance I needed was given to me. I see that your teacher is your guide and protector. During the incarnation as John, I was a poor man and a fisherman. I was young and ambitious, I wanted to travel and see the world. The first time I saw Jesus; I was shocked by his presence. He radiated love, compassion and light. He came to us, the fishermen, to ask us to help Him, demonstrate the word of God. We could not believe what he said. Why us? During the following days He demonstrated to us the powers of prayer and the use of Divine guidance. After that, we knew that he was the Messiah. When He said to us "follow me," we did without any doubt.

His teachings opened our minds. He made us see the world as a different place, and all people as our brothers. He explained patiently any questions we asked. His knowledge was tremendous. I was most inspired by His teachings and healings. He never discussed personal matters with us. His life was private. His love and respect for his mother was an example difficult to follow.

The demonstration of His death on the cross was the last sacrifice he made, to teach us, that the spirit is alive and will keep on living forever. This demonstration, as sad and devastating as it was, was a demonstration of faith. The resurrection was a fact, and the recordings true. His glorious presence appeared before us three days after the crucifixion. I saw him with my own eyes.

After He departed from us, we were in mourning. We cried, without knowing what to do. The bible describes what happened, but the emotional state of His followers was something very difficult to put in writing. As time passed the lessons were learned. We needed to be practical and pass this knowledge onto others. Because of that, I decided I should write Revelations. I understood that what I saw, was part of the future. Now is the time to let these revelations be known. I am your friend in Christ, John the Divine.

JOHN THE DIVINE AND HIS VISIONS

The lesson for today will be about the visions of the prophet John the Divine, and why he was able to see these visions. The faith and dedication that the apostles had in Jesus, was such, that it allowed them to transcend time and visualize the future. That is what John the Divine experienced. The purpose of these visions was to prepare mankind for a future that will come to them in the blink of an eye. During the time John was a disciple, his desire to be of service, was expressed in a sequence of visions. Some of them were terrifying and others showed him a futuristic place on this planet where people treated each other with love and respect. There were times he was confused.

The death of our Master Jesus, and the necessity to record these visions, led him to write Revelations and describe the best way he could, his visions of the future. Jesus said: "The meek will inherit the earth." In that phrase he was referring to the souls who will be living on this planet during the millennium. The time to awaken to these predictions is now. The development of the souls on this planet need a new awakening and that will be through the Cataclysm. The souls of millions of people will pass to other spheres, and the ones remaining on the planet will be responsible for the regeneration and the future of a new civilization.

The work you were appointed to do, is the continuation of a job you did many incarnations ago. You are the soul of one of the followers of Jesus.

At that time, you did what you could to sustain the faith of many of His followers. Your name was Amitrios, and you converted to Jesus's faith after you witnessed one of Jesus's healings. That life was dedicated to writing and documenting parts of the life of Jesus. This life, you were assigned to write about the visions of John.

Question- Is Revelation the last chapter of the Bible because we have not found more scrolls, or is it because these are the predictions that mankind needs to know now?

Answer -The book of revelations was written to explain what will happen on this planet in the future. There are other writings about the teachings of Jesus, which have remained hidden to man. During the period in which the book of revelations was written, most of the apostles had run away from Israel. They were in fear of being persecuted, as Jesus was. They wrote about the life of the Savior, as best as they could remember, and they decided to hide the manuscript for future generations.

John was one of the apostles that were blessed with the gift of visions. When he was growing up, several times he had visions, and he thought he was daydreaming. John was a fisherman and the calm and vastness of the sea, provided him a lot of time to think and ponder. When John met Jesus, he thought he was a wise rabbi. He listened to his teachings and was completely captivated by his knowledge and presence. The desire to follow Jesus was easy. He wanted to learn and travel. He was young and ready to transform his life.

At the time, there was great unrest in Judea, and the fear of the Romans, and the pressure of taxes and laws imposed by the Romans and the Rabbis made life very difficult. Following Jesus was to him, a kind of liberation. He saw the possibilities of a new way of life. He did not know that everything would change so drastically and so soon. The time he spent with our Savior was to reconfirm his expectations of a better future for mankind. Without realizing it, all of these things happened in his life, because they were meant to be. All these visions were part of a plan, and reason why he was there at sea, when Jesus approached them. John's visions became stronger and more meaningful, after the crucifixion. When John decided to write about the visions, he was protected and guided and his writings were protected for future generations. Now is the time to review and study what the prophet really saw. I am Tumargeo who blesses you.

SPIRITUAL GUIDE, SAINT AUGUSTINE

I am your spiritual guide, Saint Augustine. I am here because I know you want to renew your wish for service, and that is the reason you have been disciplining yourself.

To write daily, activates the cerebral condition that helps you listen. Your wishes will be granted.

In the year 1256, I was a simple monk who was dedicating my days to write papers concerning the church. To learn how to be humble, I had to pray and listen to many sermons. Since then, I realized that only listening and discerning when you recite the words of God, you can find the truth. In my particular case, many incarnations later, I was able to "listen." My soul could not believe that it was possible to hear the Divine voice. I couldn't believe that in this physical plane we could have the opportunity to hear a voice, without sound, from another spiritual plane. When I began my meditation, and listening to my spiritual guide, in my heart I felt an infinite joy! It was like a great door made of iron, opened wide in order to allow me to understand. Then I understood the truths we are learning, are in the direct plane where we find ourselves. The other thing was, I began to feel a new joy and patience to know that spiritual growth is infinite. I realized then that the teaching of the Catholic Church in its totality was not a fountain of Divine instructions but human instructions. That was very disconcerting to me and I began to study books of other countries and other religious creeds. Several times I asked my teachers, why was there so much diversity in religious creeds. My teachers answered that because the civilization of this planet unfolded on the base of racial evolution of the inhabitants, each race and region of this world has a different concept of their Deity and in that diversity God expresses as Love, Light, Law and Life. That is the way we are all able to advance spiritually, and see the parallels of Divine expression.

AN UNIDENTIFIED SOUL #1

I am in your aura and was chosen to speak to you. During the last stage of a terrible disease, I was approached by a priest and asked if I wanted to have the Holy Rights. The act of was like cleansing balm that helped me to release the fears that I had at that time. I was in a state of coma for several days, but I was aware of people who came to see me.

Question: Were you able to hear the people talking to you?

The response to your question is yes; I was surprised to hear and to be able to understand what they were saying. It is a sad state, and a difficult one, when you cannot communicate your thoughts to those that were there to see you. Now that I am aware of the process of dying, and I know that our etheric body is the one aware of the surroundings, it is easy to understand why I was able to hear. Gilda thank you for letting me express my thoughts and I hope this will be of help to many others that will experience the same fate.

AN UNIDENTIFIED SOUL - #2

I am the spirit of a soul who lived on your planet and is at this time in the six sphere. I came to you, because my guide told me that you were meditating, and I should listen and learn. During my life, I was constantly aware of a calling, and a desire to do service. I received my first calling on a day that I was very sad and disappointed about the situation of my relationship with a member of my family. At that time, I recalled saying that if that was my cousin, asking for help, I would tell her to go to hell! As soon as I thought that, I heard a voice saying: I am your guide and I want you to reconsider!

That was my awakening. At first I thought I was imagining this inner voice. Then I begin to think about it and realize that I was being too harsh and that I could really help her. Since that day, the "voice" has been with me, and I am learning to not only listen but to heed to its suggestions and clean up my act. I am a follower of Christ and I bless you.

THE SOUL OF A SURVIVOR

I am a soul who lived on this planet during the cataclysm that happened twenty six thousand years ago. As I recalled, the weather was beautiful, and we lived in a community of people, that were evolved to the degree of a concept of a community. We were happy, industrious and at peace. We lived near a river, and we had all the resources needed for a comfortable life. One day the sun was overcast, then rain and winds began to come with increasing force. We ran to the hills, and looked for shelter. The river grew in force and dimension and soon changed it's course. We were able to see how the water was carrying all kinds of animals, trees, huts etc.

This terrible storm, increased in intensity and great tremors of the earth started and a growling sound, was felt from the bowels of the earth. The force of the winds pushed us against the earth. Many died of fear, injuries, and at the end, of starvation. Only the strongest, youngest, and fittest were able to run to better shelters, and survive. That terrible weather lasted for a long time. One day, the clouds disappeared and the glorious sun came out again. We were exhausted. We began to inspect the terrain and what was left of our community. Everything looked different. So many trees lay on the ground. The river was farther away and several small hills were in front of us. Why has this happened? We never knew the answer to that, until after several incarnations. From data we learned the concept of the renewal of the planet.

We painfully survived, and tried to pass our knowledge onto the new generation. These tales of old were lost, until the studies of geology. Today, societies are aware of the cataclysm that happened before. They are more scientifically prepared to understand this phenomenon. The time is near for a new renewing of the energy of the planet and the beginning of new generations of more informed and knowledgeable humans on this planet. Thank you for listening. I am one who survived the last cataclysm on this planet.

Gilda M. Schaut

THE SOUL OF GEORGE

I am in your Aura and I came to tell you why, I am in the predicament in which, I find myself. I am a twelve-year-old boy. My parents think that I am a good boy, but I steal and drink, and even try to look at porno on the computer. I know that they suspect something is wrong but they can't find out, what it is. I am an artist in the way, I allow my parents to believe how good I am at following their rules.

How are you doing in school?

I am a B student. School is not a problem for me.

Why then do you do these things and tell me about them.

I am a spoiled boy and I want to do these things because I can.

Have you thought about the pain that your parents will feel when they find out?

Yes, it has crossed my mind. Yes I care. I think I am telling you this, because I am starting to feel scared.

Is it because of peer pressure?

No, it is I. Sometimes I think, I am bad soul and I pray that, somebody listens to me.

I am listening. You are not a bad soul. You need to think about your future and the joy that will be, to have a clean mind, heart and conscience, when you grow to be a young man. How proud your parents will be of you. Remember to make good choices and thank the Lord for all the blessings, you already have. I always will be here waiting to listen.

Response: Mrs. Gilda, thank you. My name is George and I will remember you often.

SOUL OF MARK

I am the expression of light that you call a soul. I am reincarnated in a physical body and my name is Mark. I am twenty-three years old. Thank you for listening. I am attracted to your aura because I want to learn how to be a medium. You know how to listen and how to concentrate. All my life I have had the desire to write and express the thoughts that came to mind.

Question: Where do you live?

Answer: I live in a state in the north. The reason for my awareness and the reason my guardian let me come to your aura now is because I am able to see and learn, the physical aspect has no relevance. I am Mark and I thank you for your help.

SOUL OF AMU

I am a soul that lived on this planet a long time ago. The reason I am here is because; I want to let you know that "time" is the idea that keeps us experiencing one act after another. At the time I was on your planet, the concept of exact time did not exist. We were a colony of about 300 people living on an island. We were aware that the sun came out every day, and the moon at night. We observed the growing of plants, children and the change of seasons. The concept of these events was what gave birth to the idea of "time." At that time, we recalled things from our past and explained it to others. It was quite difficult, but language developed slowly. To put things into perspective, we communicated with designs. Today they are called hieroglyphics. To us, that was the most exciting creative media, and we were very proud to be able to achieve this as a way of communication.

Question: Where did you live?

Answer: We lived in part of what is today the Mediterranean Sea. At that time the configuration of the continents was different. We were a group of Aryans, and we did not belong to any larger group of people.

Question: Why are you able to see all this progress ?

Answer: I am a soul in the twentieth sphere. My degree of evolution allowed me to recall the knowledge of my past incarnations.

Question: Can you see forward, with regard to time?

Answer: Time is relative. There is no concept of "time', when you are in your soul experience on the other side of the veil. You only experience time in relation to your existence as a human. The evolution of "time" has been a magical concept.

Gilda, It was a pleasure to talk to you. I am Amu, one of the souls who first populated your planet.

THE SOUL OF A JEALOUS HUSBAND

I am the soul of another person that wants to talk to you. I am in the ninth sphere, and I am ready to come back to earth. I was a man and I took a life. The reason for this terrible act was jealousy. I became enraged and blind with the idea that the only way to stop this relationship was by killing this man. After many years of terrible pain, and time to think about, what I did, I passed away and I did find myself in the position to see my past life, and to understand why my wife was infatuated with this man. To her, he represented the man I could never become. He was more educated, considerate and loving. He did not expect anything in return. I was the husband, and because of that, I thought I had the right to expect physical love, obedience and the compete confidence in my judgment. I realized that I was wrong and should have been more kind and considerate. This lesson is one of many, I have learned during my last incarnation. I am ready to begin a new life, and I am planning to be a better human being. I am the soul that thanks you for listening.

THE SOUL OF HELMUT R.

I am aware of the presence of your teacher Tumargeo. I am in my higher self. I am Helmut R. and I am a teacher at the German Institute of Research for Biogenetics. My research is in the reconstruction of nerve filaments and the improvement of movement and communication in the nerves that connect them. This experiment is an advanced development that will revolutionize the world of paralytics and other humans who suffer the terrible consequences of nerve severance. During my career as an M.D. and researcher, I observed that part of the healing process is not physical but spiritual. This thought stayed in my mind, so I began to see if I could reach that part of the cell which expresses the innermost part of the soul as light. It occurred to me that we all have a desire to heal ourselves and restore our own sources of wellness. How do we do that?

The process of healing is one of a cooperative effort between the cells and the soul. Sometimes this process happens during our sleep within the unconscious mind. The reason I went back to the process of basic functions the body uses to demonstrate health is because some people heal and some don't. Why does this work for some people but not others? Through genetic engineering, I discovered that the process that reactivates healing is a rearrangement of neutrons and other parts of atoms. This process changes the charge of the atoms and therefore the function. When I was able to see this visually, a connection happened in my mind! This was the basic change needed to restore the process of healing. This discovery has been kept a secret until now, because this understanding would call for changes at every level within the medical field. My participation in this discovery is only as a tool for the betterment of mankind.

Gilda, I am surprised and awed that you are able to hear me so clearly. This process of mind communication is new to me. Your teacher explained to me the necessity of these records and the results of your writing, as a demonstration of the power of mediumship. Thank you for the opportunity to express myself. I am Helmut R. who blesses you.

Gilda, The research M.D. who spoke to you yesterday is here today. He will continue his communications. I am Helmut R. and I came to express my gratitude for the acknowledgement of my work. The research started as a discovery and a puzzle that we were not able to understand. The many equations we needed to solve this puzzle were hidden in the most innermost part of the atom. Because of the recent discoveries of the tinniest particles called neutrinos, we were able to establish the connection we were looking for. The response of these connections was so amazing, that we were not able to believe that we finally found the answer to our dilemma.

We don't know what caused the reactivation of the healing process, but we understand how it manifests. The regeneration of a cell is due to a process, which is definitive, the product of changes in the innermost part of the atoms of that cell.

The process is too complicated for me to explain now. The result will revolutionize the process of healing and the length of time for recuperation in many diseases.

This wonderful news will be known this year. The application of these discoveries will be put into practice as soon as the Academy of Medicine approves of the procedures.

I am Helmut R. and I bless you.

SOUL OF ANDREW

I am the soul of a man who left this earth many years ago. My name is Andrew and yes, I was convicted of a crime of passion. During my formative years I learned that the love you give to others is like a cushion that helps you to protect yourself. This was my reasoning and as the years passed I found myself involved with a nice lady. She professed to love me, and I believed her. The truth is that she had a lover, and was after my money. We were together for about 12 years. The second year of our marriage we had a son, and later on two daughters. The truth came out; when in a rage she said that she had never loved me and that my son and daughters belonged to somebody else. The rage had blinded my senses, and I killed her. That was a painful satisfaction. The years I spent in prison were not as painful, as the remorse I felt. Only after I died, was I able to know the truth. Hortense, that was her name, was in love with the man that became a friend of our family. During the years of marriage, I trusted him, because he too was married. When I came to this side of the veil, I went through a long period of waiting and rehearsing in my mind all the terrible lies in my life. Then one day I thought about Hortense, and I asked where she was. Because there is no sense of time on this veil, I did not realize that she was here too.

The answer to my question came through a messenger of light, who appeared all of a sudden and said, "follow me." He took me to a desolate place, where there were several people trying to plant some crops. There she was, as pretty as I remembered her. She was so surprised to see me. We were allowed to talk. She explained to me that after they took me to prison, her children wanted to know why I had committed the crime of killing my wife. I never did let them know the truth, because I was so hurt and felt diminished. She explained to me, that the son was the only one who belonged to her lover. The two girls were mine. She was real sorry for all of the sorrow she caused not only to our family, but also to the family of her lover. To forgive is, an act of Divine Grace! I was not ready to forgive her and I returned to the same place. I did have lots of time to think, and I decided that the road to perfection is hard but the way we choose our course is the outcome of our future. At that same instant, the guide appeared again and said he was my guardian angel, there to answer my questions. That was like awakening to a new life! I had so many questions, and all of them were answered. The wheels of karma were responsible for many of my encounters and when I understood why I had to marry her, life took on another meaning. The sense of culpability, or guilt, began to leave my consciousness, and I felt like a big burden had been lifted from me. The love and compassion I was able to feel was tremendous and new vision of a better tomorrow came to mind.

I am a soul who came to you after a long period of time and I told you my story because I want everybody to know that the laws for humans are incomplete and unfair. Thank you for listening, God bless you.

SOUL OF CARMEN

I am the first one who is waiting to talk to you. Yes, you have many souls around you. My name is Carmen and I was alive during the Roman Empire. I was living in one of the provinces, and I was aware of the laws of the land. My father was a magistrate of the Imperial Palace. He decided to allow me to learn not only to read and write but also to learn, diction, rhetoric and the basic knowledge of the universe. Because we lived in a land conquered by Rome, every citizen was accountable to the state. The reason why we were counted was because of taxes. Each family had to contribute to the Roman Empire. I was privileged, in the sense of my family's wealth, but at the same time, I was conscious of the imposed discipline and restricted laws, that prevented our people from expressing their nationality.

Question: Where did you live?

Answer: We lived in Byzantium

I thank you for the opportunity to talk with you. I am Carman.

SOUL OF CATHERINE

I am a soul who was Catherine Cookson in her previous life. I am in a place of peace and light. The reason I was able to write all of those books is because I used the power of mediumship. Yes, you sense that! I was a medium and I was able to listen to every word that was sent to me. Writing the first book came to me as a test. I was depressed and without hope. I was resting one day, when all of a sudden a voice came to me and, as clear as a bell the voice said: Pick up paper, a pen and start writing. From then on I was guided all the time. My life was dedicated to write about the life of many souls who had experienced terrible times. The stories that I wrote were in part about those people. They came to me through meditation and helped me write their stories.

I know that you are a medium and listen to the stories of many people also. Gilda you are not only a medium but also a soul of light who has been chosen to write the truth of human evolution and to record the stories of souls who have crossed over. It is important that they be told at this time. The world is changing and people will listen to you. Thank you for listening. I am Catherine Cookson.

THE SOUL OF ADMAN

Adman: I am a family man. I am a religious man. My wife and I are Muslims. We have three children. To us Mohammad is like Jesus is to you. The concept of faith is what I don't understand.

Question: Why do people believe in different Gods? Why are we considered evil because we love God and his prophet?

Answer: The reason people believe in different names for God, is because we learn this concept from our families, and according to the country where we were born, we speak different languages and evolve different beliefs. GOD is one; GOD is Love, Light, Law and Life. The act of terrorism to impose your faith is not what your prophet wants and taught you to do. These acts of violence are the product of the minds of some corrupt leaders of your faith that want power and domination over the minds of the people.

Adman: Thanks for your answer and explanation. The Koran said: "Love one another." During the years when I was growing up my father showed me the importance of being good. He said listen Adam; life is too short to waste time in fighting or quarreling. The essence of life is to help others and be happy. He was right! Gilda, that is your name. I want to thank you for the conversation we had and ask you to pray for the resolution to our problems. I am Adman; I am in the sixth sphere. I am thirty-seven years old.

THE SOUL OF DANNY THOMAS

Gilda: The reason that you needed to pray and give thanks to the people, who have been the light of this world, is because you read the article about St. Jude's Hospital.

Marlo Thomas and her father are two beings of light. They came to this world with the assignment to help children with cancer. Their dedicated lives have been a blessing to thousands of children. Their work will continue to exist even after the cataclysm. Their united effort is known worldwide.

I am Danny Thomas. I am in your aura. I see that you are surprised. I came to tell you that the will of God is to pursue our purpose. In doing that you help us to help those in need.

During my life, I was led to work with children. As a teacher and a father, I realized that the most precious gift was the health of a child. During a year of great stress due to the war, I found out that a lot of children were affected with cancer. This was the beginning of my career as a leader in finding a cure and treatment for this terrible disease. I was aware of the necessity of a hospital specializing in the cure of children with cancer. I was in no condition to offer money, nor the knowledge needed to start this project. The inner voice was so clear. I was led to a person who was able to make all of my dreams possible. Doctor Henry helped me to initiate a project that would flourish, and fulfill all of my dreams. I was blessed with a wonderful wife and child. Marlo was my soul mate. She came to this world, to help me not only with my project, but to assure me this would be the purpose of her life too. I am so grateful for the many souls that through hard work and devotion have saved the life of so many children. Thank you Gilda for listening to me and to know that we are guided by the will of God.

THE SOUL OF A RESCUE WORKER IN HAITI DURING THE EARTHQUAKE

I am a soul of a person who was part of a team of rescue workers during the earthquake in Haiti. The devastation and misery was like a nightmare. Where people's homes and businesses once stood were now only piles of rubble. The streets were blocked with disabled cars, trucks and all kinds of debris. The stench of rotten food, dead people and animals permeated the air. The frustration of trying to communicate with these people and get their help to work with us was one of the worst problems that we had ever experienced. Their idea of why we were there was for us to provide to them anything they needed or wanted. They didn't have the idea of cooperation nor the discipline needed to alleviate their own problems. There was a lack of a basic sense of organization on their part and this created a major barrier to the proper distribution of goods and planning for shelters.

Compassion and the desire to help was the only reason I volunteered. This was an eye opener for me, because I did not realize before, how different, less educated and evolved other societies could be. I am a volunteer, who blesses you.

THE SOUL OF A PRIEST OF THE CATHOLIC CHURCH ~ UNKNOWN NAME

I am the spirit of a priest of the Catholic Church. During my life, I dedicated most of my time to help others and to listen to the confessions of my parishioners. My faith helped me to live a life of dedications and service. I thought I was right teaching what I knew to others. After I passed, I realized that not all the souls who were with me in this new place believed as I did. I talked to many other souls and each one said, they were there because they needed to review the actions and thoughts of their past life. I realized then that GOD is not a judge of people, that we are our own judge, and the past deeds that we try to see from this new perspective, doesn't have to do with the position in society that you previously had or the education, or social economic place. This new knowledge opened my eyes and made me understand that during our earthly life, we are guided to believe through the eyes of society and the place we acquired in this society. Titles, honors and degrees of education don't count on this side. Each soul has to reconcile his own mistakes and atone for them. When you realize this, you are able to see parts of your past life and feel the damage you have done with your thoughts or actions. I regret not being able to convey to you the importance of these statements.

The evaluation of your "sins" is most difficult part of our journey in the after life. Now I do believe in a GOD of forgiveness and a redeemable life that await us in the future. Yes, I do believe in reincarnation. This idea was in the back of my mind, but I never wanted to let it grow because it is not part of the dogma of the Catholic religion. Now I know that it is the truth. I have seen part of other incarnations in my past and it is a logical explanation, as to the growing of the soul in the evolution and the opportunity to repay with kindness for the mistakes of a previous life. Miss Gilda, I thank you for the opportunity of explaining this part of a process called "Evolution of the Soul" that I was not aware of. I am a priest who passed away one year ago.

THE SOUL OF OSCAR ~ TWIN TOWERS

I am the soul of one of the victims that died on September 11, 2001. My name is Oscar and I was a server in the dinning hall. I remember the impact and tremors that followed, then the idea of an earthquake. Several of my coworkers ran to the door and tried to exit to the hall. Seconds later, we saw a light that reflected on the windows and we realized that we had a fire. The noise of the alarms and the confusion was such that, no one knew how to behave. The noise and anxiety increased, when somebody told us to exit, because an airplane had hit the building. I ran with the others to the elevator and then to the stairs. The light was shut off and we started to descend. We were on the fourth floor. I thought of my family and that helped me to control my emotions. I have to live for them. They needed me. I was almost to the ground floor, when the second shaking of the building happened. The masses of people on those stairs and the panic were indescribable. Somebody yelled that the second tower had been hit. We reached the main floor. There we saw the firefighters and their equipment. We were almost free. Then a big explosion happened and it ended thousands of lives. I found myself looking at that inferno from above. I was wondering if I was dreaming. I saw the next building in flames and the implosion, of that one too. I could not believe what I was experiencing. Then I realized that I was alive! Yes, I thought that I was alive and that vision was just an idea of what had happened. I tried to find other people like me and there were so many! We stayed around there and we could not comprehend what had happened. After a long time, we realized, that we could not go back home. This massive group of people were displaced and guided to a special place, where many other souls served as guides. We were instructed telepathically to wait and follow our guides. There were people like us; very normal people and I thought that this was a program of the Federal Government to help us. Man, I was wrong! My turn came and our guide took us to our new place. This was not the building that I expected. This was not New York, and I started to doubt myself and where we were. Somebody in the group asked where we were. The answer was: You are in the Sixth Sphere and you are in your etheric bodies. The realization of the finality of this statement came to us like thunder. The presence of a personal guide appeared in front of me and I was guided to a different place. My mind needed explanations. I surrendered myself in sorrow and thoughts of concern for my family and my coworkers. I remained in that state of awareness for a long time. Emotional pain was the source of all of my thoughts. The sense of time was lost, and all of a sudden, I woke up to a new environment.

The light changed, as did my surroundings. I asked why and the same guide stood in front of me and said it was time for me to know the truth. He asked me to follow him and I was now in front of a screen. The film of my life was now on the screen. The recollection of many acts of love and kindness that I had given and received was all there. Also there were my negative thoughts and actions. I realized that we are the judge and the one who understands, why all of these things happened to us. My life was cut short, and I knew that I was supposed to live several more years. At the end, I saw the terrible episode of the destruction of the Twin Towers. My heart was full of pain. I cried and cried, not only for me, but also for my family, friends and the sadness that there are people in this world who don't respect other human lives. That was like a cleansing of my soul. I realized that life is eternal and that, only God knows the reason, why all of these terrible things happen.

Today, I am talking to you from a very different perspective. The recollection of many past incarnations has allowed me to understand the progressive development of the soul of humans. These cumulative experiences give the advantage, to be more compassionate and caring. Also, we are more appreciative of the acts of kindness of others. The evolution of the soul offers us the opportunity to study, to be more useful to others, to be in a better position to express a better life and to be a better human being. This law of free will is universal law that is applied, when we are in this plane, or on a physical expression on a planet. I have learned many physical lessons, since I have been here. The most important is to know that we are one with God and his creations. I am Oscar, and I thank you for patience and understanding. God bless you.

THE SOUL OF ANTONIO ~ TWIN TOWERS

I am the Soul of a fireman; I was in New York on September 11th. I belonged to the rescue squad that went to the aid of the people in the Twin Towers. My name is Antonio R. We entered the building of tower #1, and immediately realized that the automatic system was in place. The alarms and the water sprinklers were going full speed. The people in the building were in a state of panic. I remember telling my friend Rosco, if we make it, it will be a miracle.

We proceeded with the basic requirements. Then we tried to organize an orderly exit. People were too scared to obey orders. During a period of about 20 minutes, we proceeded with the extending of the hoses and the spraying of burning materials. Then our chief told us that the second tower was on fire. I could not believe it. Time was like a movie. I was the spectator of chaos. The urgency of the moment gave us an adrenaline push, and we were trying our best to help contain that fire. We went to the service stairs, and from there climbed to the 52nd story.

People were crying and praying. The stench of the gas from the plastics on fire was overwhelming. I remember a person who told me: Son, God bless you, and he disappeared through the smoke. It was then, that we felt the terrible explosion. The whole building began to collapse. At that moment, I knew we were in trouble. I regained consciousness minutes after. I was in my etheric body. I could hear the wail and screaming of the people. In a second, I was on the front of building #2 watching, how the fires consumed that building too. Then I saw Rosco he was at my side. He looked petrified. I talked to him, and he responded: "I knew it, I knew it." We were aware that we hadn't made it. I stayed there until the 2nd tower collapsed. I saw thousands of people run for their lives. At that moment I thought, we have been attacked, but by whom? Everything was like a fast movie.

Then I began to think about what has happened to me. I looked around, and I only saw the debris. I felt my body, and I thought: "How did I survive?" I didn't feel any pain, and I can see, think and move around. The pain in my soul was like a wall that was around me. I was part of that disaster and my mind was confused. As a firefighter, I was use to complying with orders. This time I was alone. Then, I remembered a prayer that my mother taught me when I was a child. The love and comfort of that very moment brought tears to my eyes. I realized that only God could save his children. At that moment, the whole scenario changed, and I found myself in an impressionably large depot and there were thousands of people there. The impression I got was that I was going somewhere. A man dressed in a particular outfit came to me and said my name. He told me to follow him. In an instant we were in another place. This place was a secluded part of a park. There was a podium of sorts, and a screen, like that of a movie theater. The visions I saw of my past life were overwhelming, I cried. I was very aware that was a movie of past events of my life. I was able to see my family and their sorrow. I could see my fellow firemen and how, they too were leaving the earth, like me. I asked the guide "why, why did God allow this to happen?" He said to me: God is his creation. He gave man free will. These acts of revenge are the work of sick minds that want to impose their faith and beliefs, upon the rest of the world. It is then, that I understood that the Arabs had done this.

When this episode ended, I realized that the guide was talking to me, without a sound! I was listening to his words, as you are listening to me. Dear Lady, thank you for listening and for documenting these moments. I am Antonio R, one firefighter who died on tower #1.

THE SOUL OF GEORGE

I am another victim of 9/11. I was working in the 2nd Tower. My name is George and I worked for a money market company. The working day had just started; we were busy uploading the computer when a big bang shook the building. During these few minutes I thought it was an earthquake. Then I realized people were screaming and we ran into the halls. There we learned that an airplane had hit the 1st tower. Our first idea was that it was pilot error. We then tried to go to the other side, where we could see what was happening. Panic started pervading all the people of the 69th floor and I remember asking myself if this was really happening and what should I do?

Soon we heard the fire alarms go on and everybody started running to the exits. There are several exits and all of them were full of people. We started our descent and a cold feeling engulfed us. Many were debating to wait and see. Many decided to go down.

Almost all the people were silent and tense. The more we went down, we encountered more and more people and desperation were on the faces of many. We reached the 46th floor. Then a big impact shook the building and we knew that this was happening in our building. After that I remember praying ...

The lights started going off and the emergency lights took over. A lady said to me "please if you make it, call my husband" and gave me his name and number. Somebody who came to join us told us that the building was not only on fire, but airplanes have impacted both buildings. This last news was like a wave of fear spreading through us all. Many started pushing their way out. Panic was rampant and to stay safe, you let the scared people pass. Three more floors down, I realized the building was trembling. This was the last sign of doom ...

Then I was awake and walking. I remember looking up to see where the airplanes had hit the building! I wanted to know what had happened. The explosion and implosion of the building was a sight to remember. I saw so many people screaming in the streets. Then I saw a policeman. He was carrying a man in his arms. This made me think, why am I not hurt? The reality of being on the ground floor and walking out without a scratch was too much!

It was then, that I began to realize I was not alive! I desperately wanted to tell others that everything was all right, that we were alive! When I realized that nobody heard me. I tried to help. I ran to the nearest victim, who was a lady that was in shock. Paramedics were there and she regained consciousness. She did not know that I was there! I could not explain what was happening to me. Then all of the sudden a guide came to my rescue. He was a tall, young man and he let me know that I was in a transition state and soon I would be finding my way. His presence was like a breath of peace. I instantly became aware of a multitude of people walking and I joined them. They all looked sad and tired and many took one path, others another, many kept walking next to me. I was thinking of how I would get back home! I had no idea of where I was. The image of my wife and daughter Susan came to mind. Do they know what happened? Maybe they will try to contact me.

In this vast valley I walked what seemed like hours. I stopped and I realized that I wasn't tired. At this place I looked around and I saw many animals. I wondered where I was. The tall guy that talked to me at the beginning appeared again and explained that I was in a different sphere or dimension and all those animals were in their etheric bodies, as I was also. I could not believe it! I approached one of the animals. It was a nandu (ostrich) and it looked at me like I a was solid man. I asked why I was seeing all of this and able to hear, smell, walk and think? The guide told me that when we enter this new dimension we carry with us all these bodies. The only one left on earth is our physical one. Then I understood that I was dead. The finality of this thought was overwhelming. That means I will not be able to see or hear my beloved ones again! The guide told me that was not the truth, that in due time I will be able to see and talk to them. I did not believe it. Then during a period of recollections, I was taken to witness a healing. That was you and your guide praying. What I saw was unbelievable. The rays of light expanded yards and yards from your aura. I realized then that I could talk to you and you can listen. Your teacher allowed me to express myself. Yes today, two years ago I was just another man working in one of the towers. Tell the people of the USA, that we deserve peace and we deserve freedom because we are aware of the joy that this brings to our soul. I am George, who wishes you many blessings.

THE SOUL OF DUARTE

I was chosen to talk to you. I am the soul of a magistrate, who came to this side of the veil, many years ago. I took a long time to accept the idea, that I was dead. I was thinking of the past and creating with my mind, stages where I could justify my way of thinking. My name is Duarte, and I realize that all my surroundings never change. When I asked why I found the answer. My idea that life stops, when you leave your physical body, was the reason for this mental image. I decided to find out, why I was here. It was then, that a guide approached me and explained to me the news that changed my life. It was like, to be born again. My mind was open, to this new fountain of information, and I began to learn my relationship to past incarnations and which roll we play in the family. It is only then, that I recognize the false, thoughts that keep me in the state of inertia. Lady, I am telling you this, just in case a reader sees this, and remembers this experience, when his time is ready to come to this side. The truth will make you free! Thank you for listening and I congratulate you for your work.

THE SOUL OF A HINDU MAN

Greetings, I am a man who is 46 years old. I live on a mountain with my wife, two daughters and one son. All my life I have been told that, God is the source of all there is. What I don't understand is the disparity of races, and the bad feeling between people of different races. I have a feeling that you understand what I am asking. I am Hindu, and in this country there are several casts. This is one of the things that worried me.

Question: When we leave this earth, will we go to a place similar to this?

Answer: Dear friend, the concept of different casts is an invention of the human mind. There are no casts. Every human being is a unique creation of God. His spirit abides in each soul. When your soul leaves this planet, a new awareness of whom you are, will awaken your mind to a place of peace and light. You will be able to meet many other people you knew, and see for yourself that those beliefs were created to divide, and dominate others. You are a good soul and you care for your family and neighbors. God be with you.

Question: Dear Lady, if I died, do you think God will allow me to visit my family?

Answer: Yes, you will be able to do so in your etheric body, which is a copy of your last physical body.

THE SOUL OF LAVINIA

I am a soul who was watching you write the thoughts of others. This intrigued me. I am guided to come to you because I need help. During my life, I was a teacher in a school in Alabama. There, life was hard and the people were poor. When my time came to come to this side, I said to myself: "Girl, you are too young to die." I was thirty-seven years old. My pupils cried, because they loved me and appreciated my kindness. Now that I am here, I see that the years you live are not important. What you accomplish in the relationships with your family and friends, and how you treat other people is what is important.

I am in the sixth sphere, and I see many people, like me, who are learning new ideas of what life is all about. I am alive and I am planning to find out more about this process of reincarnation, that I was not aware of before. I was a Baptist. The ideas of the devil and many others need to be revised. They can damage the minds and souls of many. I am aware of the blessing of Light, Love and the assistance of beings of light, which are always ready to help everybody. Thank you for allowing me to express my thoughts. I am Lavinia.

THE SOUL OF ALBERT

My name is Albert and I am in the eight sphere. During my life as a metal worker, I encountered many men who think almost the same way that I used to think. If you are a good provider for your family, and work hard, what you think or do doesn't have any importance. How wrong I was! The value of our thoughts and the impact of them on family, friends, or other people is of the most importance. During my marriage, I treated my wife with contempt and I always expected respect and to be obeyed by her. That was not right. She suffered in silence because of the children. They learned a false concept of relationships. I am at this side of the veil now, and after a long period of consideration; I was taken to a place where I was able to see my life, since I was born. There were many things I had forgotten and many things that I did not want to remember. When I was watching the way that I had treated her I felt her resentment and pain. Then I realized that the only important things in the earth life are thoughts and good actions. All the rest is nothing. This recognition has allowed me to rectify my beliefs and to apply it as knowledge for my next incarnation. These patterns of experiences are like chips in a computer. It will stay in my mind's bank forever. I am Albert and I bless you.

THE SOUL OF DARWIN

I am in a place of light and I would like to communicate with you. I was assigned to write the development of the human race, and I did so, from the viewpoint of genetic adaptation. I am the soul of Darwin and I came to tell you, the real evolution of a race, here or on other planets is the evolution of the soul. When the soul is capable of experiencing love, compassion, and understanding, only then do the cells of DNA re-arrange and become capable of expressing a refined body and mind. During my research, I was completely sure that it was a physical adaptation that caused evolution. How wrong I was! The evolution of the soul is the only motivator for change in behavior.

The soul is the one who moves the body and mind, to achieve different patterns of life in humans and mammals. The mind is the tool of the soul. The brain is the computer. The emotional body is a tool to cushion the impacts of ideas that are too soft or too hard to express. The control of ones emotions is one of the most difficult tasks to accomplish. I am explaining this to you, because I can see that you can understand. These characteristics are not equal through the Universe. There are different kinds of humans on other planets, who evolved in different ways.

The purpose of my studies was to explain why the process of evolution took place. Now, I know better. I have to realize that, at the time; that idea was unrealistic but possible. Scientists are aware only of facts, and according to their findings, they agreed with my reasoning. The time has come, to rectify these studies, and the future generations will see, the power of the soul is a co-creator of changes in the forms or bodies that express their beings on the planet. I am Darwin and I bless you.

SOUL OF RAUL

I am the soul of a merchant who dedicated my life to sell arms. My name is Raul Espinoza. Please listen to me. When I came to this side, I first had to accept that life is eternal. I also had realized that I was not in my physical body, but in a ethereal one. This ethereal copy of the human body is for the purpose of identification. As long as we remain in this body, teachers, members of our family, friends and acquaintances will be able to recognize us. I also learned to recognize all of my mistakes and the mistreatment of other human beings.

I was born in Bogotá, Columbia. My family taught me good principles and provided me with a suitable education. During my youth I experimented with drugs, which led me into selling arms. I realized that the way I was living my life wasn't good, but I was only thinking about the comfort that I could provide for my family and myself. That was my way of justifying what I was doing.

The reason that I am telling you about my life is, because I know that you chose a path that dedicated a good portion of your life to help and educate others. I witness how you receive these messages. Your hearing is as clear as a telephone. There is not compassion in those people who promote drugs. I sense a great culpability.

During my years as a married man, I never thought that my trade would affect my children. They knew what I did for a living. They were ashamed of my roll in society contaminated with drugs and weapons of destruction. They wanted to have nothing do with me. Teresa my daughter told me that she would not be at my side when I die. I began to feel pain in my bones and soon found out that I had cancer, and that is what caused my death!

When I crossed over to this side, I was so surprised to see that I was alive! At first I felt an emotion of happiness and then of sadness and pain, when I realized that I was alone without my family. I was surrounded by a lot of people who were going from one place to another. I asked where I was, and the answer was: The place of remembrance! I asked for help, and a being of light with a white tunic and a golden scepter suddenly appeared. His name was Orion and he is my guardian angel. Orion guided me to anther place and there I saw parts of my past life, like in a movie. This three-dimensional movie was in color and was about people, and their choice to use drugs and weapons. I saw in horror, how these innocents died because they chose the wrong path in life. I felt a great sense of culpability.

Now I know that all the negative things I did were creating negative karma that will have to be repaid. God doesn't blame us. We ourselves have to recognize our mistakes, and pay for them in future lives. After this process, I know God in his infinite grace; will give us the chance to renew our lives with new opportunities to the service of others. Thank you Ms. Gilda for listening. God Bless you.

SOUL OF CARL

I am your brother in Christ. I came to you because my mentors told me you are one able to listen to me. My name is Carl and I am twenty-three years old. I live in a country where liberty is a bad word. All of my life I have been tied to mandates and orders. These restrictions are like a burden on my soul. When I was two years old, my father took me for the first time to a mosque. From then on I have been always told what to do.

Question: Why do you feel this is so hard?

Answer: Because I am able to see that there are other humans in this world, that don't live the way I do. I am a Muslim, and according to the Koran, I am to obey the orders of the Mulas. They are the ones who make the rules and arrange our lives.

Question: Are you in this dimension, or at the other side of the veil?

Answer: I am alive! Yes, you can say that I am liberated of my physical body. I can still think, remember, see, and feel the pain of my brothers and sisters. I can understand why I was not able to be objective, when my family and friends surrounded me. I think I was content, knowing that I had a loving father, and mother, and the company of my sister Acme and brother Isbar.

I wish and hope that the time ahead of us will bring peace and a new way of thinking to the people of my country. God bless you for listening. I am Carl in the six sphere.

THE SOUL OF A PRIEST OF THE CATHOLIC CHURCH ~ JOSE RODRIGO

I am the soul of a priest who lived in Spain, at the beginning of the 1600th century. My name is Jose Rodrigo de Santiago, and I was chosen as an exemplary monk at my convent. During my short life, I was able to express the same mediumship qualities that you have. I started praying for the sick, and it was then, that I realized that the energy of healing was passing through my body and exiting my hands. Healing, this divine grace, helped me to continue with my prayers and ask for understanding for those, who were in need.

When I was 20 years old, my superiors chose me to go on a pilgrimage to Compostela. There I found my mission. At this place, I realized what God had in mind for me to do. I had a vision of our Lord Jesus Christ, and I heard: "Dear brother, you life is of light and your actions will be blessed by God." During those moments, my soul felt as if, I was soaring in Heaven. The radiant light that surrounded me, made me feel like, I had no physical body.

After that experience, my superior assigned me to a Parish as curator of that church. My life as a monk and my service to God, was a test of service. My mission was accomplished. Now I know that the dedication and prayers of my soul were an example to many of my successors. Today I am called "San Joseph of Compostela."

The truth is, that my soul was guided, and my mission accomplished.

I came to tell you, that your life too has been guided and you too came to this planet with a mission. Your mission is almost at the end. I will pray for your soul and the prompt and successful reality of the publication of your books. I am Santiago de Compostela, your friend in Christ.

SOUL OF MARILYN B.

I am the sister of a friend and my name was Marilyn. I am in your mist and I was summoned to your aura to tell you about my death and removal of my soul, due to an accident. The day I was driving, the car behind me was not able to stop in time. The life of my children and the sorrow of my dear husband, I know how much the family had to suffer. I am not completely aware of the process of evolution. I do know that I am in the transition period that humans call purgatory. I am aware that you are a medium and you can understand what I am saying because I see your aura pulsating and changing colors. We are all spirit and we are all part of the All. Go to my sister and to my beloved husband, I send them all my love. Tell them that the reason I am here is because I have to go to a course of instructions to understand why the soul is the vehicle of the "I Am." You know that already and you are still in your physical body! Dear sister pray for me but do not be worried about my soul, I am in a place of love and light.

There are thousand and thousands of souls, all in a state of transition. The reason I am here is to learn and be guided. The angel of light that is my guide is named Romie, and is standing at my side. I am constantly provided with everything I need, the love and affection of God, the light and the beautiful surroundings. The things that you think are needed in your plane are not needed here. Life as I know it now is only the expression of my soul in the fourth sphere of space and I am one with God. I am aware of the presence of beings of light, who guide and teach us. I do think my physical body is now my etheric body. My mind is the recapitulation of memories. I am being instructed to revise these memories and when I learn how to reconcile all the actions and facts that made up my being on earth; then I will be ready to go into another dimension, and know why I made so many mistakes, or why as a soul, we are not all equal. I am grateful that you have listened to me, give my love to my husband and children.

SOUL OF ROBERT

Gilda, I am a soul, who has committed many bad things during my previous lives. When I came to live on this planet I was aware that this was not a place where I wanted to live. My parents were poor and with minimal education. In their struggle to survive, and provide, for my siblings, and me they turned to God and asked for help. They died very young and we were left alone. It was my responsibility to take care of my brother and two sisters. I wasn't ready to work or provide for them. I found myself at times begging for food. Then a man asked me if I wanted a job. I was fourteen years old. He treated me with care and kindness. His name was Albert. After two years he let me go, because he didn't need me anymore. My siblings were too small to work and the city where I lived, took charge of their lives. I am ashamed to tell you I felt such relief. My next boss was a bad man that took advantage of my situation and worked me near to death. During a heated discussion, I picked up a shovel and hit him in the head. He died three days later. I was charged and sent to prison for ten years. I asked myself why did this happen to me? During the time that I was in prison, I met many men and listened to their stories, and why they were there.

One of them told me that before I came to this planet, I was alive in heaven and had to return because I had to pay for a Karmic death. I did not understand what he was taking about. After I finish my confinement, I was free. The recession was over and it was easy to find a job. I died alone, because of a very high fever. I was thirty-two years old. I am now in a place that God assigned to others and me, like me. During all this time I have regained the memories of my previous lives and now understand why my life was so arduous. Dear Lady, thank you for listening to my story and for believing (like I do now) That God is love, life, light and law. I am Robert, your friend in Christ.

Two Days Later

I am in your aura. I am the same soul who you listened to two days ago. I am Robert, yes!. I came to tell you what I have learned about the mercy of God. As I told you, I lost my parents and my siblings during that incarnation. After a long period of rest, at this side of the veil, an angel of light appeared in front of me and he said: "by the mercy of God, you will be able to see your parents and siblings." As in a dream, my parents and siblings were in front of me. They looked young and healthy. They embraced me and they said that during the time that they were on this side, they had learned a lot about reincarnation and how to control their minds. These two facts, allowed them to express their higher self in a better way, and to be able to prepare for what they had to do in their next incarnation. They said they knew what had happened to my siblings and me. It was a very emotional encounter. I needed to know about this, and I found such a relief in my soul.

Question: What about your brother and sisters?

Answer: They are in a different place where I have no access now to reach them.

Dear Lady, thanks for listening to me. I am Robert in the eighth spiritual sphere.

THE SOUL OF A FATHER AND TEACHER

I am the soul of a man who passed to this new dimension about one hundred years ago. The place was New York, and the cause of my demise was cancer. During my long illness, I had lots of time to think about my life. When I arrived at this side of the veil, the reality of what saddened me was intriguing. I was like living again in New York, without the pain, but with all the other people, housing, stores, etc. This went on for a long period. Then one day I recognized a friend that had passed away, years before me. He greeted me and started conservation. This seemed odd. I was dead, and in another place. I asked him why he was there, he answered that he was attracted to this place according to the thoughts he had entertained. I wanted to know more.

I decided to explore and I walked to the edge of the river, and there was this man waiting for me. His name is Jonathan and he is my guardian angel. He answered most of my questions and asked me if I wanted to move on. I said yes, and I found myself in a different place, surrounded by people, and there was a sound that harmonized everyone's auras. I felt a sense of peace and contentment. Then my guide asked me if I wanted to find out about my past life.

Instantly, I found myself in an amphitheater, and there in front of me, big as real life, was the story of my life. When I realized the many mistakes I made with the power given to me, as a teacher, father, and husband, I was ashamed and full of sorrow. The pain that I had caused was so intense that I asked how I could repay these people.

My guardian angel explained to me, that the actions that were made in anger will be repaid by kindness, and the ones that showed contempt to members of my family, will be repaid by being in a position of dependence. The idea of reincarnation crossed my mind. Yes, said my guide you will have many opportunities for retribution. I am the soul of a father; a teacher and I thank you for your kindness.

CARL SAGAN

QUESTION: Is the other side of the veil as you expected?

ANSWER: In the process called "death," the soul evaporates from the physical body. I am Carl Sagan, your brother in Christ. I do know that your Teacher guides you and you wanted to know if I was OK. The condition of life on this sphere is of constant change. The mind produces the images which surround us and because of that it is like a constant movie.

The only reason why I was not able to correct my instability is because as of yet, I am not able to assimilate the process of reincarnation.

When I arrived here, I was exposed to a revision of the process of my life and it was an incredulous spectacle! I know that it is not possible to remember every detail, but I do know that the most important was the time dedicated to my profession, to my studies and to trying to understand the Universe. I know that I wanted to do thousands of things and I never did have the time or opportunity. I know that I still have a lot to learn and I see I do have the ability to communicate through vibrations of decibels almost imperceptible for the human ear. This is incredible! The voice that you listen to is nothing more than the acoustic projection of my thoughts. Your mind receives them and transcribes them in your language. I have to confess that I have never seen something similar. I am your friend in Christ, Carl Sagan. I will talk to you again. Au revoir!

QUESTION: Are you happy to be able to ask so many questions and find the answers and reference in the place you are at?

ANSWER: I am Carl Sagan and I want to express my gratitude for your prayers. As I told you, I am surprised and reverent to find out that life is a continuous endeavor and the reason for that is the ever evolving soul that must be expressed through us.

The consciousness of GOD is his creation.

We are part of that evolving consciousness.

The light that fills the atoms is nothing else than the LIGHT OF THE SPHERES! Yes!

I have seen and finally found the explanation to the mysteries of life.

The perception we as humans have of atoms is the structural part of the reality. Ye are Light! How true is that statement!

The potential for learning and for explaining theories that puzzles humankind is at our fingertips.

The illusion and mystery that seems to surround religious ideologies is nothing more than a step to express knowledge that has been kept from humans because we are not ready to accept our place in the Universe.

QUESTION: Can you elaborate on that?

ANSWER: The evolution of most humans is not sufficient to let them understand and believe that GOD IS. I do see that you are most aware of this process of evolution.

QUESTION: You must find it fascinating to see how the law acts in the Universe.

ANSWER: Everything that I so painstakingly studied I encountered on this plane as a matter of fact.

Without going into details, I will tell you that the most awesome sight of the Cosmos is the view of the expanding Universe. The realization that as humans we are able to comprehend that idea is awesome.

QUESTION: Are you able to see planets of our Solar System?

ANSWER: The solar system or SOLOGA is the most beautiful sight you will ever see! In the next incarnation I will be able to not only teach but to manifest the ideas and teachings that I am learning at the present time.

I see that we have to say good-bye. God Bless You.

QUESTION: Are humanoids on other planets?

ANSWER: Yes. The realization came to me when for the first time in my life I dared to think that we were not alone in the Universe.

The Constellation of Andromeda alone has so many inhabited planets that it is impossible for us to imagine.

QUESTIONS: Have you been able to learn anything new about this? Where are you now?

ANSWER: It is my most pressing desire to pursue the study of this subject. I am not allowed yet to travel extensively through the Cosmos.

QUESTION: Are you aware of any big changes on our planet in the near future?

ANSWER: Yes. It is a known fact that Planet Earth will be affected by a distortion of it's axis and that will produce great changes in the outer crust of the Earth's structure. This will happen during the second part of the millennium.

QUESTION: Is there something that you want to say to us as humans?

ANSWER: I will accept the challenge. I do want to convey a message of most importance. The resources of the planet, like water, air, and soil, are the most important basic substances for the people who live on the planet. The balance, cleanliness and rightful use of these resources are most important. Each one of them is absolutely needed to maintain equilibrium in nature.

Gilda, I do thank you for the opportunity to express myself and I want to send my love and appreciation to my colleague, John who always knew the truth and never told me. I am Carl Sagan.

QUESTION: I want to ask you to please tell me how to be a better expression of GOD!

ANSWER: Greetings. I am Carl Sagan and I want to explain to you how and when I realized the ONENESS of GOD.

The soul is an expression of GOD that represents an infinitesimal part of the Universe.

As such, it is formed of light. Because that light is part of the consciousness that is God, we are ONE.

Yes, the light is the all-encompassing media that unites all creation.

QUESTION: Is the light the same in other constellations?

ANSWER: The question will be: Is light the common denominator and the same throughout the universe?

Yes, it is. The physical expression of the stars and planets of each constellation are different because they express different degrees of evolution.

QUESTION: What about the Black Holes?

ANSWER: Black holes are duplicate realities of different polarization. In that case, the system of attraction is like a magnet that is trying to pull away a force as big as itself.

QUESTION: The effort Earthlings are making to communicate with Extraterrestrial is not working and it has been explained to me by my Teachers the reason why it is so. Can you suggest a more reasonable and effective way to communicate with our more advanced brothers?

ANSWER: Our space brothers are aware of the effort that you mention. They are aware of your Earthly desire to interchange communications.

The reason for their muteness is because humans are not ready to accept other teachings, other forms of humanoids, and other forms of expressions in the Universe.

Our concept of GOD and creation is childish and the basis for that knowledge is based solely on holy books. The spiritual side has not been addressed because that would cause tremendous emotional and monetary catastrophes on the planet.

Religious believers have sponsored the idea of creation.

Science is the faculty to understanding, through the mind, the true process of creation.

QUESTION: Then to be able to know the truth, will we have to wait years for scientific evolution, physically and spiritually?

ANSWER: The understanding of physical matter has changed greatly because of scientific discoveries.

The challenge that the space program is providing and the new metaphysical revolution will prepare the consciousness of future generations for a change that not only is possible but is a must!

I am Carl Sagan and I want to finish this communication with this thought: The advancement of the human race will be a fact and the next generation will be able to transmit and receive message throughout the cosmos!

Yes, the evolution of each soul encompasses progress in different scopes of his/her personality.

The element of concentration and dedication that you put into your pursuits of metaphysics and spiritual values, are applied to the study of the physical expression of GOD.

LASSITER

Did Carl Sagan belong to the Extension School of Instructors in a previous incarnation? Are you aware of his mission as an astronomer, teacher and heralder of new concepts for this planet?

I am Lassiter. I am one of the students of the School of SOLOGA. Gilda, the question you ask about the School of Extension Instructors is knowledge that is reserved for advanced souls who guide and instruct leaders in the field of Astronomy. Planet Earth is a small planet, young in evolution and knowledge. The progress attained until now, by Sagan, is not enough or sufficient to allow souls of his evolution to partake in these advanced studies.

Why is this information available to mankind then?

The knowledge of the Universe is available to the minds of humans as an incentive to develop their inner souls. In the case of Carl Sagan, he was a soul who attained a good degree of space knowledge and the recognition of fellow humans. The purpose of his life as a forerunner of intergalactic awareness is in no way a demonstration of spiritual development. The source of spiritual understanding is not the intellect. In this case he was an instrument of knowledge and a medium to promote new ideas and understanding.

I am your friend and co-worker in the realm of Light and I understand your surprise. Your past incarnation was one of friendship and your life was well-developed around theories and studies of the occult. When the time comes that you will be able to learn why you are able to talk to me so easily then we will be able to see each other and renew our friendship. I am Lassiter, your friend in Christ.

MELKEDISECK

The purpose of mentioning my name, Melkediseck, is because I am in charge of part of the Cosmos that includes your Solar System.

The Constellation of Andromeda is my base home.

The Lactean or Arimea (Milky Way) Constellation as it is called by other beings of light is where your solar system is.

The evolution of your planet is in great danger and that is the reason for this publication. We will assist you and your teachers and we'll help you to discern the facets of progress and changes that will be mentioned in the future. The realignment and synchronicity of the planets will be a fact.

The cataclysm and violent atmospheric changes will be a fact. The eruption of volcanic lava *will* happen.

Most of the continents will be in peril of one source or another.

Gilda, this is not a warning. This is the statement of an advanced Master who prays for the souls of your planet.

I am Melkediseck and I bless you.

ARCHANGEL URIEL

I am the Spirit of Light, Uriel. I come to bless you and to tell you that your mission this year will be to overcome rancor and express forgiveness. You can advance in the path of light if you have no thoughts of rancor.

Gilda M. Schaut

QUESTION: Even if it is justified?

ANSWER: The person who knowingly commits an unjust act is the person who has to account to the law of cause and effect. If you do not participate in that act then you are only a spectator; you should not judge.

ROMAN GLADIATOR

You are a mirror of light. I am in your aura and I bless you. I am the spirit of a roman gladiator who lived in the year 7 BC and who was present during the coming of Jesus to this Earth. At that time the Jewish custom allowed families to travel from one town to another and from one village to another to look for work or comply with their religious life.

During that time, the Praetorian Chief gave an order to count the inhabitants of the region of Judea and Galilee because that region was full of transient people, and it was not easy to collect taxes. This was the reason why Joseph and Mary went to Bethlehem to subscribe their names as residents. I am Auculcus and I have, in my astral memory, this explanation.

QUESTION: Did you see Jesus?

ANSWER: I was a roman soldier and as such my obligations or duties did not allow me to mix with the common people. That explanation was only to let you know why Mary and Joseph went to Bethlehem.

I am your Guardian Angel Gabriel and I am guiding you to listen to your inner voice.

Jesus had a childhood full of love and dedication from his parents. His religious instruction opened his mind to a new way of seeing things and when he was able to listen to his inner voice he recognized that they were mistaken and that he was a Divine Messenger. In his I AM he understood his mission and saw that his destiny was to teach to all the people of Planet Earth and not only to Jews. His words were listened to by many and his truths were a fountain of love and peace, which brought many to reflection.

Gilda, you must listen to your friends, brothers, sisters, sons and relatives in the same way that Jesus knew how to respect the religious ideas of his parents. You will have to respect those who are around you for they are not capable of understanding nor feeling what you know. Smile then, because they have not a worry in the world thinking that they are right. God Bless you, the peace of the Lord is with you.

ARCHANGEL GABRIEL

I am in your aura and bless you. I am the Spirit of Light, Gabriel. Your mission is of love, understanding, and teaching. You should understand that each person has his own path and in it he can choose several alternatives using free will. Not to think of a spiritual progress would be a sign of spiritual rigidity which in turn would make the inhabitants of the planet, robots. Your reading of Urantia has given you an understanding of how difficult it was for Jesus not to demonstrate his glorious origin and intelligence. He decided to demonstrate with examples and parables. His life was an example of love and brotherhood and in your case, you will have to demonstrate what you learn.

SAINT TERESA OF THE ANDES

I am in your aura and bless you. I am your friend in Christ, Saint Teresa of Los Andes. Yes, I do know that you are surprised. Your Guardian Angel Gabriel gave me permission to come to your aura. I was the one that inspired you to sing. Praise be to GOD. Praise be to his name. You listen very well and sing it just as it should be.

Gilda, I want to tell you that the privilege to know what you know is due to many, many years of service. You can remember the past if you want to and ask your teachers what you did in other incarnations.

In the vineyard of the Lord

We are one in his kingdom

Dear Sister in Christ, ask help from your teachers, they are anxious to guide you.

SAINT FRANCIS

I am your brother in Christ, Hillarion. I am a disciple of San Augustine. The purpose of San Francis's life was to demonstrate to that community that divine power could be manifested in all human beings. The light of Christ radiated through these beings of advanced spiritual life to show others how GOD is manifested in all his children. San Francis chose or elected in that life to demonstrate that material possessions corrupt and especially corrupt people with lots of money by making them forget the ones less privileged.

Let us pray. In that way you will be able not only to share your thoughts but the divine light, which passes through you. AMEN.

RICHARD

I am your Higher self, your husband Julio asked for this communication on behalf of Richard.

I am the spirit named Richard. I am in the space sphere called: transitory station. Your husband told me that you can hear my voice. I never thought that was possible. I don't know how you do it. I only see that your aura is of light and that it has a crown of stars in the center. Gilda is your name and you have a violet ray of light which circumscribes your aura.

Who were you when you were alive?

On Earth, I was a minister of the Evangelical Church. I knew much about theology and I always believed that I would go to heaven. Gilda, as a Minister I did know how to lead a straight life and because of that I thought I deserved to go to heaven. What I did not know was that the soul progresses accordingly with what one does in respect to their plan before they reincarnate. I did not execute several goals.

The concept of a life of dedication and prayers is not worthy per se as to know how to discern and be appreciative of what is good and correct.

I did sin of haughtiness.

I thought that my truth was absolute. I also sinned of indulgence. I ate and drank too much. Thank you for your attention and God Bless You. I am Richard, Julio's friend.

LUNDA

QUESTION: Is there something in the vibrations of this house that causes trouble for those who inhabit it, past and present?

ANSWER: I am the spirit of the ghost that you think you imagined. I am one with the thousands of spirits that pollute the Earth. I have the opportunity to speak to you and express my disappointment. I thought that you were a being of light and that I would have the chance to liberate my soul.

I am in this place because I was humiliated and looked down upon all the time. My husband treated me like a dog. His children were the only souls that helped pull me through.

My name is Lunda. I lived in this place years ago. The presence of your soul gave me hope and I was waiting for the opportunity to talk to you. I want to know why I am here and why my soul is bound to this place.

QUESTION: May I ask assistance to help this soul?

ANSWER: (The spirit of GOD is with you and the presence of the Angel of Peace.) Lunda, your soul is troubled because your thoughts about your husband keep appearing in your conscious. Your question is why am I still here? You are here because your thoughts are violent. Yes, you rejoice yourself with the idea of having revenge. You rejoice when people get mad or disturbed. You don't want to change. I can help you. Let us pray.

The light and love of the Universe is expressed through us. Peace be with you and with everybody who lives and comes into this home.

QUESTION: May I help Lunda?

ANSWER: I am the spirit of light and peace. I am Archangel Gabriel. Blessed be the Mother of Christ. You want to pray and help your daughter, Erika. She needs to understand that the Light of God is always present. The presence of this entity in her home is attracted to the vibrations of the children. Lunda was a mother and she mistreated her children. She doesn't know that her soul is in a state of transition. Do you know what coma is? Yes, it is a state like coma, but for the soul, and it will remain until sufficient people pray for her.

QUESTION: Does she want forgiveness? Is she aware of her wrong doings?

ANSWER: Lunda exists in a state of transition. She is not aware that she can be helped.

QUESTION: Has anyone prayed for her before?

ANSWER: She thinks she is still alive, she is afraid of people and she does not want to be helped.

QUESTION: Why are Erika and I aware of her presence?

ANSWER: Because you and Erika are mediums.

QUESTION: What should we do?

ANSWER: Gilda, I know how much you want to help. Yes, you can pray to Mother Mary for Lunda.

I am your Teacher in Christ, Tumargeo.

QUESTIONS: Did Erika envision the spirit of Lunda in her dream? What about the children's voices?

ANSWER: Your daughter Erika is a medium. She did see Lunda in her etheric body and did hear the sound of the children. The constant presence of this entity in her house is because she used to live in this same spot many centuries ago. She was married to a farmer and had three children, one boy and two girls. Her husband was responsible for her present condition. His name was Jessie and he was abusive and of a bad disposition.

The three children died of a disease that was incurable at that time, pneumonia. Yes, the year was 1896 and it was one of the coldest winters in the history of Minnesota.

The reason why she became insane was due to the sadness and the solitude of her life.

She did not understand what happened to her and her children. Her life was of many sorrows. She died at the age of twenty-seven years and she took with her all the rage and disappointment of this incarnation. She lived in a world of fear and cold. Her thoughts are the cause of her constant regret. Pray for her soul and the souls of her three children. She is aware of your presence. She will come to you for help. Let us pray.

QUESTION: What can Erika do to protect herself and sleep peacefully?

ANSWER: Erika is a soul that wants to help.

Gilda, I am Lunda. I am in your aura and see your light. I want to tell you that I see the light that comes from your head when you pray. I am in this house alone and I cannot forget my children. My children were taken from me, yes, the three of them. My husband left me and I did survive the winter. I was scared and lonely.

QUESTION: How did you feed yourself?

ANSWER: I had potatoes. The winter was long and cold. I knew how to catch rabbits and minor animals. I was afraid most of the time.

QUESTION: How long did you live alone?

Gilda M. Schaut

ANSWER: I am alone. This house is old and the winter is almost here. I am afraid of the cold and I do not know if I will live through the winter.

QUESTION: Do you want to go to a warmer place?

ANSWER: You are a funny girl! You think that you can walk and go wherever you please? I am alone and I remain alone.

Gilda, I find your light and I am drawn to you. I am ready to listen.

QUESTION: Lunda, would you like me to guide you to a place of light where you can see your children again?

ANSWER: Lies, Lies! Yes, he was a LIAR! He told me that he would help me and then left me all alone.

QUESTION: Do you want to see your children again?

ANSWER: No, I do not. I think they are dead. Yes, they died of cold. You are lying, see?

Lunda, listen. Life is Eternal. That means forever and ever. You are alive, I am alive, and your children are alive. We are one in the love of GOD.

Lunda's Child Speaking: I am the older. I do want to see my mother. I died of cold and my father buried my body next to my sister. Today I am alive and in a place of light. Mother, I want to see you again. I am your son. I will pray for you.

QUESTION: Early a.m., at five o'clock, there was a great noise. According to Erika the angel statue on her kitchen windowsill was standing upright on the counter, another on its head and the shade was still closed. What happened?

ANSWER: I am your Teacher in Christ, Tumargeo.

You want to know what happened last night? The spirit of light that protects you is asking you to pray for Lunda. That entity is so desperate and wants you to help her. She is scared and last night she began to move objects to show all of you her "powers." The desire to manifest her ideas is translated in these acts.

QUESTION: Why with the angels? Does she believe in angels?

ANSWER: Lunda's reasoning is, if I show these mediums that I am capable of moving these figurines then they will know that I exist. She does not believe in beings of light.

QUESTION: How can Erika and I help her?

ANSWER: She sees you when you meditate. She has an enormous curiosity and she knows that you can listen. You can help her by listening and answering her questions.

QUESTION: Lunda, I know that you can listen to me and you were the one who moved those figurines last night. I want to listen to you and help you.

ANSWER: I am Lunda. I am at your side and I see you as a circle of light. You don't believe that I have a body, but I do! (Etheric body).

I am twenty-seven years old. I am tall, with a dark complexion and dark hair. I lived in this valley for ten years.

I got married with Jessie in the town of Northside. Yes. Northside was a town in the upperland and near the river. I was young and healthy. He was older and mean.

We arrived to this place and built a cabin. Yes, this old cabin has two bedrooms and a fireplace. The top part is made of barks and mud and the walls are made of timber.

The first three years we suffered much cold and hunger. He was a good trapper, but he did not want to leave me alone, because I was with child.

My first child, a girl, was pretty. She grew well until she was two years old. Then the second one was born. He was a boy, yes. Jessie was happy.

Then the winter came and the cold and snow. We barely were able to survive. Jessie became sick. I did not know what to do. He became cruel and weak. I had to care for the children and fetch water. The cold and lack of food destroyed our family. I hate this place. Yes, I did have another boy. He was weak and died small. I am not making this up!

The summer came and we went down South. There we met other families. He wanted to find a new place for us to live. We looked and looked but nobody wanted to share their land. We came back and the reason for my rage is that he was so mean.

Learn how to treat our children nice I said, but he did not do so.

He yelled and spanked. That is all he knew.

Winter came again and Thelma, yes, that was her name, became with fever. Soon after, John caught the same cold. The pain and suffering was terrible.

Jessie wept. Then he left the house and I did not see him ever again.

Gilda, you are a good person and you too know pain. I beg of you to help me. I am alone in this house and the winter is so cold.

Where is Jessie? Why did he not come back? Why is the weather so mean? Can you help me?

Gilda: Yes Lunda I can. I will answer your questions and you will be free again. Life is like a long journey. You have been staying for a long time in one place. It is time for you to go to a better place where you will not be cold any longer. Do you want that?

Lunda: I do understand, but you are a foolish girl, Gilda. I can not travel alone. There are bears and cats, and I do not know how to defend myself.

Gilda: Somebody will knock at your door. He is your friend. I will send him to travel with you and protect you. He is a Good Samaritan that will take you to a better and sunnier place. There you will meet other people and you will find help. I will pray for your safe journey and when you arrive there, I will listen to you again.

Lunda: Gilda, thank you for thinking of me. I hope your man is nice and treats me nicely. When will he come to fetch me?

Gilda: Whenever you want. When YOU are ready.

Lunda: Gilda, I am so poor. I do not have money or food. How am I going to feed this person?

Gilda: My friend has food for him and for you. You only have to take your clothes.

Lunda: Gilda, I will take the ax and the fire rack. I am trying to think. It will be useful to take the pot and the beans (kidney beans). That will be useful. The day will come when I will talk to you again. Yes. I am willing to leave this house. Gilda, you are a good girl.

QUESTION: May I know if Lunda decided to go?

ANSWER: I am afraid. I am at your side. I do not know if you can see me. I do not need anybody. I am hiding from my husband. He is Jessie and he hasn't returned for a long time.

QUESTION: Do you remember that you are waiting for my friend, the one who will guide and protect you and together you will travel South?

ANSWER: Lunda: Yes, I know. I am thinking. Do you know that if I leave this house I do not know if I would be welcomed in another place?

Gilda: Lunda, my friend is a very good man and he will take you to the house of a family who is ready to take you in. Yes. You will be helped by them, they are expecting you.

Lunda: Think. Thinking. Yes, I see in your mind the rays of light. I am not so intelligent nor pretty, but I know how to work. I am very sad because life was not what I wanted.

Gilda: Lunda, you are young and will find a mate who will help you to fulfill your dreams.

Lunda: I am not stupid. I am twenty-seven years old and soon to be twenty-eight. What will happen if I go with your friend and he asks me to offer my body? I do not believe that I am so young!

Gilda: You should believe me when I said that my friend is a good person, he will not ask you that.

Lunda: Do you know that you can think in colors? Yes, that is what you do. Every time that you think, you have a color that vibrates in your aura.

Gilda: Lunda, thank-you for expressing your ideas. I wish you the best. When will you be ready?

Lunda: I am thinking. You wish me well. I don't trust anybody.

Gilda: Do you want to meet my friend only for a minute? After you see him you can talk to him, then he will be gone.

Lunda: Yes, I want to see him.

I am Lunda and I came to ask for help. You know how I feel. I have to decide if I should stay here or leave. I have a dog. It is a tan color and his name is Nappy. I have a male rabbit and three female ones, which provide me with food, when I need it. I have a lot of work. The water I drink is the one I have to fetch at the stream. Yes, it is near. I have two coins; they are not worth much. Do you think I could sell this house and the rabbits?

QUESTION: Do you see other people who you can sell your house or animals to?

Lunda: I asked you! You are clever. I don't know anybody.

Gilda: I think you can sell the house if you talk to somebody and explain that you need the money and that you are leaving.

Lunda: Gilda, I don't know anybody!

Gilda: Do you want to see other people?

Lunda: Gilda, you are so clever. When you told me to sell the house you were thinking of me talking to strangers. I do not want to go South. I will wait and live in this place until I know who the person is that you said is your friend.

Gilda. I am your Guardian Angel. You are protected and guided. Yes. You will be able to speak with him.

I am the spirit and guide called Murghen. Yes. That is my name. The etheric body of your protected soul is in your aura. Lunda knows that I will be the one who will help her.

I studied the art of divination in the School of Antiquity and in that incarnation I learned to distinguish between good and bad.

I learned to discern and to listen to the voice of other discarnate beings.

I had three sons and I was not able to provide for their necessities.

I was in a trap of my own ideas and I accumulated karma. I want to assure you that the infinite love of GOD is the one that unites us at this moment to be part of this spiritual healing.

Lunda knows that you want to help her. Let us pray for her soul.

I am your Guardian Angel, Gabriel. I came to bless you and to tell you that your prayers are being heard.

Remember when you prayed for Lunda? She asked for help and now is in your aura.

Lunda: I have to think; yes I know that you are listening.

You should understand that I am not alone, I have a dog and four rabbits. Gilda, I want you to find that friend of yours and tell him to come. May I take my dog and rabbits? The cold will come and then it will be impossible to travel. I am scared. But worse than that is to stay in this place and to put up with the cold.

QUESTION: Lunda, do you want to listen to my friend only one time?

You don't have to even open the door!

ANSWER: I will try. Do you think that he can talk to me in the same way that you talk to me?

Gilda: Yes, he can. If you want to see him, look and see him. He is outside waiting.

Lunda: Gilda, he is standing outside! He is tall and he carries with him a walking stick. Yes.

I am looking. He is a man taller than my husband. Yes.

He has gray hair and a gray beard.

I think he is much older than I am.

Gilda: Do you think he is strong?

Lunda: Yes, he is strong. I can see his muscles. He is waiting and looking at the house.

Gilda: Can you ask him if he is my friend and if he can tell you why he is there?

Lunda: I am scared. He is so strong. I think that I will ask his name. I do want to know how many days he wants to travel and where we are going.

My name is Murghen. Yes.

I am ready to listen and to be of service.

Gilda: Will you help this lady travel?

Murghen: Yes. I came to protect her and her dog. She is a young lady and needs protection.

Lunda: I remember when my father was alive. He use to take me through the woods. My father was tall and strong too. Gilda, I think that he (Murghen) is a good person. Yes. I will listen to him.

Murghen: I am Murghen and I am your guide and friend. I come prepared to guide you to a place where winter is mild and where you will find another house better than this one. The dog will come with us and the rabbits too. They are your family and you love them.

Lunda: I can't think so fast. I think I should open the door. I did. Yes, I did!

This is my dog; he is a good dog. (I think I will tell him my name).

My name is Lunda. (Yes, he is tall!).

I see that he carries a basket and a rod. He smells like the forest. I am so impressed. I want to cry. I want to know how many days we will travel.

Murghen: Yes. (I will tell her, but first I want to tell you; bless you and the work you do).

We will go through the river, and we will walk until we see the first fork of the river. There we will rest. The food I have will be sufficient.

Lunda: (I can ask for myself). I am happy and I am ready to fetch my ax and rack and the beans. The sun is just coming and the day will be long.

Gilda, I want you to stay in touch. I want you to know how I am doing. Tell me - when will I see you again?

Gilda: I will be always ready to see you again. Have a wonderful trip. God Bless You All.

Tumargeo: I came to tell you that Lunda is in a new place. She wants to talk to you.

Lunda: Gilda, I am Lunda. I see you as a circle of Light. I am the same Lunda that you listened to and who traveled to this new place.

I am happy to know that I will be able to keep on going on this path.

I did find a new house. It is in a meadow and has a door and two windows.

My dog keeps me company. Your friend is good and strong. He took me down the river and shared his food with me.

The river is called MISSISSIPPI and I am in a small village.

QUESTION: Have you seen other people?

ANSWER: Yes. I was talking to a woman with a family who lives nearby. Her name is Ester and she is a woman of thirty-five years or more. They have three children and they are working the land. She gave me flour and flowers. I know that you find this strange but the flour is made of corn and with that I can make bread. The air is warm and the light bright.

QUESTION: Did your Guide leave?

ANSWER: Yes. He is not here anymore.

QUESTION: Do you want to tell me something else?

ANSWER: Yes. I want to see other people. I have to go through the other side of this meadow where there is a road. I know that I can do it. Soon I will go to town and I will have to talk with other people. I think that now I will be welcomed. You have a guide next to you. He is saying that you should listen to me. I see you in rose color. I do have to go. I will visit soon. I am your friend, Lunda.

ISHMAEL

I am your Guardian Angel, Gabriel. I come to bless you and to present you with a Being of Light who wants to meet you Gilda. I am Ishmael. Your color is violet and you have a circle of light.

I am in the ninth spatial sphere, and my assignment is keeping count of the many souls who pass to the other side without knowing where they are. The work is hard and I have with me several beings of light that work diligently to guide and help these souls. The process is simple. As soon as a soul appears in the etheric realm, an angel guides him to a place of rest. There he finds a peaceful place where he begins to awaken and with his thoughts to demonstrate his emotional and mental capacity. According to this awareness, this soul is taken to the place that he has to go. There, he starts a process of purification. During this process there are thousands of volunteers who will help to answer all their questions. This is the period of transition. In this state, the mind only remembers what it did in the last incarnation. The purpose of this process is to put order in the thoughts and to make that soul see by itself its actions, because each action is the product of a thought. During this period, that soul has the privilege of living in a place similar to the one he lived on Earth and learns little by little the different aspects of the ethereal realms. His communication is real. I will leave you with my blessings. Amen.

ISABELLA

I am in your aura and I expect to be listened to. I am not your Teacher but I am a soul who wishes to learn. My name is Isabella and I died many years ago. The tragedy of my death is that I did not believe! Yes. The awakening in the realms of Light was the most surprising thing! I have to recognize that you are very fast and good at listening. I think and you immediately write my thoughts. I wish I had believed as you do. The sad part of this is that there are so many millions of ignorant souls that do not know.

How do you know?

The truth is that I was a priest in a previous incarnation. The knowledge came to me when I started questioning my own beliefs. The Beings of Light appointed to help me were wiser than all the wisest people I have ever known. They helped me to understand the process of reincarnation and the Law of Cause and Effect. These two principals are the basic parts of the awareness of each soul.

Gilda, if I can describe Light and Love as I know it now I would tell you come and join us. But we are on different planes of existence. The ability to transcribe my words or thoughts is one of the most fascinating things I have ever seen.

God bless you. I am Isabella and I am in the sixth sphere.

Eugenia Ruiz de Mirasol – Year 1826

I am the soul of a lady who learned to write and to recite in the year 1826. My name is Eugenia Ruiz de Mirasol. In the year of our Lord 1842, my fiancé was planning our future and he ordered the construction of a house in the town of Sacramento. When we got married, we were very happy and I dedicated my life to reciting and singing. This artistic disposition led me to esotericism. I discovered that you are a Medium and I decided to talk to you. I am not in your sphere but I know that you can listen to me. Remember what your teachers told you? Yes, you can and you must help other souls.

Did you have children?

Yes. My daughter's name was Marisol and the older boy, Alfredo and the youngest, Armando. They were my love and my reason to be alive.

Where are you now?

The development of my soul has allowed me to learn in part what you know. I am a speaking medium. I am actually incarnated and I am 22 years old. At this moment, I have not been able to express my virtue because I have not been able to leave aside my family's religious creeds. I am in the sixth sphere and do appreciate your consideration.

4 year old boy

I am in your aura and I bless you. I see you as a light that radiates violet color rays. I am a being who is in the 3rd sphere in space. I am 4 years old and I can't find my family. I learned how to communicate with you and now I can do it quickly.

Do you know that this is very interesting?

You think too and you want to know my name.

My name is Peter, I am four years old and I am waiting for a mother to bring me to Earth.

Did you like my homework? Yes. That was my homework. I have to go.

All the light of your aura I can see. Gilda I will see you soon.

IRMA

I am a soul who is watching you. I am in the 4th sphere in space. I was on your planet ten years ago. My name is Irma. Yes. Pray for my soul.

I know that I am "dead" and I do know that there are helpers, but I can't make myself recognize the sins I committed.

I am ready to find a new human body to induce her and carry on with my life. Yes, to reincarnate. I want to atone for my sins. I will be born defective and the mother will suffer for my sins.

Gilda, I thank you for your support. I will tell my Guardian Angel that I am ready.

JOHN - AN EXPLANATION

A spirit resides in the house of my daughter, Erika. His name is John. He awakened her by rapping hard on the wall to capture her attention. This following dialogue with him is why he remains in the house alone. The reason why John remained by himself is because he did not want to receive help.

Where are Irene and the children? Will she be willing to come and see him?

I am the soul you call John. Yes. I am the man who lives in the house where your daughter is staying.

Do you want to see your wife and sons?

You don't know where they are!

My guide and Teacher can tell me where they are. The souls of your wife and children are waiting for you. Yes. The reason for this delay is your unforgiveness. Do you remember? Your wife Irene was ready to bake and she went to the barn to pick up some apples. The day was cold and the sun was covered with clouds. She lit the candle because the barn was dark. She tried to put the fire out but she couldn't. The fire spread like lightening and it was already too late when you came to her rescue. You lost your wife, your animals, your barn and everything in it. The help of other people who came when they viewed the fire was too late. You suffered minor burns but your spirit was sad. The reason for living (the love of your wife) was gone. Irene died soon after and her soul knew that you blamed her for this misfortune.

What happened to the boys and where are they?

The boys were playing in the courtyard and they called and called for their Father. John was 12 and Troner was 8 years old. You were about 2 miles from home. The anguish and anxiety filled your soul with rancor and in your mourning and solitude you wished her in hell! That cold winter John caught the Flu and his brother soon followed. They died of pneumonia.

John, what did you do after that?

I am John and I don't want to remember!

If we tell you that you can see Irene and the boys again, would you be willing to say yes?

They died. I was left alone.

This Being of Light that you said is an Angel, is he the one who will bring my wife to me?

Yes. He is the Angel who is very pleased to help you.

Are the boys coming too?

Yes, they will too!

JOHN: They are here! Yes, the 3 of them. She is younger than I remember her and the boys are healthy! She is telling me that the period of separation has been too long.

Irene: I am Irene. I am in the 3rd spatial sphere in this vast land and I was lost and lonely for a long time. Sorrows and tears were my companions. My sons came to see me as soon as they could but they went away.

Do you know why you were there?

When the fire caught my dress I tried to put it out with the rug that we used for cleaning. It wasn't only the dress, but also the grass, the animals, food and the grains! My soul cried when I remembered the sounds of terror from those animals! The sin of dying for the error of judgment that I committed that day is branded in my soul. My soul was released and I found myself in a place very similar to the one from which I came. The walls were the same and the view was the same. One person, a relative long dead, came to see me. He was the one who told me that I was in another dimension. I started to question my sanity. Why was my husband not here and where were my children? For a long time I waited until one day I went for a walk and I met a lady dressed in a blue gown. Her name was Gloria. Yes. She said that she was willing to help me. That was the beginning of my recovery. I know my soul traveled through different places. Gilda, I thank you for your help and prayers. I am Irene.

CORNELIUS OF CESAREA

I am the soul of Cornelius and I come to instruct you.

The sun was coming up, when I climbed to the road. My spirit was anxious to serve the Lord and I asked for guidance.

The light which surrounded me was so brilliant that I thought that I was dead!

The vision I had was in a state of trance and what I saw was my divine self. I know that you understand what I am talking about.

The Judaic Law forbids us to eat sacrificed meat without the benediction of a Rabbi. That law was imposed to protect the owner of the sheep from the ones who were stealing and killing animals indiscriminately.

At that moment I understood that that is the law of GOD, the one we must follow, and that the animal meat is not impure because it is God's creation. I am your brother in Christ, Cornelius the Roman.

Are nuns and monks more attuned to GOD because they pray and meditate for long periods of time?

The understanding or concept of GOD and its expression on this planet is of a different nature in every religion.

The guidance of the teachers is the same, regardless of the interpretation of the rites or creeds.

The evolution of the soul is not in regard to their human religious beliefs, but to their deeds and choices that each soul makes in each incarnation.

The reason why humans put so much emphasis on their religious practices is because they want to demonstrate to others that they are the only ones who know the truth! The realization of this mirage will cease to exist the day humans realize that doctrines and creeds are the invention of each civilization.

What about the prophets?

Prophets were enlightened men who had the power to foresee the future. The scriptures are in part truth and in part, events that never happened.

Do people of other planets evolve spirituality in a similar manner?

The evolution of a humanoid soul is unique to each case and is different on each planet. The different aspects of development are in direct proportion to the amount of knowledge and amount of incarnations that each soul has had on each planet.

There are planets in which ever being is in a state of apelike existence and the concept of divinity does not exist.

There are others, in which the grade of evolution is more advance than that of Planet Earths'. Some of their inhabitant's can sense and express their oneness with the Most High!

Solutions. That word implies the answers to questions. Yes. You can find out answers to a lot of questions, which will help mankind.

Be aware that not all the answers will be given to you.

The reason behind that is because we realize the misuse of this in the hands of unscrupulous minds. God bless you and rest. responsibility to guide our children. This responsibility ends

AMELIA EARHART

What happened to Amelia Earhart?

Greetings. Gilda, I see that you are able to read my thoughts and to communicate with me. The story you watched on television was accurate and I am impressed to see how the media pursued the trail of my last voyage. The purpose of achieving a goal in life was most important to me during that lifetime. The idea to demonstrate to others that it was possible for a female to circulate around the globe was my ultimate goal. What happened during that last part of my journey was this ... I was over the ocean and a change of weather threw me off course. I was forced to land on an island and my airplane was damaged. The radio worked for a couple of times and then I did not have any means of communicating with the outside world. I was stranded and alone the last days of my life. The weather was hot, humid and raining most of the time.

Were you injured?

Yes. My arm and part of my face was cut and the door that came out upon landing cut my leg above the thigh. The medicine chest that was in the rear was expelled with the impact and I could not find it. That was the moment I began to think about GOD and my life. The injuries became infected and soon I was running a high fever. The nights were scary and lonely and the lack of water and food soon proved to be the cause of my death. I lasted for two weeks. The ocean took most of the parts and pieces of debris from the airplane. That is the truth. The soul came out of my body like smoke and the peace and release I felt was indescribable. Gilda, thank you for asking me to come to you and tell you what happened to me at the end of that "life."

Where are you now?

I know that you would want to see this place! It is the most beautiful place you could ever imagine. I am still in the process of learning and my soul is in the 12th sphere.

AUDREY SANTO

8-11-98 5:58am broadcast MN/St. Paul television. Girl has been in a coma for over a decade. Thousands of people (Catholics) flock to her home in Massachusetts to see her. The statues in her room cry tears and there are marks on her body that resemble the crucifixion of Christ.

What can you tell me about these miracles? Why do these wounds keep reappearing? Does touching this girl bring about healing? Is it a hoax?

Greetings. Gilda, I am in your aura and I will answer your questions. I am San Augustine. Yes.

This girl, Audrey Santo, is a soul that came to this Earth with the purpose of demonstrating faith. In the Coma State, she is not aware of her wounds. This is testimony of her passion for the life and passion of Jesus the Christ and she wants to speak to you.

Audrey: Dear friend, Gilda. My soul recognizes the splendor and faith that you feel. We are the forerunners of the Millennium and we offer our testimony of love and faith because GOD has allowed us to demonstrate his miracles. The wounds that our dear Jesus suffered are my beatitude and in them I rejoice! The answer to your question is: I am not dead. I am alive and I want to demonstrate the power of faith and love for GOD in the only form that I know. Yes, Gilda, I will live for a few more years. The physical body is nothing but the outer cover of my soul. My soul and yours are brilliant and pure expressions of the Light and Love that is GOD.

CHAPTER 7

Stories From Soldiers

PRAYERS FOR SOLDIERS

Gilda, in the next two weeks, your mission will be to pray for those, who are at war, and need your prayers. Most of them are not aware of Divine help they will have, when their spirit is released from their physical body. The Muslims believe in a heaven that is the product of their mind. The rest of the soldiers like Americans, British, German, French, etc. think that they know, but their ideas are product of the several different Christian ideologies that they belong to. These souls are destined to wander and emotionally suffer, after they pass to a new dimension. When you pray for them, they will receive a direct assistant, their confused minds will detect the ideas of comfort and light, that will inspire in them the desire to ask for help. Through these specific prayers you will see, after several writings that this mission is a real soul mission. I am your teacher Tumargeo, who blesses you.

SOLDIER OF CONFEDERATE ARMY

Greetings, I am a soldier of Confederate Army. I am one of many who fought to give the liberty and freedom to the state, and to build this big nation. This is the year of eighteen ninety-four, and I am in the State of Virginia. We are a group of forty-five men and one sergeant. We don't have many supplies. Each one of us owns a musket and a canteen. We are traveling south to a new post. The time is like still. This forest is dense and protects us from the enemy. I see that you don't believe me. I see all of my friends, and they are trying to find something to eat. Rations are scarce. The sergeant is relentless in pursuing the enemy.

Gilda: Are you unhappy in this situation?

Soldier: What kind of a question is that? I am a soldier and I am supposed to obey.

Gilda: You did not answer my question.

Soldier: I am thinking. I think I'd rather be at my home, with my family.

Gilda: Do you think your fellow soldiers want the same that you do?

Soldier: Yes. This is a long and tedious war.

Gilda: Let us pray. Please pray with me, and show me the way. It is so easy to surrender to the will of God. You have been under the will of man for too long. Let the love and light of God guide you. Ask and you will receive. Ask for peace.

Soldier: That was a beautiful prayer. I want to be in a peaceful place, where we don't have to hide anymore.

My name is Castor and I am also a soldier in this regiment and I was listening to your words and prayer and I also want to return home and thank you for your prayer.

SOLDIER IN AFGHANISTAN

I am a soldier in the war in Afghanistan and have been here for two years. My name is Robert and I am twenty-three years old. This country is mountains and dirt. The people who live here are not like us and I think that they don't deserve the time we are spending here in training them to liberate themselves from the Taliban. Yes I am mad, because I have seen how many troops have died or have been injured and the situation that we are facing hasn't improved. How long will we be here? What is our goal? There are too many unanswered questions. The morale of the troops is not what it used to be. I see that you think that praying can change the situation. I don't think so.

Gilda: Please listen to me, I understand that you are tired, frustrated, and far from home. You are not only your physical being but you are a spiritual being also. The connection of that spirit to the All encompasses part of God that is spirit and will allow you to be released from the place where you are. Believe Me! Ask in prayer, and it will be answered!

Robert: Lady, you are talking like that, because you are sitting comfortably in your home, and nobody can hurt you.

Gilda: Think for just moment, if you leave your bitterness aside, and be sincere with your own self. Don't you want to be at peace? If you say yes, try to be calm, and ask God to help you. The quality of time spent in prayers is the one that renews and clarifies the mind, spirit and the purpose in life!

Gilda, this is Tumargeo. Your desire to help those who are in a state of mind that can be altered only by themselves, in the next dimension, is one most needed and is commendable.

Prayers that contain truth and knowledge are answered because they are able to awaken their particular soul to further investigate their life and the connection with the source of their life.

SOUL OF CARL

I am in the Army and I was assigned to patrol the streets of Beluja. My name is Carl and I am 22 years old. The day I was killed three of my fellow soldiers were with me. We're walking on the right side of the road. A convoy of trucks and artillery had just passed us. We came to an intersection and stopped. As we pass through the intersection we came upon two houses. Part of our job was to make sure that they were free of insurgents. We went into the first one and nobody was there. As we started to enter the second house, one of our soldiers was shot in the shoulder. We took cover as best as we could in the house, and applied pressure to the man's shoulder to stop the bleeding. We also tried to use the radio to contact the paramedics and our battalion for backup but all we got was a lot of static. We started taking heavy fire. They were able to overrun, shoot us and run.

In an instant, I was awake and touching my leg, it was fine. I looked around and saw my two companions. They were as surprised as I was. We are okay. The first thing that came to mind was to go and warn the convoy that had just passed us. I went back to the road but found it deserted. I was puzzled as to what had just happened. I returned to the house and explained to the men that we were on our own. We decided to wait for assistance. After a short period of time we decided to go out and see if we could reconnect with our battalion. To our surprise, the road was empty. Our confidence started to diminish. We decided to wait until It got dark out and then try to escape. Night never came! My friend started us praying. As soon as we started a guide appeared before and he offered to help us. We ask questions, and all of them were answered. He explained to us where we were and that life is eternal. We were extremely happy to know that we are alive and not wounded. He took us to join several other soldiers who had died in a similar way.

Ms. Gilda, I wanted to tell you my story, because there are many parents, spouses, and children who are worried and distraught because they don't know where their love ones are. We are fine. Our life is different and without pain or fear I am new here, and because of that, I can explain my surroundings. I know for sure the feelings of love and peace is beyond understanding. I am a soldier that died for his country.

ROGELIO

I am the soul of a soldier who died during the Second World War and lived in Spain. I have asked permission to talk to you. You know that I saw you and I thought that you were an apparition. I saw you like a light and asked to talk to you. My name is Rogelio and on Earth I lived in the City of Molina.

When I passed to this side of the veil my spiritual guide taught me how to pray and believe in the spiritual life. Gilda, if you only knew how important it is not to look for excuses to find the time to meditate and pray. During my time on the planet I studied metaphysics.

The grief of my existence made me do acts that depressed me and I only wish to tell you that the most important thing I ever did was to appreciate the love and friendship of my loved ones. Everything else does not matter. When it is time to recollect, only the love given and received has importance. Gilda, keep on meditating and helping your kin. Your friend in Christ. Rogelio.

THE SOUL OF ARCHIBAL (DAY ONE)

I am a soldier in Afghanistan. I came to you because I was summoned to do so. I am thirty years old and my name is Archibal. In my command there are six soldiers. My mission is to scout, evaluate, prepare and distribute ammunition and supplies to two different groups of men. One group is made up of the fighting forces and the other of medics. The place where we are working is in a valley that is surrounded by mountains. The visibility is clear. The only advantage our enemies have is that they know these lands and we don't. Even with our superior arms and ammunition they can sneak up behind you and kill you. I was ambushed two days ago. Two of my companions were shot dead. I escaped and hid behind some rocks. From there I could see the enemy and how they were moving. They did not seem to be aware of my presence. I am worried that I will not be able to reach my platoon. What shall I do?

Answer: Thank you for letting me listen to your plea. I see that you were guided to talk to me because I know the truth. Life is eternal. The reason why you can see your enemies and they can't see you is because you are in your etheric body. You left your physical body behind. I know how difficult this is for you to acknowledge the truth. Your life will continue in another dimension. I am ready to listen to you again later. Your sister in light, Gilda.

THE SOUL OF ARCHIBAL (DAY TWO)

I am the soldier who came to talk to you yesterday. Yes, I am Archibal. I am here to tell you that you were right. I am dead! The realization of this fact occurred to me as soon as you told me. I was so surprised to see that I was able to see, hear, and move just as when I was alive. Then, the guy that was with me let me know that we should move to a new location. As soon as he said so, I was in the middle of a group of soldiers who were in this enormous place waiting to be called. I saw my friends and at that very moment, I felt joy. Then a voice called my name. Immediately, I found myself in a different place. This was a theater of sorts and on the screen I could see parts of my childhood. I recall seeing my mother kissing my head, and promising me she would be praying for me. I was three years old. The light and love of this new place engulfed me and a sense of peace came over me. The rest of the view was about all of the good and bad actions of my life. The recollections of the past experiences made me realize that life is a learning experience. The fact that I am alive is a great bonus. I don't understand yet, why I am here, and what my life will be in the future, but I am grateful for this new finding. Thank you Gilda for listening. I am Archibal, and I am in the third sphere.

THE SOUL OF RUPERT

I am the soul of a soldier who was sent to the City of Bahrain. I did not understand why the two soldiers whom were with me, all of a sudden disappeared. We were walking through uneven terrain, and the sand and rocks were always in our way. (I am not making this up!) I looked for several hours, but I was not able to find them.

I started to become scared, and decided to return to my base. I walked for hours, without seeing anybody. Then, I stopped and asked for directions. The minute I finished asking, I found myself in another place. This time I was one of many soldiers. I asked where I was, one of them told me we were waiting to be called. My name was called, and the man who appeared in front of me, told me to follow him. He told me that I was in another dimension and was I ready to see my past life. I could not believe it! Here I was, in my own body. I could hear, see and touch, and he was saying that I was dead! Then he explained to me, that the soul is eternal, and I was in a state of transition. In this state, we retain our senses, mind, and memories of the period we lived on earth.

Then in an instant I was in front of a mural, with a screen in it where I saw parts of my past life. The reality, color and sound were like, a movie. I saw myself when I was two years old. My mother was taking me for a ride on a merry-go-round. Then I saw myself when I was ten years old, at school. The teacher was telling me to pay attention! I saw my older brother John. He always helped me with my homework. My sister Elizabeth was the youngest and I loved her. We were very good friends. I regret not being able to tell them that I loved them. I saw my Mom and Dad, trying to be strong, but they were so sad when they found out that I was dead. I don't know why my life was so short. I had so many projects that I wanted to complete in my future. When the showing ended, my guide told me that I was ready to assume my real identity as a soul.

In an instant my physical appearance changed, and I was transported to another dimension. This new dimension was a place where my soul had been attracted like a magnet, according to my soul's evolution. I felt a sense of silence and peace, and then I was able to see that I was in a great vast valley. Here there are all kinds of people, like me, who are alive, walking, thinking and doing almost all the things they used to do on earth. The only difference, knows that we are in a process of development of our souls and sooner or later, we will go to another place.

Question ~ Do you work, or read, or do exercises?

Answer ~ Those are funny questions. The answer is No. We don't have the need to do all those things. When we think of a pear, as an example, the pear appears! Yes, the instant manifestation of thought is one of the most intriguing things that happen in this dimension. We are here, to learn how to think and manifest the ideas. This is a process that some find is rewarding and at times can be dangerous. The value of these lessons is to acknowledge that all creative processes are part of the infinite intelligence of the Cosmos, who is God! I have learned that positive thoughts are uplifting and keep us in a pattern of soul progression. Negative ideas; attract negative patterns that delay the process of moving forward in our soul's development. Life is good and full of beautiful sights in this wonderful place. I am in the sixth sphere, my name is Rupert and I thank you for allowing me to talk to you. God bless you.

Message to my Family

Gilda, I am in the Navy and was assigned to this ship about six months ago. The reason that I am contacting you is because I want to send a message to my family. My name is Robert Cupertino and I know that my family misses me. I want to let them know that I will return to them. Pray that this war and this assignment will end soon. Thank you for listening.

Soul of Allen

I am a soldier that was taken prisoner in Afghanistan. The day they caught me I was patrolling the streets in our Humvee, with three of my friends. We were passing a shop door, when from inside three Afghanis with machine guns assaulted us and took control of our vehicle. They motioned for us to get out. They immediately tied us up and took our weapons, radio and all of our possessions. They took us to a ransack house, and tied us to a centralized pole. We have been here for three months. They allow us to go out only at night to do our necessities. We are continually guarded buy two Afghans with weapons. The food is really bad, but we understand that it is our only choice. They gave us water two times a day. They pray in front of us and they're waiting for orders of what to do with us. We pray that somebody is looking for us.

My name is Alan and I am the one who is talking to you. Gilda, we were watching you! When you were praying, the light surrounding you was intensely beautiful and increased several yards around you! The love and freedom that we were experiencing was incredible. Yes, we are free! As soon as you said, "let us pray" a tall guardian angel appeared in a mist and helped us to understand that we had died three months ago. Our ignorance of the afterlife was what was keeping us there. My friends send you their thanks and appreciation for your intervention. I am Allen and you will be in my prayers also.

SOUL OF RAYMOND

I am the spirit of a soldier who is in your aura. My name is Sergeant Raymond and I was assigned to assist in a reconnaissance mission of a particular mountain in Afghanistan. It was about four p.m. when the enemy began an invasion of our troops on a lower part of the mountain that we had been assigned to "recon." We were in a higher position and had the advantage of reconnaissance aircraft that would inform us of the enemy's actual position. Once informed, we opened fire with mortars and far reaching munitions, which caused them to disperse. We thought we had been free of their presence and moved our position to what we thought would be a more secure place to stay for the night. At about nine forty-five p.m. we were ambushed and all hell broke loose. It was a firefight with a lot wounded and casualties. My rifle was taken away from me and I was hit on the head several times. My mind went blank. When I awoke, I found myself in a different place. The landscape looked like the North Carolina Mountains. The trees were green and healthy and the aroma of the grass and flowers smelled great. I couldn't figure out why I was there. I was born in Chicago and never been to North Carolina. After I walked a short distance, I found two soldiers, and asked them where we were. They told me they didn't know, they had arrived recently too. Then I saw one of my pals that I had been with. I was so happy! His name is Richard. He came to me and said: How did you get to this place? I said I didn't know. We tried to remember when we last saw each other. It was then, when we both realized the night, when we were attacked, we had lost our lives.

Immediately, a young man appeared, and asked us to follow him. The landscape changed again. This time I was alone in a courtyard, where I saw a screen, and in that screen, like in a movie, parts of the most important events in my life, were projected. I recognized my negative actions and how those affected other people. I realized that we are our worst judges. I felt in my own soul, the pain that I emotionally inflicted on those persons. Then

I saw my family. Sadness overcame me and I realized that I would not see them again. My guide said that I would be allowed to pray and help that way, not only for members of my family, but for others also. After that episode, I found myself in another place. This they told me, will be my place of rest and learning. I am in the fourth sphere or dimension, and I'm aware that I am aware that I am alive. The recognition of this fact brought to my mind the idea that the promise Jesus made is fact. Life is eternal. I am grateful for your cooperation with these writings. I am Raymond and I thank you.

SOUL OF ROBERT

I am the soul of a soldier who died in Afghanistan. I was sent to patrol on the outskirts of Tarikh, and was carrying a machine gun and portable radio. I was in a group of six soldiers when we were attacked. I was hit by gunfire, as was Carl and Jones. The pain was unbearable. My thigh was blown wide open, and I was loosing blood so fast that, at one point I lost consciousness. Then I found myself in in a vast plain, and did not recognize the place. My friends were not there, and I asked myself: where are they, and why am I here? I saw my body and realized that I could walk, think and breathe. For a moment I thought I was dreaming. Then I remembered what had happened. At that moment, I saw a man standing near me. He was my age and seemed friendly. I asked him where I was, and he said we were in the fourth dimension. I could not understand what that meant. He patiently explained that this was the place where I was supposed to come, after I left my physical body on earth. It was then that I realized I had died. I asked him his name and why he was there, and he said his name was Arnaund, and he was one of the many helpers that were there to receive the newly arriving souls. I asked him about my friends, and he explained that two of them were badly injured and the other three had escaped. During this conversation I realized that he wasn't talking or making any sound! Then I understood that he was communicating his thoughts telepathically, just like I am doing with you. He guided me to a new place, and I realized that I was not alone. There were people from all different parts of the world. Nobody seemed to be surprised to be there.

My name was called and immediately a new guide approached me, and mentally asked me to follow him. I found myself in a place surrounded by a fence and in the center was a podium. There appeared an image of my parents. They were crying. I became very emotional. They were remembering all of the good moments that we had shared. I saw my sister and her husband. They have two children. I will never see them play again. Then I remembered my cousin Alfred. He also had joined the Army. My older brother was there. He had taught me how to fish, hunt and be a man. I was overwhelmed with emotions. The guide told me that I was the love of my family and that they had guided my soul into the path of righteousness. I really was blessed. A great peace came over me. Then I realized that I was alive, only in another place. Like the Bible said, In the kingdom of God, there are many mansions.

Question: Where are Carl and Jones Now?

Answer: The two soldiers who were in that battle with you were taken to a MASH hospital. They received the needed medical care and they are in the process of recovering form their injuries. No, they are not in the USA. My name is Robert and I thank you for listening to my story. God bless you.

SOUL OF PATRICK

I am in your aura and I want to talk to you. I am a soul who passed away during the war in Kuwait. I am a soldier that understood and spoke some Arabic. I was assigned to search for Intel on soldiers that had defected from Saddam's regime. During the interrogations of these defectors, we determined that they had pretended to be deserters, when in fact they were not. We had to meet these soldiers in places that were not safe. We were lured into a remote cave for a meeting and were killed. My name is Patrick and I am twenty-two years old.

Question: Where are you now?

Answer: When I regained consciousness, I found myself in a remote place, similar to where I had died. Immediately, I realized that I was alive! I had a feeling of euphoria, while at the same time sadness that I would not be able to be with my wife Karen and my parents again. This feeling lasted until I met other soldiers who had also died. They told me not to worry, that the help I needed was coming to us. The aid came in the form of another soldier, who said to me, that I was assigned to his care and guidance. This guide called Peter led me to a new place. I quickly realized that I was moving really fast without the weight of my physical body. My physical body had been replaced and I was now in my etheric body. The etheric body is a replica of our physical body we left on earth. Peter showed me a lot of soldiers and people who were there. Some were happy; some had questions and wanted to know more. I want to know more and I will go to another place to learn. Thank you for listening.

SOLDIER SCOTT L.

Gilda, The purpose of your meditation today will be about the support and prayers for the soldiers who are in the Middle East. They have been chosen to fight an impossible war. Their love for this country is the reason that so many volunteers have been sent to the front. Let Us Pray.

I am a soldier who was sent to a place in Europe, to relocate later to Asia. There are problems that are not disclosed to people of our country. The powerful influence of the Chinese indoctrination is felt in several small countries in Asia. This way of thinking limits and oppresses those who are of low self-esteem and little education. This campaign to let them see, that they can survive, live a better life and be free is a losing battle. There are a few of us, who speak their language, and are able to gain their confidence. I came to tell you this, because the mismanagement of power is a human way of thinking on this planet and its being used to enslave others.

I believe in what I am doing, and that is why I am here. God Bless you for praying for us, I am Scott L..

Gilda M. Schaut

SOUL OF PAUL

I am the spirit of a soldier who was wounded in Iraq. I am 32 years old. I am a platoon leader in charge of a section of the city. The soldiers who work with me are usually younger and inexperienced. The basic training is good, but they don't know how inhospitable and evil this place is. Yesterday, I was leading a group of eight soldiers. We had been directed to patrol a neighborhood that was full of ordinary people; men, women and children. After patrolling for three hours, we regrouped. During a short break, I was alerted by one of my men that they had found a house that they thought to be housing the enemy. We decided that we were going to divide our group and secure the area surrounding the house. Intel informed us that the enemy was inside, armed and ready to die for their beliefs. After several minutes, we blasted the door, and found three females screaming and showing us their children. It was at this same moment that an enemy soldier armed with a machine gun exited the house attempting to escape and started shooting at us. He was killed on the spot, but in the process he was able to get off rounds that wounded me and two of my men. This is the war that we have to face every day. The purpose of this communication is to make people aware that this is a condition that occurs almost everyday. The enemy is made up of cowards that hide in homes of the city. They use their own people as shields. They have no morals.

Thank you for listening and keeping us in your prayers.

I am Sgt. Paul.

SOUL OF EDWARD

I am in the process called discernment. Yes, I am the soul of soldier who died during a battle in Iraq. I came to you, because I wanted to let my family know that I am better off here, then crippled for the rest of my life. My name is Edward and I was in an ambush with six of my companions. All of a sudden, two Iraqis with machine guns had attacked us and three of us were severely wounded. The other three went for help, and to peruse the attackers. For me, help was too late. Richard and Paul, we're taken by the paramedics back to the base.

The first time I awoke on this side, I was still in my fatigues. The place was the same place where my body was found? After I made sure that I was okay, I called to the others, but nobody came. I searched the surrounding area but I couldn't find anyone. I tried to retrace my steps in hopes of returning to my unit. I found a group of soldiers, walking in the same direction I was and asked them where they were going. One of them indicated that they were trying to find their headquarters, so that they could be reassigned to a new area. That made sense to me and I want along with them. The only thing that was different was a sense of peace and lack of fear. During the march, I asked one of the soldiers how I could find out about the status my companions. The Sgt. in-charge said that they had tried to communicate with them, but were unable to reach them. A strange feeling started making me feel insecure and afraid. I decided to pray in silence. After I said "Our Father," a new soldier appeared by my side, and said that he would take me to where my friends were staying. In a second; I was at the side of the bed of my friend Richard. He was badly wounded and had lost an arm. Then I saw Peter and he was in a comatose state. I asked another soldier there, how I got there. He explained to me, I was able to travel that fast, because I was in my etheric body. It is then, that I realized that I was dead. The soldier who was my guide disappeared, and I found myself in a different place. We were with lots of people but not soldiers. This is the place where I went for discernment. Thousands of questions came to my mine; as soon as I formulated a question, the guide appeared and gave me the answers. I am still here, but little by little I am beginning to understand the process that the soul goes through and that, life is eternal. Thank you for listening to my words and praying for all of us I am Edward in the fourth sphere.

SOUL OF WALTER

I am a German soldier who was attacked by the enemy during the Second World War. My name is Walter and I am 17 years old. During the war, I was assigned to patrolling our barracks during the night. One night I was attacked buy two American soldiers. I was struck from behind and knocked unconscious for what seemed like a long time.

From then on I was near the barracks waiting to find out what had happened to my friends. At the same time I was wondering when I was going to be able to walk again. It felt like my legs were completely broken. I was born in Wiesbaden and at some point my family left our home because they were afraid of the rioters during the war.

Question from Gilda: Do you want to live a normal life again?

Answer from Walter: This is depressing place is all that I know. Yes I would like to go home.

Gilda: Let us pray.

The minute you finished your prayers, two men came to me and helped me to stand and let me know that they were going to be my guides. Then they told me that I was fine and I would be able to go to my home that I had longed for. This is like the movies. I am here and I can see that everything has changed. The road to my home is now a four way separate highway. The buildings are new, and Germany is like a different country. My guides told me that now I am in my etheric body, which is the projection of my body, in my last incarnation. I now know that I was physically dead and now I am alive. My guides will now take me to a place where I will be able to see my previous life, and be again able to continue my journey.

Thank you Gilda for offering your time to help me regain my mind and to believe that God is the one and only source of life and love in this world.

Gilda, I am in your aura and I beg you to listen. I am a man that was killed on a battlefield. I am an American and I know you are able to listen to me. The first impression after I passed to this new "land" was to try to find out where I was. The place looked to me like the one I was in before I expired. I then realized that I was alone and my physical body felt light and almost ethereal. The horror of knowing the truth caught me by surprise! I am dead. Why I am able to still think, see, and talk to you is a mystery. I want to understand why I am here and when I will be released. Pray for me and I will be listening.

What is your name?

My name is Karl and I am 23 years old.

What do you want to know?

First I want to know if I am alive or dead?

Karl you are alive because you are in your spiritual self and ethereal self. You are conscious of your being and the reason for that is that all creation is a constant expression of GOD. You are God individualized.

Where am I now?

You are in a transitional state and in another dimension. To be able to progress in your understanding you need to ask to be guided. There are light beings that will come to you and explain the next steps.

Karl: I don't see anybody. The landscape is barren and there is not a soul around.

Karl, did you have any religious instruction when you were grown up?

This conversation is not helping me. I don't believe in the unknown.

Do you remember somebody in your family who passed away years ago?

Yes, that was my cousin Albert. He was ill and he died 6 years ago.

We will pray and ask to see your cousin. Let us pray.

Karl: In the middle of your prayers I saw a light and I heard a sound that increased vibration. All of a sudden a being of light appeared and came closer. I understood that he wanted to tell me that the presence of my cousin was not necessary. What I need is to listen and open my mind. Then another being appeared! This was an angel because I recognized his presence as such. He said that you called him and he will be my guide and companion. I can't explain to you my gratitude. These beings of light encompass an enormous area and I feel like I am lifted from my body and carried though space. They are telling me that you are a forerunner and your mission is to help souls who are in need. In the meantime I saw a change in my environment. I am no longer at that place of battle.

Where are you now?

The perspective is amazing! I use to think that nothing compared with the grandiose view of the Grand Canyon. Where I am is a valley full of tress and water and at both sides are these tall mountains. I am in a new dimension and I realize that this new facet of my life is a period of recognition of my deeds and a searching for the meaning of life. The guidance and love that surrounds me is incredible! The most amazing thing is the mental communication. I am able not only to talk to you but to countless other souls who live in this place.

What do you call that place?

This is not a place on the planet. I am in a valley and as far as I can see there are hundreds of tress, rivers and flowers. I think the purpose of me being here is to learn how to mange the projections of my mind. I recall a time when I was only able to see a barren landscape. What I have found out is that my mind can project these pictures and suddenly I am in the middle of it.

What about your guides?

I saw them. They are teaching me about the things I ask.

I want to know why you offered your help to me?

I am a medium and my training is part of my mission to help others, the ones who want to be helped only. I have learned to listen to my guides though many incarnations. I am glad if I was able to be of any help.

What happened to your memories?

When I first came to this place, the first thing I wanted to know was why I was here. Then I remembered the battlefield and there I was again. The thought of remembering it is kind of scary. I don't want to go back to that place.

Karl, your past life was not only your life as a soldier. You were a son in a family. You went to school and had friends or girlfriends. If you want to recall parts that are nice in your past life you can. You don't have to be afraid of going back there; ask your guardian angel to guide you and protect you.

I am Karl. I want to talk to you and let you know what I have learned since the last time we talked. The minute you left another being of light came and began talking to me telepathically. I assume it was my guardian angel. I realized then that what you told me was the truth. I have lived on earth for 23 years and I should remember who I was. His love, patience and understanding made me realize that I should not have to fear anything. The recollection of every important act of hat life came to me in a second and I saw my life projected on a screen. Then a strange thing happened. I was there at the same time and I was aware of watching! The realization of good and bad that has happened to me was a very rewarding experience. I can say now that I understand why I was living, and what the purpose of my life was. I want to go forward to learn and experience the potential of my soul. The angel left me with the feeling of accomplishment and self-worth that I thought I had lost.

Are you still alone?

I am alone but I am thinking that soon I will meet somebody. It is strange that nobody lives in this beautiful valley.

I am the one you call Karl. I am in your aura and thank you for helping me. The minute I saw you I recognized you. This place is a vision of Eden. The trees are so tall and they sine. The sky is always blue and the sir is cool and breezy. The only source of light is the presence of love that surrounds all living creatures in here.

What have you done since we talked last?

After the reviewing of my past life my guide explained to me that the purpose of seeing the past was to evaluate our mistakes. This angel gave me a recollection of all the good and bad deeds I have made. To see one's self judging others is one the worst acts because we don't know why that person is taking that attitude. Now I know that some of the things I did were acts of revenge and that was a way to express my anger towards that person.

Did you feel sad for the roll you played during the war?

Yes. I realized that I was inflicting pain and misery in a different part of that country.

What country is that?

A. I was killed in Afghanistan. I understand that the war was a means to make them understand that you can kill innocent people in the name of GOD. During my short stay in that area I saw so many families desolated by the attacks. Many were females and children, running away from the Al-kigh-da Regime. Not all the people who live there are bad.

I am a soul who already has been in your aura. Yes I am Karl. I am aware of your mission and I see that your aura changes colors and patterns when you greet me. I am in the 6th sphere and I am ready to learn a new method of communication. As you can see I am able to talk to you and other souls who are in this place. I realize that the concept of loneliness is one of surrounding ourselves with a wall of mistrust. During the first day of my stay in this beautiful place I was all by myself. Then as I recalled my past life and realized that life is a never-ending expression of the divine light, I began to see other souls. They are as real as I am. They approached me and I realized that all of them were aware of where they were and happy to be here! Then they told me of a program to learn new mental skills. One of them offered to guide me and we went to a reunion of souls who were eager to learn. There were several teachers. One took the podium and gave a dissertation about the importance of perception. This was a new subject to me and I learned a lot. The second teacher spoke about mediation and the effect of this discipline to the soul. I have never made a connection of mind and soul and see how important it is to think positive. The art of mediation is a practice which is learned during several incarnations and this knowledge opened the heart chakra and allowed the light to pass through. The reality of these teachings and the awareness of the pupils is so impressive you can see the light! We practiced this discipline and an urgency of love and oneness surrounded the group. Maybe these are the experiences that will stay with us forever. Gilda, thank you for listening to me. You are the one who first was willing to see that I was not dead. I am alive and happy.

Do you want to let your family know that you are happy?

I know that you mean well but they are not ready to understand where I am or why. I am ready to learn because I was prepared to listen in previous incarnations. Thanks again, I am Karl who blesses you.

OSAMA BIN LADEN

Question: Is Osama Bin Laden alive, and where is he? Why is he so intent on causing so much pain to his people and others?

Answer: Osama Bin Laden is a leader of a group of Muslim people that believe that their faith should be the only one on this planet. He is a soul who came to this world to help his people, but instead he chose to help his own ego. His perception of good became distorted and he decided to increase the number of followers to his religious beliefs, and start a religious war. In his mind he considers himself a religious leader.

Yes, he is alive and in disguise in the mountains of the border of Afghanistan and Iran. His followers consider him a soul sent by Allah to purify their race.

Question: Everything has a beginning and an end. When will the majority of the Arab people realize that this man, Osama bin Laden, is a bad leader that doesn't help his people?

Answer: Osama bin Laden, is a religious leader of a fraction of the Islamic population. The leaders of the governments of the Islamic faith, are not in agreement with his tactics. The majority of Islamic believers are normal people, with a different ethnic culture than the people of western countries.

These differences will not change during this span of time. The future of this planet is the reconstruction of not only the lives, and material things, but also the desire to live a life with a higher degree of acceptance of the different races.

After the cataclysm, the knowledge that we are not the only ones in this universe, will act, as an enzyme that will unify the inhabitants of this planet in knowing there is only one omnipotent God, the Creator.

Osama bin Laden is today a symbol of a leader of a group of people who are desperately trying to prove that their ideas are right. He will not be successful, because it is impossible to convince everybody that doing unfair acts can produce good results.

THE SOUL OF GEORGE

I am the soul who lived during the war between the North and South of the USA. My company was stationed in Virginia. During one of those battles I lost my life, I was only seventeen years old, when I passed to this side of the veil. I encountered several other solders that had suffered as I had.

I couldn't understand why I was alive. Then I realized that the most important thing to remember was to know that life is eternal. I understood also that all of our actions have consequences. I wasn't capable of understanding the difference between my previous life, as a human and the life I was expressing at the other side, where everything was like memories from my mind.

After a long time I realized that many of the soldiers started to disappear. I asked why? And a voice told me that they were not on earth anymore. That was a big emotional shock to me. Then I wanted to know how I had arrived in this new place. My spiritual guide answered: You are not dead; you are alive in another dimension. To know the truth, open your mind and understand that life is eternal.

My guide took me to a place of peace, where I was able to see parts of my life as a boy and later as an adult. I cried when I saw my parents praying for me. After that I found myself in a place similar to the house in Virginia and I was comforted to know that several of my soldier friends were there in the same condition. I was one of the many who fought for the idea of liberty.

Now I am reincarnated and I live in another country. I know that this is the truth and I will keep on trying to offer others the opportunity to be free. I am George, a soul who died in 1762.

THE SOUL OF A SOLDIER

I am a soldier in the war against Iraq. I am being sent to the front for the third time. My job is to patrol the streets of the city and to teach the new soldiers how to protect themselves. Yes, I am alive and I was granted the privilege of speaking to you. The idea that this war is the solution to terrorism is wrong, because these people really believe in Allah as their Savior. The reason they hate us is because they think we are not part of their culture and their unique beliefs. They have been told that they are the only ones in the world who know the truth about God and religion.

Their lives and customs revolve around what Allah tells them to do.

I understand that other countries have other faiths and customs, but they are not aggressive or extremist, as these are. I believe that peace will come, when we recognize the futility of our mission.

I am a soldier, a Christian and a believer in the will of God!

SOUL OF CARL

I am Carl. I am a soldier in the English First Battalion. The isolation of this place is unbearable. I am in a prison, and the Taliban has kept me tied down to a pole for a long, long time. The food isn't enough to feed a bird. I've lost a lot of weight. There are other soldiers here with me. At least we are able to chat and remember.

Gilda: Carl, do you think it is possible to get out of there, and regain control of your life?

Carl: Yes, everything is possible!

Gilda: Let me help you, we will pray to God to set you free, and that can be an example of love and gratitude for the other soldiers that are with you.

Carl: The minute you said, "let the love of God ..." I saw a tall man come to my rescue. He spoke to me with power, he said: Soldier your days of sorrow are over. The light that is God is surrounding you and your friends and allowing you to know that you will be able to resume your free lives. Remember when they took you prisoner? Two days later, all of you were dead. The Taliban ordered the execution. The reason you thought that you remained in this cell is because you did not believe in the ethereal life. Yes, now you know. After that, we experienced a marvelous reshaping of our etheric bodies, and the entire landscape changed. We are now on a terrain similar to England. What a joy! I thank you, so do my pals, for your love and prayers. We are indebted to you, dear lady. I am Carl in the third sphere.

Gilda: I am your Teacher. The results of your prayers are the rehabilitation of so many souls, and the freedom to continue with their lives.

SOUL OF MARK

I am one of the soldiers who talked with you before. After a long time, I am able to talk to you again. Since I spoke with you last, I have restored my past memories and realize that I have lived on planet earth thousands of times before. This was a proof of reincarnation for me. I am studying why we have to go through this process, and how each time we learn more about one's relationship with God. I know now that is not important what religious belief you were raised with. What's important is to express the best of your soul and to act as patient and loving as you can. Dear Lady, thank you for listening. I am Mark, in the seventeenth sphere.

SOUL OF GERALD

Dear Gilda, I am one of the soldiers who have come to you to tell my story. The day I joined the service; I was convinced that this was what I wanted to do. The honor of serving my country and the opportunity of learning were two very powerful incentives. After training I was sent to Iraq. I've been there for almost a year. The ideas I had of the world have changed completely. I realized how blessed we are, to live in a country where we respect each other, we're free to speak and to vote, and we have so many opportunities that you don't find in other places.

The realization that in a small part I am contributing to the development of peace and a better way of life for these people makes me feel good. I have seen many injustices being committed, and I pity the ones who commit violence against their own people.

The purpose of this letter is to let you know, that regardless of what you read in the papers, this war was necessary. Many people are dead, and maybe there will be many more. The people of Iraq and of the Middle East deserve a better way of life.

I am Sgt. Gerald Thompson, and I thank you for your time.

SOUL OF CARL

My name is Carl, I am twenty years old, and I am in Iraq. I have been here only two months. The lieutenant in charge is an experienced soldier and he inspires confidence and a sense of respect. I miss my home. I am the oldest of a family of five. I came to this place thinking that this commitment will release my father of so much work to provide for the rest of the family. My three sisters are in school, and the older boy is in an institution for the mentally disturbed. This fact, affected all of us. My mother has suffered a lot, and we know that there is no cure. Dear Lady, pray for my family and me. We are regular Americans and our desire is to see this country free of the menace of the Taliban. Thank you for listening.

The Souls of George and Paul (Part One)

I am the soul of a soldier who is here because a guide asked me to follow him. I know that you are a "being of light," and you can hear me. My name is George, and I am 34 years old. I am in the engineering corps and was assigned to go with six of my pals to a remote place, between two mountains. We are in Afghanistan. This place is all rocks and sand. Three of my soldiers died yesterday. We were attacked by a bunch of Arabs, who wear these pantaloons and scarves on their heads. They came upon us by surprise and we were outnumbered and we surrendered. We were prisoners but we were able to escape. Paul and I ran for our lives. We only stopped, when we're about 5 km away from them. We almost couldn't breathe. Why am I telling you all of this? It is because for a strange reason, we can't find the rest of our patrols. We ask you to please help us.

Response: Dear George and Paul, you are alive! Yes, you are seeing around you, the projection of your mind. You are in your etheric body, which is a copy of your formal physical body. Life is eternal. Your guide is waiting for the both of you.

George: I am still here? I can't believe what you told me. I can see the soil and the mountains! How can I see Paul?

Response: Because you have the vision in your mind, and the control of your senses.

George: How can I get out of here? We have been stuck in this place for days!

THE SOULS OF GEORGE AND PAUL (PART TWO)

I am the soldier named George. We came to you to ask for help. Do you remember Carl? Yes, he is here with me. After we talked to you and listened to your explanation and we arrived at the conclusion that we were "dead." We couldn't understand why we were able to see, listen, and feel the world around us. Your explanation makes sense. We asked our guide to take us to a different place, and all of a sudden, we were in place full of soldiers. They were all waiting to be called. We waited and when our name was called, we found ourselves in a completely different place, according to our beliefs. I remembered the second I was there, the time my mother explained to me that we part of the creation. God, our creator was the one we worshiped, and we understood that our religious beliefs we're part of this basic concept. I was not a person who went to church when I was growing up. Life was not easy, and I lived day-by-day just working and trying to get by. My lack of understanding in these matters was because I was not interested in religion. Then I saw a screen, the size of a wall and in it were pictures of parts of my life. It was so real that it brought tears to my eyes. I realized then, that I was not the best guy in the world. The pain I inflicted on to others, came back to me, as a real personal pain. I was so ashamed! Then, they showed me some of that good I did. I was so surprised to realize that other people reacted that way to my kindness. After this evaluation, the screen disappeared and I found myself in a totally different place. This was like Virginia, the place where I was born and raised. I am still here, living a different life, looking forward to being more informed about the nature of our spiritual life. Thank you for listening; I am George and the third sphere.

THE SOULS OF A GEORGE AND PAUL (PART THREE)

I am Paul. Greetings! I went through a process similar to George, but the difference was in the way I was taught about religion. My parents were Jewish, and the way they live was a demonstration of their religious beliefs. I believe that we are part of the creative process that is God. There is only one God. Because of that, I passed the process of recollection, and found myself in a different place. I was aware of the presence of relatives that passed away before, and they're loving welcome. This is a place, where people are free and worshiping God, in any way that they please. It is a vast park, full of trees and flowers. Life is good. I thank you for opening our minds and spirits into accepting and understanding that life is eternal. I am in the sixth sphere.

THE SOUL OF A LEONIDE

Greetings, I am the spirit of a soldier who died during the Korean War. For the longest time I was convinced that I was a prisoner of war. I was experiencing all the misery that you go through, when you are in a dirty cell with ten or more men. One day, after a prisoner came into the cell. He was older, and he began to pray. He did not pray out loud. Never the less, we realized, that he was praying. That simple act triggered a remembrance of our younger years, in our minds. It was then, that I decided to pray in silence too, and asked the Lord for guidance.

At that moment, I saw myself in another location. In that new place there were many people of different races and gender. I understood they were waiting. Soon afterwards we were called by name and a guide appeared, and they left the group. Then my turn came. I was taken to a large room, where there was kind of a drape on the wall; on it I saw parts of my past life. I could not believe what I was watching. My parents, young and healthy, were smiling at me. I also saw my brother and two older sisters. Then I saw my teenage years. I was a hard working lad. I helped my dad in his shop. Times were difficult and jobs were scarce. I was forced to go into the army. The love and support of my family, was like a balm that helped me to survive in that jail. Then I realized that the reason that I was seeing this was because I was dead!

I asked my guide to explain to me why did I have to endure so much pain. I was not a bad person. He told me that I had many opportunities to ask for assistance and recognize that we were all God's children. Then I realized that, I never in my life gave

any importance to the spiritual side of myself. That was one of the most important lessons that I learned in that life. I am Leonide, a soldier. Thank you for listening.

SOUL OF ROBERT

I am the spirit of a soldier who came to you days ago. I am in Iraq and I am a paramedic. The day I talked to you I learned that it is possible to communicate mentally with other human beings. This was the first time in my life that this had happened to me. Because of that, I want to learn more about what you are doing. This process of telepathic communication is like a new way of thinking. Many times I wanted to reach out to my patients, and find out how they were feeling. Sometimes it's frustrating to see somebody hurt and not being able to communicate with him or her.

I thank you for the opportunity you have given me to express my thoughts. Yours in Christ, First Sgt. Robert

SOUL OF MANUEL

I am a soldier, and my soul is in a place I call "in transit." My name is Manual Pindera and I am in the fourth sphere. My guide told me that you would help me. I belong to a group of soldiers, whose mission was to patrol the center of Baghdad.

I am 21 years old, and I left my physical body due a wound that I received while on training patrol. In the beginning I couldn't understand what had happened to me. I found myself in a strange place not understanding where I was. Then my thoughts started to come back to me. I saw several soldiers who were talking about where they had been. The strange thing was that I could understand what they were thinking without talking to them. One of them recognized me and let me know what had happened. His recollection of the past event was so clear; I couldn't doubt that he was telling the truth. It was then that I realized I was in another dimension. I know that life is eternal because I am Catholic. My parents have other sons, but they always will remember me as the one who didn't return. When I realized I was alive, it was a beautiful feeling. I decided to find out if somebody could guide me. In an instant my guide appeared. His name is Ignacio and he is a being of light. He explained to me the process of adjustment and how I will be able to see my past life. That was like a revelation, because I was able to see all the love and dedication of my parents in the eternal relationship that connects us.

Gilda, I know you listen to people like me and collect these cases. I wanted to tell my parents that I am okay and happy to be in this dimension and hoping that I will see them in the future.

God bless you.

SOUL OF DONALD

I am an American soldier stationed in Afghanistan. I am with eighteen other soldiers, and our mission is to advance, and verify the target. This mission is very dangerous, because we don't know where the enemy is hiding. My friends and I, approached a building, that we thought was abandoned. The truth was, that there were three Afghans, and all of them were armed with machine guns. I thought that we were in hell. The sound and terror was such, that in a second, we were all out of there and running. This happened a long time ago, and we have not been able to find our platoon. We are tired and stressed, and looking for any help possible.

Gilda: What is your name and the names of your pals?

Roland: My name is Ronald and my pal's names are Donald and James, and we are in the middle of nowhere. We would be grateful if you can bring us help.

Gilda: What is happening now?

Ronald: We see a tall soldier approaching us now. He is greeting us and explaining to us, that we are in a different dimension. He is asking us if we would be willing to follow him, and look for a safer place to stay. I don't believe it. He seems like a real person. I tried talking with Donald and James. They are tired of staying where we are and agree to follow this guy to a better place.

Gilda: What happens next?

Donald: You won't believe this, as soon as we agree, the landscape changes, and we are standing in a spacious terrain full of trees and small ponds. It looks like the place where we went on vacation in Colorado. This is incredible! The person that guided us here is no longer dressed as a soldier, and explains to us, that we were alive, but in our etheric bodies. He went on to tell us that life is eternal and involves the progression of experiences in different bodies called incarnations. We just finished one life on the planet earth. He also said that the mission we were sent to ended and now we were ready to experience our real life, as the soul expression of God.

Dear Gilda, thank you for releasing our souls, minds and etheric bodies of that nightmare. We are Americans and believe in God and country. In a way, I am glad that I had the opportunity to serve my country, to be a good son, and to live in a privileged country. I am Donald.

CHAPTER 8

Books and Discussion

DISCUSSION OF "THE ATOM-SMASHING POWER OF THE MIND" BY CHARLES FILLMORE

The book you are reading was one of the most frequently read books by the followers of Unity. His work brought light and understanding to many Christians that at that time, did not know about the other bodies mankind has, but only knew about the physical. His inspiration and resolution to write about that subject came to him after he experienced the revelation of his own healing. Charles Fillmore was an advanced soul, whose purpose in life was to awaken the divine ideas, in the people who were ready to understand.

The book that you are writing, is for the purpose of explaining events that are happening, and the reason why they are taking place. The acceptance of new ideas or realities is part of the growing process that mankind needs, in order to progress in understanding the evolution of the soul and the evolution of the planet where we live. At the moment, there are few people ready to assimilate these new concepts. People are so absorbed in the realities of their daily lives that they don't want to consider a different future. The basic teachings of Metaphysics and the spiritual instructions of different religious faiths in this world are not sufficient tools to prepare the masses for the impending cataclysm.

The renovation of every concept and idea about the presence of God will be one of the greatest changes in the dynamic thinking of the new generations. The confirmation of life on other worlds, and the possibility of a cooperation of ideas and a better future for this planet will be like a balm of healing in a wound.

To be prepared spiritually and physically many will try to improve their commitment to their religious ideas, others will try to accept their faith and be resigned to any event.

Gilda, I am one of your mentors, my name is Thomas. I came to tell you that your mind is ready to listen and cooperate with our space brothers. They know there are many souls like you that at this moment are aware of the future of this planet. They want to assist you and convey their thoughts to you. They know of your mission and they are ready to help you accomplish your goal.

Discussion of "Miracles and Other Wonders" By Charles E. Sellier

How is a person, who is in a wheelchair, able to help a teenager who was stranded in a wind and snow storm?

Answer: The presence that assisted the girl was the astral body of the invalid lady. The voice the father heard on the phone was the projection of the plea for help; the person that was the receiver, sent the message to the mind of the father. The girl was in need, she prayed for help and her prayer was answered. When Mrs. Morgan was looking through that window, she heard the cry for help and it was her desire to be of help. Yes, she was and is a soul who is aware of the omnipotence of God; she knows that everything is possible in His name. This amazing feat is called astral displacement and happens anytime an advanced soul goes to the aide of a soul in distress. This actually happens quite often but people are superstitious and dismiss the possibility of these acts.

Question: Does this happen here on earth and on other planets as well?

Answer: Yes, the only difference would be how solid the bodies are. In other spheres, the rescuers are able to materialize, in order to help those who are not evolved enough to accept their new condition. Yes, the more you advance the less you will need your ethereal body.

Question: What happens later when we let go of the ethereal body? Do we just dismiss this body because we have no use for it?

Answer: The soul who reaches the understanding of Master, assumes a degree of responsibility and teaching degree. It becomes their duty to travel and teach their knowledge. In that stage of development the soul discards the ethereal body and acquires the sublime light that will help him to carry on the work of love and life he is assigned.

Discussion of "Marcus" by Paul Dyal

The book called "Marcus" by Paul Dyal is one of the best documented stories of the time of the crucifixion. The development of the different characters and the description of the different places where our Lord walked on earth are authentic. The illusion of the Jewish people about the restoration of their power, and Jesus as their leader, what's an unfounded idea. Jesus explained clearly that his reign was not of this world. They did not want to listen. Jesus came to change the laws, not to liberate them from Roman domination.

Question: Did Jesus feel sad to be so misunderstood?

Answer: Jesus knew that the majority of his people we're close minded. He knew also that his job was not, to be a military hero. He accepted the role as the savior of souls, not of bodies.

Evolution is based on the understanding of the soul. Because of that Jesus knew that the process of reincarnation would take care of the problems of his race. His disciples accepted His teachings and understood that he was training them to teach future generations. They knew that he would leave this earth, and go to the Father. The development of the Christian religions happened after his death, and that was based on the teachings of

Jesus, not on the Jewish teachings. The recounting of the life and miracles of Jesus by his disciples are the books of the New Testament. The different aspects of each chapter are due to the different points of view of each of the apostles. Life at that time was most difficult, and many of them were afraid of repercussions. That is the reason they departed from Jerusalem, and journeyed to other parts of the Roman Empire, to write and teach. To the understanding of today's society, all of these teachings are unique and marvelous tales. The truth is that most of the stories are very real, and they change the way one could perceive and do things in this world. Christians understood that the way to salvation was through the teachings of Jesus. His lessons were to inform man about compassion and integrity. This is what changed civilizations. The freedom of the soul is the light that shines when a person chooses to act in a positive way that is why he said "I am the light and the way." The process of enlightenment on planet Earth has taken many, many incarnations.

The new discoveries of the Internet and other visual technology are a positive achievement. They will not only enhance the knowledge in other parts of the world, but they demonstrate how intrinsically connected all of nature is. The idea of respect and care for the resources of the planet will increase during the next generations.

Many new discoveries in chemistry and biology will help with the production of new and better products for consumers. The development of a conscience in a society that needs to function as a whole, and not as enemies, will help to find the way towards mutual cooperation. All of this will take place after the cataclysm.

"THE AQUARIAN GOSPEL OF JESUS THE CHRIST" BY LEVI DOWLING

Levi Dowling was a student of religion and spent forty years in study and silent meditation, which prepared him to be the messenger to carry this knowledge, which was recorded in the Akashic record during the time of Jesus Christ.

In section XV Jesus went to Jerusalem to the temple and was disappointed to see the money changers in the House of God. He drove the merchants out and set the birds and lambs free. Jesus was confronted by the priest, and questioned about being a King. In section XV, page 105, verse 28-31, Jesus says "The King is God; the pure in heart alone can see the face of God and live." "I am the candle of the Lord a flame to light the way; and while you have the light, walk in the light."

Explanation - Jesus comes back to the temple and explains, what a Messiah is in a parable. Jesus performed several healings and spoke of kindness. Nicodemis, ruler of the Jews, went by night to talk to Jesus.

In section XV, page 108, verse 11, Jesus says, "Except a man be born of water and the holy Breath, he cannot come into the kingdom of the Holy One."

Answer by teacher Tumargeo- When Jesus spoke those words; he referred to the inner essence of knowledge that is a part of every soul. The process of evolution of the soul is in part, during the life on this planet. Because man is 80% water, Jesus said: "Except a man is born of water, confirming his experience as a human being. Then He mentions the Holy Breath, which shows his awareness of his son-ship as a child of God.

Verse 12 "That which is born of flesh is child of man; that which is born of Holy Breath is child of God."

Verse15, page 108 "And Jesus said: The kingdom of the Holy One is in the soul, man cannot see it with his carnal eyes; with all their reasoning powers, they comprehend it not."

Verse 16 "It is a life deep hid in God, its recognition is the work of inner consciousness."

Verse 17 "The kingdoms of the world are kingdoms of the sight, the kingdom of the Holy One is that of faith; its King is love."

In chapter 81, Jesus teaches a woman of Samaria. She asked who He was and this was Jesus's answer, Verse 23, "I am the one who came to break away the wall that separates the sons of men. In Holy Breath there is no Greek, or Jew, and not Samaritan; no bond, no free, for all are one."

At the end of chapter 81 verses 26-29, Jesus teaches the Samarian woman at Jacob's well. He tells her that," men must worship God within the temple of the heart." Then he tells her, "Behold the Christ has come; Messiah speaks to you."

Jesus went to several other towns, and continued to pray and teach. He was healing the sick, when summoned by the Priest. He explains to them he did not come to break the law, but to help the sick, and to teach that if they were united in the cause of right, they would win; if they were divided they would fall.

Chapter 85, page 117-118 Gilda's teacher, Tumargeo explains. The chapter you just read is the story of the Apostle, John the Baptist, when the soldiers of Herod apprehended him. John knew that his work was done. His faith and his love for Jesus were his shield. He was sent to prison for telling the truth. The disciples asked Jesus

why God had allowed this to happen. Jesus explained that John had finished his work, and those rulers will do to Him, the same thing they did to John. Verse 18, page 118, Jesus says "All these events are part of God's own plan. The innocent will suffer while the wicked are in power; but woe to them who cause the suffering of the innocents."

In Section XV, Chapter 88, there is an explanation of how Jesus chose his twelve apostles. This happened at the Sea of Galilee and the first four apostles were fisherman Peter, Andrew, James and John. Phillip and Nathaniel were teachers of Greek philosophy at Bethsaida and Jesus tells them, "the Masters have a higher work for you and me to do; I go and you may follow me." Mathew was a Roman and he was knowledgeable about the ways of the Jews, Syrians, and Greeks.

On page 121, verse 25; we are told Ischariot and his son Judas were employed by Matthew at the tribute house. Jesus tells Judas to stop his work and come with him. Jesus met a lawyer and Greek philosopher named Thomas, who was chosen because he could interpret law. In verse 30, when Jesus gets home that evening, his kindred, James and Jude, sons of Alpheus and Miriam, are there. They are called men of faith and carpenters of Nazareth. Jesus tells them, "The Masters call us now to aid in building homes for souls; homes built without the sound of hammer, ax, or saw;"

James and Jude exclaim "Lord, we will follow you." The next day Jesus sends a message to Simon," leader of the Zelotes, a strict exponent of the Jewish law." In verse 35 we are told "And in the message Jesus said, the masters call for men to demonstrate the faith of Abraham; I go and you may follow me. And Simon followed him."

Question- In chapter 90, verse 19-26, Did Jesus say to the palsy man, "I forgive your sins," and he was cured because Jesus was referring to the man's karma?

Answer- The question you ask is; why did Jesus mention the man's sins, before he cured him? The reason was that this man was born with the propensity for that disease. The family members were in debt to him, and they needed to repay him with love and kindness for the wrongs they had done to him in a previous life. Jesus saw the love and dedication of his family and forgave their sins. The soul of the sick man was liberated from the negative karma and his health was restored.

"The Da Vinci Code" Book by Dan Brown

I am reading the book, "The Da Vinci Code" by Dan Brown, should I read it with caution, because half of the story is only the imagination of the author?

Answer- The book you are reading is based on the programs of the Catholic Church to teach and manipulate the people. According to the author, the code was written

to prevent further dissention between the Protestants and the Catholics. The belief that Michelangelo was a soul, who did not believe in the after-life, is not truth. He was an inspired soul, who dedicated his life to reproducing the images that came to his mind. He was a medium and his visions were grandiose! The desire to express his love and faith gave him the strength to continue to do so, in spite of the many enemies he encountered through his life. As you have dedicated part of your life to write your meditations, Michelangelo painted the visions he received in meditation. Blessed are those who believe.

Discussion of "Hidden Messages in Water" by Masaru Emoto

Question: Is language the expression of the components of the planet or is it the expression of a particular race of people?

Answer: The reason you have different languages on your planet is because the first humans appeared on earth in different continents and are of different races. The sounds they needed to communicate were the basis for language. The development of language changed when man decided to move and conquer other places.

Question: Then why is water positively influenced by the same word in different languages?

Answer: The "meaning" of a word is the fact that influences the water. Words are the vocal or written expression of thoughts.

Question: What is the meaning of "Before the tower of Babel all people spoke the same language?

Answer: This phrase from the Bible, tries to explain that the prevalent thought before the destruction of the city was of a negative nature.

I read an article in the March-April 1989 issue of the American Scientific Journal, by Warren J. Hamerman. He wrote that the "organic matter that forms human beings generates a frequency that can be represented by sound at approximately forty-two octaves above middle C. The modern standard for middle C is approximately 262 HZ, so this means that the sound vibrates

570 trillion times a second, a number that exceeds the imagination and indicates incredible and wonderful hidden potential."

Question: Is this the reason for the music of the spheres, and why each sphere must have different music?

Answer- The explanation that you read about the vibratory patterns of physical objects, including humans, animals and plants is not totally correct. The evaluation of the vibration is in error. The realization that every object produces sound is not the cause of the music of the spheres. The harmonious thoughts of the living species on the planets cause the music of the spheres. When you are in a forest, you feel peace. You are aware of the vibrations of Peace. When you are in a big city, you are aware of the vibrations of anxiety, negativity and fear that collectively produce notes of dissonance. As above, so below, each sphere attracts souls of similar vibrations and the collections of those thoughts form a "music" or noise according to the degree of evolution of the souls in that place.

Question: Is this the same throughout the universe?

Answer: No, there are solar systems that are not ready to express this sound, and there are others that are only expressing positive thoughts and of course the music is glorious.

DISCUSSION OF "MESSAGES FROM THE VIRGIN MARY" BY STEFANO GOBBI

The soul called Stefano Gobbi, is an Italian Priest who devoted his life to the Virgin Mary. The denomination of his congregation, The Marians, is a group of priests who devote their lives the Virgin Mary. Mary is an evolved soul, who in the mind of many millions of people is the mother of Jesus (the man), and the mother of God to the people of the Catholic faith. The concept of Deity is what is in doubt in these statements.

To the Catholics, Jesus Christ is God. To the remainder of Christians, "Jesus is one with God." God is Spirit, Light, Love, Law and Life. This spirit of God is manifested throughout the universe as His creation. Because all of the atoms that form the human body are part of the creative process of God, we are one with God. At the time Jesus said "I and my father are one ", humans did not know what an atom was and knew even less about the important functions and force called life or energy that existed in each one of them. The universality of the spirit of God is a concept not easy to comprehend.

Planet earth is one of the smaller planets of this solar system. The development and evolution of this planet is very new. The different religions on this planet constitute phases of understanding that humans go through, in order to understand their relationship with God. The majority of humans on this planet think that they are the only intelligent beings in the universe! The ideas of each religion are revised and outdated according to the emotional and intellectual advancement of the different groups of believers.

Messages from the Virgin Mary

One of the major religions in the world today is Christianity. Their faith teaches that God and Jesus are one. That statement is truth. The concept that Jesus is God is not truth. Jesus is a master and the teachings and miracles he performed, testified to his powers. He knew that his words would be misunderstood. Mary his mother, is a pure and exalted soul. She came to assist the people who asked for her help. The thoughts and ideas that she sent to Stefano Gobbi are written according to the parameters of Stefano's faith and understanding.

The interpretation of the symbols of Revelations, are based on the premise that God is all powerful and that Jesus as His son, has the power to stop all these negative acts that have been happening all over the world. Stefano is a devoted soul and his beliefs and understanding are based on the teachings of the church, however the interpretations of the words of Mary are tinted by the dogmas and doctrines of his church. Mary, mother of Jesus, is the soul who has given information that will be influenced by the revision and outdating of several old fashioned ideas. Not all of the members of the church agree with these communications. The fame and power of the church can't admit to errors committed in the past. The work of Stefano Gobbi is positive, and will be influential in the revision of dogmas and new ideas for the Catholic Church. I am your teacher, Tumargeo and I bless you.

Discussion of "The Gospel According to the Son" by Norman Mailer

The book you are reading was written to evaluate the human form and the part of it that has the expression of Jesus. The life of a person at that time was based on how much they could share with others. To have a trade, meant that you would have food on your table and the respect of others. Jesus learned his trade from Joseph. The time he spent traveling to teach, he relied solely on the good will of others.

The work he did was a demonstration of Oneness with God. He demonstrated the power of healing and of commanding vibratory patterns of light, which allowed Him to cleanse the aura of individuals who were possessed by lower entities. During this period of demonstration, his soul was in constant attunement with God, which was the source of Light, Love, and Law applied in every case. In the end his demonstrations produced a uncontrolled envy in some of the leaders of the Sanhedrin. Jesus realized that His teachings were too advanced for the people of that time. His mission was to tell the truth. The misinterpretations and changes that occurred in the writings of the Bible are due to human error. Truth takes a long time to evolve in understanding. Each life gives us part of the truth that we are seeking. The knowledge you have acquired during many incarnations, has allowed you to tap into the process of the evolution of humanoids. This concept is a Universal one and includes people from other planets. During several of your communications you have talked to several of them. The degree of evolution of the majority of people on this planet, doesn't allow them to understand the process of reincarnation or the evolution of the soul. Jesus was a forerunner of Truth that is still to be proven.

DISCUSSION OF "ANATOMY OF SPIRIT" BY CAROLINE MYSS, PH.D.

Question: Is it true that you can act as a healing channel, and you do not need to be in a meditative state? On page 41 of the book it says you cannot be a healer if you are preoccupied with personal problems. It also says that prolonged depression often precedes the development of physical illness and we unconsciously create our own illness. On page 55 it says that a self motivated person is the one who is able to do whatever is required to maintain the balance of body, mind, and spirit, and each chakra is the source of an expression of being, through them we experience our relationship to the world that surrounds us. Can you comment?

Answer: Our sidereal development is one of the bases for awareness and use of these chakras. We are able to manifest the Universal Light, or Divine power only in the measure that we express positive thoughts and action. The other factor is karma. The foundation of a harmonious and healthy body is based on preplanning before we manifest as physical beings on this planet. Some diseases are part of the plan to re-establish a consciousness of oneness or as a balance for the trespasses committed by the soul who will be in charge of that body. We can understand that not all diseases are preplanned or congenital, but the ones that are congenital have a karmic source.

DISCUSSION OF "BEYOND BELIEF" BY ELAINE PAGELS

I am trying to understand what Jesus meant when he said "Truly, truly, I say unto you, unless you eat the flesh of the Son of Man and drink His blood, you have no life in you. For my flesh is truly food, and my blood is truly drink."

Answer: When Jesus was with His disciples, he knew that soon he would be leaving them. The last supper was a farewell party. The words He spoke were to remind them of His teachings. The way this phrase is written, is because of discussions and altercations between His disciples. When He said, unless you eat of the flesh of the Son of Man, He wanted to let them know that if they don't do and act as He taught them by example, they will not be able to evolve in life. When He said "and drink my blood" that phrase was to let them know that every time they drink, the forces of life are manifested in every atom. He was saying that it will be as if this living force enters their physical bodies and renews their material selves. Jesus knew that when you love and respect your physical body, you are expressing the rays of light in a better, clearer way, and that was the reason He said that the physical body is the temple of the soul on this planet. I am your teacher Tumargeo, who bless you

THE ANCIENT SECRET OF THE FLOWER OF LIFE-VOLUME I, BY DRUNVALO MELCHIZEDEK

I have been reading volume I of the books by Drunvalo Melchizedek and I have some questions, did the Martians actually invade the Earth and try to control the human population? Did the experiments that the Martians tried on humans, eventually lead to an extinction level event?

Answer: The reality is the Atlanteans reached a high level of evolution and some of the teachings of that civilization were left to the Egyptians, the Mayans, and certain tribes that lived near the border of Afghanistan. Those tribes used that knowledge to develop different teachings like astronomy, alchemy, medicine, and the basics of mathematics. The second question is the arrival of Martians to planet earth. Yes that happened; their planet was becoming a place detrimental to health and life.

The continent of Atlantis was a vast territory; it extended between what is today Central America, to the basin of the Mediterranean. In the north, was part of the land that today is the south of France. In the east, part of the land entered into the high mountains of Afghanistan. The western part was where the Atlantic Ocean is now.

Some of those islands in the Atlantic are the tops of mountains that were on the continent of Atlantis. There were seven big cities and many minor towns. Their civilization was based on the idea that One God and One Power was the creator of their race and life. They were intelligent self disciplined people. They knew how to distribute their wealth and provisions. They achieved great discoveries in the field of medicine, astronomy and in the use of metallurgy. Electricity was one of their main developments and they even used it to influence the weather patterns. When the Martians arrived in Atlantis, they were welcomed and the people were in awe. They realized that because they came from another planet, they needed to adapt to our atmosphere and use uniforms and equipment to be able to breathe. The Atlanteans were curious about them because they were able to travel through space, and had the knowledge to do so. Time and many innovations in the progress of the Martian race increased in the Atlanteans a sense of insecurity and fear, soon an idea to end this invasion of the Martians became their main preoccupation. The reason why Drunvalo mentioned the "MerKaBa" is because that secret process was used to allow humans of that time to communicate with beings in the fourth dimension or higher and ask questions, as you are doing today. The Atlanteans misused that secret code, and because of that they produced a cataclysm. Secret knowledge in the hands of ignorant people produced a terrible result.

Question: Why does Drunvalo want to teach "MerKaBa" now?

Answer: The secret teachings of the Atlanteans are one thing and the "MerKaBa" is another. The MerKaBa is a disciplined art of breathing. The discipline urges the individual to use the maximum capacity of his concentration to distribute the prana through their physical body. The unified effort of mind, body, and spirit produce a magnetic field around that person, which elevates the vibration of the particles in the aura. That difference in vibration is the one that allows the mind of the person to receive instructions and be guided. In your case, you are already in the fourth dimension, and don't need that discipline. The reasoning is that the more people who learn and are able to maintain a degree of efficiency in this, the better mankind will be able to live through the beginnings of the next Millennium. The survivors of the cataclysm will suffer tremendous losses. Their reality will be completely different than what they see today around them. To help people to understand why this will happen and what they will be able to do to adapt to the new environment, is what Drunvalo is teaching in the Flower of Life books.

Question: Does the concept of a Christ Consciousness grid, that holds the consciousness of the beings on this planet, exist? How aware are we of it?

Answer: The grid of Christ Consciousness is the electromagnetic force that surrounds your planet. This force is generated by the rotation of the planet. The scientists and astrophysicist are most aware of this force, because they have to take it into consideration when planning space exploration.

Question: Then this is happening all through the Universe?

Answer: Yes, that is so. The esoteric importance of this grid, is that according to the degree of evolution of the mass consciousness of the inhabitants of the planet, this grid is charged with different amounts of electrical particles. During an imbalance of consciousness such as what happened in Atlantis, the electrical charges were not sufficient to sustain the experimental projects, which they wanted to put in practice.

That was one of the causes for the failure of that powerful experiment. The atomic bomb is one of these kinds of experiments that can unbalance the charges of electricity in the grid of this planet. Humans of this generation are aware of the importance of preventing the next nuclear holocaust. The time will come when the nations of this planet will have to get together and discuss this subject.

Question: I do remember that you told me, under the Sphinx are remnants of the Atlantean civilization. On page 111-112, of Drunvalo's Volume I, there is spherical transparent ship one and a half miles under the Sphinx. The round image under the Sphinx, does it represent the grid of light?

Answer: This grid was built by the Atlanteans to emanate electricity that was needed to supply a set of immense dynamos, that were able to maintain the power for half of the population of the city of Kanar. During the cataclysm those dynamos were covered by one half of a mile of sand and dirt. The building of the Sphinx was a project of one of the first Pharaohs, and it has remained as a reminder of the mystery that was Atlantis.

Question: Why were only some of the enlightened people safe after the cataclysm on Atlantis?

Answer: The cataclysm that devastated Atlantis and other parts of this planet was a shifting of the poles. The change in temperature and rotation distortion produced many atmospheric patterns. The rain, storms, and tremors of earthquakes lasted for about ten days. The first impact was the worst, because people were not prepared for these terrible changes. Everything happened in seconds, and only those who at that moment lived at the margins of that continent were able to survive. The souls mentioned in the book, are those who were aware of these changes and had time to depart in one of the many air dirigibles they had at that time. They flew to the coast of what today is Spain and landed on top of the Pyrenees. They are the race that today is called the Vasques.

Question: Was I there at that time?

Answer: Yes, You and several people who worked with you. The first warning was the change of the winds. They began to speed up and soon rains and thunder began to cover the skies. At that time, the earth began to move and you and your companions were transported to a tall place, near one of the tributaries of the river Nile. For several days rain, cold, and dark was all you experienced. You and your companions survived and after walking for almost a week, arrived at a place that had water and provisions. When you looked around, the world you knew was completely changed. Great sorrow was felt by all. The remainder of that life was spent trying to find more survivors, and helping others to overcome the many obstacles in that new region. Some animals survived and they also were afraid and lost. The normalcy of day and night returned eventually, and a new beginning and a new purpose in life began again for all who survived.

Question: Were the people who lived near the Nile, the Egyptians?

Answer: The people who lived near the Nile at that time were the Nubians. These were a black race, tall and primitive. They knew how to survive by fishing and harvesting reeds and other products of that area. The civilization known as the Egyptians started a thousand years later. Gilda, your race was white and dated from the immigration of the Asians to the South, after the first period of the melting of the ice that covered part of the continent in the north, what is now Europe.

Question: page 113-114, Tumargeo, you told me that the Egyptian race evolved about 1,000 years after the Cataclysm of Atlantis, if that is so how did these souls survive?

Answer: Gilda, the book you are reading is explaining some esoteric stories. The things that Drunvalo is explaining are not stories that happened to humans. That is the story of the souls who departed from Atlantis and remained in the sixth sphere for one thousand years. When they realized that the Pharaoh of Egypt believed in one God, they decided to descend and enter into the pyramid. They were souls on their spiritual journey. These souls were attracted to the teachings of RA and they were subject to influence the mass consciousness of the people of that region.

Question: page 134-136, were Pharaoh Akhenaten and Queen Nefertiti of a different race and did that race come from the descendants of Sirius?

Answer: The explanation given in the book Volume I, as to why these souls came to your planet, at that time in Egypt is true. They were sent to mitigate the unrest of the people, and to unify the kingdom. The different formations of their skulls and skeletons was due to the custom of some tribes in upper Egypt to elongate the skulls of babies, because to them, it was a sign of beauty. The long neck was also a custom of these African tribes, and it is still happening today. The human aspect of these two souls is not the major factor of importance. These two souls were the cause of enormous changes for the people of that time. They brought peace and harmony to a disturbed society. Yes, they were souls who came to this planet from Sirius and they reincarnated to serve God. During their reign there was advancement in the sciences, agriculture, and astronomy.

Question: These elongated skulls have also been found in Peru and the Himalayas, are these remnants of the evolution that was Atlantis?

Answer: Yes, You understood immediately. The people, who survived after the cataclysm of Atlantis, became part of those new civilizations. They maintained parts of their physical structure through DNA but were no longer the advanced souls they were in Atlantis.

Question: If the civilization of Atlantis was more advanced scientifically than ours, why did they write on tablets? Did they have a written language? How did they communicate?

Answers: The tablets of thirty two pieces that Hermes Trigamentus found in Egypt was not the work of the Atlanteans. Those were part of the teachings of Thoth, and they were part of the religious secrets of the priests of Egypt. The Atlanteans were a race as advanced as yours is today. The cities were all planned, and in a way, better built than yours. They had a system of communication and they were able to send telepathic thoughts and sounds, similar to the idea of Chinese letters. The united sound of several of these characters was like your written language today. They could send written messages through space, because they built a system of antennas that conveyed those messages. Their knowledge of science, atoms, and electricity was more advanced than ours.

Question: Page 42, what do these Egyptian wheels represent, does it have anything to do with inter-dimensional travel? What about the Egyptian Neters with animal heads that are depicted under the wheels, engraved on the ceilings of the very old Egyptian temples in Egypt?

Answer: I can see that your mind is going around and around trying to figure out what the designs and the purpose of those wheels are. During the Egyptian empire, the studies of the cosmos took priority. They understood the importance of the seasons, and the pull of the moon, and their influence on humans and the crops they grew. Their civilization was related to the Nile, and the floods that brought with them the much needed fertilizers and humidity. The eight wheels that are in the temple are a representation of the phases of the moon, and the relationship with the weather patterns. The figures that are at the base of the wheels are the priests in charge of prayers and adorations needed to make these phases of the moon propitious to plant crops.

Question: Were the Egyptians aware of earths vibration and resonance at 7.8 Hz and the fact that we are in the third dimension?

Answer: The Egyptian priests were aware of other dimensions. They knew that sound and prayers combined to produce a quickening of the soul, and the opportunity to pass to other dimensions. They also knew how to use that knowledge to produce a magnetic field around certain objects, and move it to a new place. This method is called levitation, and was a common practice. They used it to build the pyramids and the temples, that knowledge was given only to certain priests, and they were subject to give their lives, if they dared to tell those secrets.

Question: Can we relearn the art of levitation again?

Answer: There are humans capable of doing that. The reason that it is not done today, is because man in general has become so incredibly materialistic that he will not believe that spirit is the force behind the quickening of the atoms. It is as simple as that!

Gilda, you are a spiritual person and you feel in your earth the pain of humanity. This state of consciousness called the third dimension is changing and will be replaced. The relation between the mass consciousness and the vibratory patterns of the earth are part of the cause of changes in the weather. The other cause is the displacement of your planet through the Universe. The influence of major stars and their attraction, will be the cause of the cataclysm. At this moment there are several million people who are already part of the fourth dimension. They are the ones who are part of the process necessary to progressively change the vibrations and begin to accept the new ideas of the future. Drunvalo Melchizedek and Greg Bradden are part of these new avatars, who have dedicated their lives to awaken the consciousness of humanity. Gilda your collaboration is of faith and love, and we appreciate your dedication.

THE ANCIENT SECRET OF THE FLOWER OF LIFE - VOLUME II, BY DRUNVALO MELCHIZEDEK

I have been reading volume II of the books by Drunvalo Melchizedek and I have some questions.

Question: Page 275, at the great Pyramid, in a special location, there was an opening called the Halls of Amenti, the womb of the earth and a fourth dimensional space. Was this built by the Egyptians and if so for what purpose?

Answer: The Halls of Amenti was a place where knowledge or instruction was given to special people who were able to understand the proper purpose and use of those instructions. There were about twelve priests in all of Egypt, who knew about these secret rites. They were in charge of the esoteric teachings, and the secrets of the evolution of the human race. The thought that it allowed a passage to the fourth dimension is not so. The priests were in the fourth dimension. The realization that life as humans on this planet lasts only a short period of time compelled them to begin teaching concepts that allowed other priests to evolve into the fourth dimension. This allowed for successors. This was built by the Egyptians as a secret place, where they taught secret knowledge and performed their rites.

Question: I have a question about the Sphinx and an underground city under the Giza complex. Is it true that the city is or was, a residence for Ascended Masters?

Answer: During the reign of Amenhotep the III, the construction of the Sphinx took place. That statue was a symbol of the teachings of the Masters of Atlantis to the people of Egypt. During his reign he ordered the construction of a city that would be as a reminder of the cities of Atlantis. There were buildings, which were several stories high, and the roads were straight and parallel to each other. Most of these concepts of construction were completely new to the Egyptian people. The concept of re-planning their cities according to the rays of the sun, and taking into consideration the source of water and provisions for their families was new to the Egyptians.

All of this was a fact and lasted for five hundred years, until it was destroyed by an earthquake. During the cataclysm that destroyed Atlantis a group of survivors remained in the valley near the Nile. They were the ones that instructed and befriended the tribes of people who used to live there.

Question: Why are they now underground?

Answer: They are underground because through the years, new civilizations have rebuilt over the ruins. The land near the river Nile has always been the place more adaptable for housing.

Question: Why does the Sphinx remain?

Answer: During the construction of the temples of Giza the priests in charge, decided that a statue would be erected as a symbol of the souls who designed the city that was under Giza. This happened thousands of years later.

Question: What about the Ascended Masters?

Answer: Gilda, I see now that you have been reading information in a book by Drunvalo Melchizedek. This story is true in part, and the Ascended Masters are now in the fourth dimension. They communicate their wishes and inspire people who are ready to listen, and they have a plan, that will help people of this planet during the transition after the cataclysm. It will help them adjust to the fourth dimension. Yes, the White Brotherhood is the same thing.

Question: Page 303, the ancient Egyptian religion and the Egyptian Sothic calendar were based on the heliacal rising of Sirius. Why was Sirius so important to the Egyptians?

Answer: The civilization of the Egyptian people began during the gathering together of a group of nomadic clans that lived around the Nile. These nomads were part Nubian, and part descendants of Aryan tribes that came down from Persia, during the aftermath of the Cataclysm that devastated the continent of Atlantis. The creation of the Mediterranean Sea and the displacement of thousands of people was the beginning of a new race, and a new purpose in life. It took centuries to adapt to new terrain, to understand the weather patterns, and to get along peacefully. During that time, the development of a conscience or a Divine Power evolved in the creation of God. They were good at growing crops and adapting to changing winds and other atmospheric problems. Thousands of years later, the first Egyptians that declared that the stars were responsible for the changes in atmospheric patterns, brought forth the studies of the Cosmos. Astrology was born and the findings of that knowledge were influential in the building of their temples.

Question: What was the influence of the Atlantean survivors during this period?

Answer: The Atlantean knowledge that survived the cataclysm was passed to their descendants. The lack of material instruments to demonstrate their advanced knowledge was one of many obstacles that prevented them from truly demonstrating and teaching what they knew. Several manuscripts were saved and passed from one generation to another, until confirmation of their advanced knowledge was finally acknowledged. They influenced the Egyptians to create dams that benefited irrigation and the building of special silos to maintain and store food and crops. Their esoteric teachings were influential in the development of the concept of One God, and the idea of one Creator.

Question: Page 418, there are concepts about Lucifer and his influence on the mass of people who lived on this planet and Mars, according to Drunvalo Melchizedek. Were the Martians and Atlanteans and some Grays influenced by the negative aspects of Lucifer?

Answer: I see your problem. Drunvalos approach to the studies of life, are only from the point of view of creative experience and the expression of geometry through the third dimension. These studies are complicated and are needed in order to explain the basic formation of atomic structure.

Answer: The creation of angels is the creation of beings of light, whose only purpose is to help humanity. During the creation of the angels of light, one of these angels called Lucifer was offered the role of guardian of the souls in the lower degrees of evolution. His role was to help them to surpass that stage of being, and advance to a stage of transition, called remorse. The role of Lucifer has been described as the one who has the power to influence the minds and souls of many past and present. The destruction of the people who used to live on Mars is not due to the influence of Lucifer, but to an erosion of the soil and changes in the climate and atmosphere of that planet.

The Grays that are described by Drunvalo as negative entities influenced by Lucifer are souls created as humans, who are in a degree of awareness that allows them to travel to other planets. Their actions are part of the process of physical investigation of people on other planets, to expand their knowledge about DNA, and use this for their own benefit. Atlantis was a society of humans who lived on this planet and they were successful in building a disciplined, prosperous, and industrious society. They accomplished diverse progress in science and technology, which surpassed what is known today on this planet. The cataclysm came and survivors remained in certain areas where they developed new colonies, and passed on some of the knowledge they had achieved.

Question: According to my understanding of the space brothers on other planets, they are not negative and they are of a higher degree of evolution than people of earth. Why does Drunvalo say that these entities are influenced by Lucifer and they are the creators of flying saucers, therefore they are a negative expression?

Answer: Gilda, I am a teacher who has come to you before, I am one of the Koan that is in charge of the process of evolution, In the beginning was God and His Word was manifested as Light. Then His Word was manifested as Sound, which was the universe. The physical manifestations of constellations, solar systems and stars are the Manifestation of Life, Love, and Law. This process of creation is one of constant transformation. The awareness of this process is given to some souls, in order to facilitate their universal progress. I know that you are a disciple of the group Sologa, because of that; your degree of knowledge in the process of universal evolution gives you the certainty of your soul's expression. There are parallel degrees of evolved souls on other planets, and those are the ones that have been instructed, as you are.

They too know that the process of evolution is part of God's assignment to the people of certain generations, who are able to demonstrate qualities of mind and spirit, that will advance that society and demonstrate God's expression, which is compassion, love, sharing, healing. Advanced souls remain as demonstrators of the process of evolution on each planet. Your work is one of confirmation of the process of evolution on this planet. Your work has been supervised and accepted and your writings will be published and successfully received by those who are ready to understand.

I am your teacher Koan, in charge of your assignment.

DISCUSSION OF THE DVD, "THE ULTIMATE LOVE STORY" BY D. MELCHIZEDEK

I have some questions about this DVD.

Answer: Gilda, the recording you watched today about Drunvalo Melchizedek's work was one of the many he has made trying to explain the theory of creation. The responsibility that he feels to share his knowledge is why he has summarized these teachings in an attempt to make them easy to understand. The theme he is explaining was about the influence of the negative and positive forces that is expressed by humans in the third, fourth, and fifth dimensions. During the process of evolution, man has ascribed these influences more vividly to their emotions and minds. The influence of Archangel Michael is one of those. He represents the positive side of humans acting on this planet. Lucifer is the negative aspect of the same actions. As you see, their reality only exists in the mind of the beholder. The majority of people who live on your planet today are under the belief that these are real entities and that they can influence you. Your belief in angels is based on your Catholic upbringing. The supreme beings that exist in other dimensions are in a degree of evolution that realizes why you think this way. During the time of transcending to another dimension, you will be able to regain the knowledge that will clarify your understanding.

HIGHER SELF CONNECTION - D. MELCHIZEDEK

I was listening to the DVD on the higher self and Mr. Drunvalo explains that it is necessary to be connected with your lower self or subconscious mind and become innocent in your beliefs in order to be able to connect with your higher self. Is this lower self-connection and meditation the only way to connect with the higher self?

Answer: The reason Drunvalo said that you need to be aware of your subconscious mind is because of the process of evolution of the soul requires a degree of perfection. This degree of perfection is the individual evolution of love. When a person is evolved to a point of no harm and realizes that every creature, animal or plant, is part of the spirit Divine, only then are they capable of being non-aggressive. This quality of the soul allows the vibrations of their being to move faster, and when this soul is in meditation, the Light will reach their aura and allow answers to their questions.

The higher self is that part of our exalted "I AM" that has already expressed life in other incarnations. This part of us is more knowledgeable and wise due to many incarnations of experience. It is necessary to be aware that only in case of necessity, would this higher self manifest in the mind of individuals who are in need of advice.

Question: Then everybody who has evolved to that degree of perfection can connect with the higher self?

Answer: Not everybody can connect with their higher self, the reason being not all people are evolved to the degree necessary to be allowed to hear from that source. It is not dependent on the many incarnations you have lived, but the positive outcome of your actions in all of them. We move from one dimension to another, and from one set of beliefs to another. The mind is the only media to record, remember, and learn new concepts. The higher self is the recollection of all the positive knowledge accumulated through all your different incarnations. This knowledge is the source of wisdom that can come to help those who want to be of service to humanity.

It is a privilege to be able to communicate with you, because you are always ready to listen and share our wisdom. I am your teacher and I bless you.

DISCUSSION OF "JOURNEY OF SOULS" BY MICHAEL NEWTON, PH.D.

Question: Do souls choose bodies whose intellectual capacities match their own development? Page 248 of the book, Are advanced souls drawn to human brains with big intelligence?

Answer: The soul who is ready to acquire a physical body, evaluates the degree of intelligence they will need to express themselves in that body. The personality is not a factor that should be confused with intelligence. To be able to express yourself as an intelligent person, a soul needs a brain able to provide the necessary cells that will allow soul to express, to store knowledge useful to teach and use as a resource for self expression.

Question: Then not all brains are created equally?

Answer: The formation of the brain is part of the creative process of a fetus. The development of cells requires basic nutrition. The mother will be guided to ingest the required foods and nutrients. The process of incarnation is a developmental process that includes the soul, the parents, and the teachers assigned to the progress of that soul. Each case is different.

DISCUSSION OF "THE BIRTH OF A NEW HUMANITY" BY DRUNVALO MELCHIZEDEK

The lesson for today will be about the impact of the melting of the ice and the consequences of that fact. Yesterday you were watching a program about the upcoming cataclysm. The reason Drunvalo Melchizedek mentions the melting of the ice, is because that phenomena started several years ago. The scientists in charge of that project have known about this impending menace, but are not able to communicate their findings to the media. The ice age that was mentioned in the DVD is not what will in this next millennium.

The reason is the earth is in a cycle of renewing her vibrations and expanding her aura. The climate will change drastically all over the planet, but will only be cold with ice on the surface of the highest mountains, and in part of the new locations of the poles. In general these climate changes will benefit the planet.

The melting waters of the South Pole will inundate the lower part of South America.

This great displacement of waters will increase the surface of the Atlantic Ocean and great masses of water will change the coastal areas.

On the Pacific side there will be an imbalance in the Humbolt current and the effect will be felt as a hurricane and several of the coastal cities and seaports will be destroyed. Nothing can stop these tidewaters until a time when a balance is regained between the earth's solid mass, and the oceans counterparts. This will last for about two weeks and the low weather pressure will be enormous.

DISCUSSION OF THE BOOK "LINEAGE" BY NANCY BEESON

I just finished reading "Lineage," and I want to understand the concept of these balls of light. According to the author the balls of light are the energy that help to form the crop circles in England.

Answer: The book Lineage is the recounting of experiences of a group of people researching the crop circles in England. Their mission was to acknowledge the participation of the extraterrestrials and the message they wanted to convey. The balls of light that they were able to see are energy that has a direct purpose and is programmed to execute a specific design. This is a tool used by the extraterrestrials to send earth people a message that they are coming, and their power is indeed real.

Different designs have different meanings:

The Hand of God – page 78 is a design that describes the position of a planet in their solar system. This specific design shows the other four planets out of the orbit. This planet is in the constellation of Ursa Major. The extraterrestrials who come to design this project are the ones that have been communicating with you from plane Unide.

Question: What are the EC rays of light? Are these from the spaceship or the extraterrestrials?

Answer: The author of that book experienced a personal awakening and these rays of light that she calls EC, are part of the vibration of the dimension she was able to enter. The purpose of the disclosure of these rays to her was because she needed to restore a physical balance in her body.

Question: May I be shown the meaning of three other crop circles? On page 122, there is a Pie crop circle, page 171, The Doorway to Christ Consciousness, and page 172, The Sun and Moon circle.

Answer: The Pie crop circle is one of the examples of precision and of Divine Geometry. The dimension of that circle was impressive. The division of the circle in twelve exact parts is the explanation of the solar system where these extraterrestrials come from. They belong to the constellation of Ursa Major and they will be here after the cataclysm. The Doorway to Christ Consciousness was a design to explain the different degrees of consciousness in different parts of the universe. This visual representation was executed by the same extraterrestrials from Ursa Major. The Sun and Moon circle shows a square in a circle and is the representation of a geographical location on the planet Unide. The diverse division of the square and the center square signifies that they belong to the Intergalactic Federation. Their visual means of communication through these emblems is what you people of earth will be able to learn and understand in the future. The Doorway circle is two circles next to each other plus a cross. Inside the larger circle is a pentagon, page 176, July 25, 2007 at West Kennett Long Barrow. This circle is the representation of a solar system that belongs to the Pleiades. This group has also been appointed to come to the aid of planet earth, they are acknowledging the Christ Consciousness with the cross.

We are Orlin from the Peiades and Osimo.

"LISTENING TO EXTRATERRESTRIALS" BY LISETTE LARKINS

Question: I just read the book "listening to Extraterrestrials" and I wonder why I don't hear the extraterrestrials talking to me?

Answer- Lisette Larkins mission in this life is to spread the word that extraterrestrials exist. Her experience is one that happens to many people, but they are afraid to research and try to make sense of what has happened to them. She was appointed to write, and teach in simple language, what she experienced and what she did about it.

The telepathic abilities that she possesses are equal to yours. The reason you have had no opportunity to meet extraterrestrials during this life, is because you assignment was different and it was not necessary. Your belief is proof enough that you are sure of their existence, plus you have received communications from several extraterrestrials that are preparing the rescue operation to help after the cataclysm. You need to continue with your writings about the different planets and their civilizations.

I am your teacher Tumargeo, who blesses you

DISCUSSION OF A BOOK BY STAN ROMANEK

Stan Romanek was abducted by ET's who came to study the basic reactions of humans on this planet to the presence of ETs. He went through some physical examinations and scrutiny by mental telepathy. The reason for these abductions was to let people know that the presence of aliens is a reality, and to try to convey the idea that they are coming in the near future. The book he wrote was the culmination of a difficult emotional and mental process. He was not persecuted by the ETs; he was selected because he offered his life on this planet for that purpose.

Question- There are drawings and equations in the book, can you explain their meaning?

Answer - Those are mathematical equations of planetary orbits, and the method of finding distances between two points in the cosmos. There is a symbol that is a visual description of vortex of light, that speeds like a tornado in your atmosphere, but this happens in space, between the space occupied by suns, planets or stars. ETs are aware of their existence and they use them as passages between two different parts of the universe. These "tunnels" are of immense proportions and spin in a way like a funnel. Their advanced knowledge of centrifugal force, allows them to maintain a course and arrive to their desired destination.

DISCUSSION OF "PLANET X AND THE KOLBRIN BIBLE CONNECTION BY GREG JENNER

Question: May I know the truth about the planet X and the Kolbrin Bible?

The Kolbrin Bible was written by monks, who collected several episodes of the life of Jesus. They were nomads who lived at that time near Jerusalem. They were aware of the tyranny imposed by the Romans and by the Jewish laws that maintained a firm hand of their adepts. When Jesus was crucified, the voice of the masses reached far away places. The nomads brought these tales to the monks who lived near the mountains. They were the ones who put in writing many episodes that sometimes are not mentioned in the new versions of the Bible. The planet X is the description of a planet that will invade this solar system; the real truth is that in the next millennium, a new planet will be visible in your solar system due to the expansion of the galaxies. The position of planet earth will change in relation to the configurations of stars visible from your planet, and when this happens, Planet X will be seen by the survivors. I am Tumargeo and I bless you

DISCUSSION OF "BEYOND THE HEAVENS" A STORY OF CONTACT BY MAURIZIO CAVALLO JHLOS

In this book that I'm reading the author says that, Clarion belongs to a binary system, and is one of the planets where an evolved civilization is not only aware of our planet but they have a group of their people living in big caves under the Brazilian Amazon. Is this the truth and why are they contacting certain people like the author of this book?

Answer: The book you are reading is one of many explanations of the extraterrestrial abductions that take place on this planet. During the past twenty years the Clarion people have researched human DNA. They know everything about your physical being, mental and emotional bodies. They need to understand why you have evolved in a different way, and are able to be more appreciative and understanding of the multiple relationships you encounter during your lives. They are mentally and physically more advanced than people of earth, but their relationships are void of the empathy and love that you have developed. They want to create hybrids that are capable of manifesting emotions and introduce this into their civilization.

Question: Where is this planet located?

Answer: This planet belongs to a solar system in the constellation of Riga. Their planet is similar to this planet only in size and temperature. Their civilization was based on the development of the mammals, you call squirrels. The transformation over many millions of years, and the purification of their animal instincts, has allowed them to express in humanoid form. They are seven feet tall and they don't have hair over their bodies. Their heads are proportional to their bodies, and they are athletic and hefty specimens. Yes, they have retained a nice face, big eyes, and they are capable of hearing and making sounds, they also have vocal chords. They used to have language to communicate with each other, but today they only communicate through telepathy.

Their mouth is small and they only eat fruits and vegetables.

Question: Why did they choose Brazil?

Answer: They chose to live in the Mato Grosso; because that is the place they found food and climate adequate for their bodies.

Question: Do they know of the impending cataclysm?

Answer: Yes, they know that the time is near and they are preparing for that time. They belong to the Intergalactic Brotherhood and they will help in the reconstruction of society.

In the book on page forty the author says he knew the Lord of Nahaeb, or recognized him, because Anthares, (the one who is born before the time), the watcher of Akahsca was the venerable white dressed figure lost in the gardens of my childhood.

Answer: This paragraph is the memory of the author and one of his astral flights. In that vision he understood the figure he saw, was a Lord he recognized as Nahaeb. Then he explains that this was Anthares the keeper of the Akaska or Akashic records, something he knew since he was young, several incarnations past.

Question: He says that Lucifer was the ancestral symbol of human intelligence, which penetrating matter and becoming conscious was possessed and enslaved by matter itself.

Answer: The author is trying to describe his idea of what the ancient idea of Lucifer was. In reality the figure or personification of Lucifer is not a reality. The vision of possessing people and the description of the negative souls, who possess them, date from ancient times. They are part of their conscience, during the time they are alive on this planet, and then become memories in their subconscious minds.

Question: On page fifty, it says the main cause of the dinosaurs extinction was, they had survived the apocalypse of an impact by Venus but were destroyed when the pole shift occurred and left our planet with no magnetosphere to shield them against the cosmic rays.

Answer: The extinction of the dinosaurs happened because at that time an impact of a major portion of a meteorite hit this planet, producing a change in the climate for several days and nights. Due to the days of darkness, the photosynthesis of plant life was affected causing decomposition of plants and the basic nutrients the dinosaurs needed, this was the cause of their demise.

Question: Did this happen on part of the planet?

Answer: Yes, This happened in that part of your planet called the Yucatan peninsula. The reason why bones of dinosaurs are found in other regions of your planet is because most of the sites where they lived were shifted during a great cataclysm, which changed the position of the continents and caused a drastic sudden change in temperature. The dinosaurs could not survive the colder temperatures without the vegetation and of course the vegetation was dead because of the frigid temperature.

Question: In the book, page seventy two, third paragraph, the author speaks of an impression of seven gigantic figures sitting on the thrones.

Answer: In this vision the author saw a representation of his own idea of what the creative process was. In reality his imagination created this place and his fears made them appear so big and powerful. Anthares is his spiritual teacher, who came to him like an enormous figure and explained to him the concepts of God, that are expressed by the most evolved beings in the universe. Gilda, this part of the book resonates with your knowledge and past experiences. You know what advanced societies of other planets know and accept as God. This is part of the process that reaffirms you soul's purpose.

DISCUSSION OF "THE KEY" A TRUE ENCOUNTER BY WHITLEY STRIEBER

Question: Why can I hear beings in other dimensions, but I am not able to see them?

Answer: During your mediation you say "I am in oneness with all Creation." This concept is one that allows you to hear your brothers and sisters in other dimensions. Not all the people on this planet are aware of that. During your progress in the realms of God, you were guided to learn a specific gift. That gift is telepathy, and you were accepted in a group of chelas or pupils, in the School of Divinity, where you learned how to hear. This happened during one of your incarnations in Egypt. The reason why you cannot see the souls of the departed beings is because you have not been trained to do so. Your faith allows you to know that they exist, and they are there, but it is not what you are supposed to be doing.

Question: Am I under mind control?

Answer: Greetings, I am Saint Augustine. I came to explain the meaning of mind control. When you are doing something, you have a choice; continue on or you say to yourself; I will do this later because ...! There is a divine voice in your mind that tells you; this is important and you should do it now! That is the Divine Mind that guides you. The way you should choose your path is the way the spirit within you increases in knowledge and your aura spreads in luminosity. The small voice within is the guidance necessary to help humans during their journey on this planet. When you go to the other side of the veil, then the clarity of this voice is real, and you will be amazed at the easy and splendorous way of being. I am your teacher Saint Augustine and I bless you

Question: What is conscious energy? On page forty six, the Master talks of conscious energy being part of the electromagnetic spectrum and detectable by machines that can record signals. On page 54, Mr. Strieber asks the Master what psychics are and he answers, speaking of the existence of an energetic organ in the body, which is generated by the nervous system, and extends above the surface of the skin. It is effectively everywhere in the universe and nowhere specific. He says this field is an organ just like the heart or the brain, and with it you could see into other worlds, and see the past or future. Is this true?

Answer: The power of God is expressed in us as energy. This energy is produced by the vibration of our souls. Each individual who is born into this planet brings with him the total balance of his past energy or degree of evolution. This expression of the soul increases during their life, according to their good deeds and actions. The word conscious means that these actions are conscious acts of kindness. During the thousands of lives of each individual the accumulation of these acts give us a concentration of power, and grant this person the blessing of protection. Conscious energy is the result of progressive positive choices accumulated during all the lifetimes spent in a physical body.

The lessons come to the pupil or chela when they are ready to understand and accept the teachings. In your case, you were aware that this inner force was hidden in your soul. You woke up to this concept when you were a child. Evolution is the degree of knowledge of the soul.

Question: Are you aware of the process of imprinting?

Answer: This is a conscious desire to chose a positive action. When a person decides to act, think, or do a positive thing then an imprinting of this action takes place in their etheric body. Your etheric body is the result of the imprint of your positive actions during this last incarnation. Yes, we take the etheric body with us to the next sphere. This body has a vibratory rate that is key to finding our new place in the afterlife.

Question: Are there imprints of diseases in the etheric body that manifest in the physical body?

Answer: Yes, there are. During the formation of the body, before the fetus begins to expand, the organs of the body that will be affected by hereditary diseases are marked in place. The DNA that forms the basic data for the future of a physical body, is imprinted with the different positive and negative attributes.

Question: Can we overcome or change any of these negative imprints?

Answer: Yes, Many humans change their negative habits to restore balance, poise and light to their auras. To change imprints of hereditary diseases, it is necessary to consult a special doctor in DNA manipulation. This is a new field of knowledge on your planet, but with time it will be developed to eradicate several of the most difficult hereditary diseases.

Question: I understand the etheric body is only the vibratory energy around the physical body that accumulates from the many positive experiences of the last incarnation. What happens to this body when we go to the other side of the veil?

Answer: During the time of "Remembrance" this etheric body provides the majority of information. Yes, it is sort of like a movie. Then, when the soul is able to see itself in the good and bad deeds of that last incarnation the etheric body disappears. The soul regains the power again, to record and learn a new way of life, according to the place where it is attracted. At the time, the soul recovers their past memories, the perception of the soul changes. For those that did a majority of positive deeds, it is like a veil taken off their eyes and they find themselves experiencing a life that is like a dream come true. For the ones that had more negative deeds, their new experience is to see themselves surrounded by souls that are similar to them and enduring fear, darkness, and the influence of lower instincts.

The book "The key" is one of the best teachings tools recorded! The master who came to instruct Mr. W. Strieber was trying to clarify in his mind, several concepts that will be a part of the New Age. The human aura is a body of light easily detectable by electromagnetic gadgets, you remember when you had your aura picture taken. The aura is the expression of the soul at any given moment. It becomes more luminous, during prayers, healings, or during emotional times like when two souls of similar vibrations meet or when a person is overcome with joy or sorrow. The etheric body is not the aura.

Question: Who is the Master speaking to Mr. Strieber in the book, "The Key"?

Answer: The Master that talks to Mr. Strieber is Kutumi. He is a Master of the constellation of Riga. He came to talk to Mr. Strieber about several points of evolution, with the intention of clarifying old concepts and teaching new ones.

DISCUSSION OF "DESTINY OF SOULS" BY MICHAEL NEWTON, PH.D.

Questions: How much energy reserve did I leave behind when I came to live on this planet?

How much reserve energy will I recuperate when I reach the other side?

Is this Divine energy that enables us to have a better mind, body and understanding of our progression through incarnations?

Answer: The book you are reading is a book that will prepare you to analyze the process of soul progress through the Cosmos. You were aware of this process before your present incarnation. There are no coincidences. You needed to read this book in order to remember and connect this knowledge, with the expressions of souls you were able to contact.

The process of reincarnation allows the soul to experience part of the karma, which needs to be paid. According to your acts here on earth, you will be judged. Each incarnation allows us to be more aware of the process of perfection, which our souls need to advance to better lives, and a glorious understanding of our relationship with God. As a consequence of this new acquired understanding, we are allowed to restore energy that will become knowledge of the soul. We are then ready for new experiences in the next incarnation.

Question: How is this related to the new assignment that your soul should commit to in the future incarnation?

Are we able to select our new assignment or is it given to us, according to which sphere of understanding we are on.

Answer: The quantity of energy acquired during the process of incarnation is not a factor in the appointment to a new life on a planet. There are different factors that a soul knows and can offer to the people who live on that planet, which would be cause for a soul to be sent to that particular incarnation. The lords of karma can see these energies, and provide the soul with a task to learn and express their qualities. Nobody orders a soul to a specific assignment before they incarnate. The selection of a place is a result of a personal study of your best knowledge and where that knowledge will be most useful.

Question: Why are souls who are more advanced with good karma and knowledge of the soul assigned to planets of less evolution?

Answer: Teachers are souls who want to pass along the knowledge they have acquired. Not all knowledge will be granted, only that which is needed at that time in the development of the soul who needs to learn. For example, a teacher of kindergarten doesn't teach all that she knows; she will only teach what the pupil needs in order to be prepared to assimilate new understanding.

Question: The author mentions several levels of soul evolution, as 1, 2, 3, etc. Is this related to the vibration that allows a soul to be in a different sphere?

Answer: According to the author's understanding, this process of awareness of the soul is characterized by numbered levels. This is not the same as being able to live in different or higher spheres. What allows the soul to progress through the Cosmos?

the knowledge that is acquired through trying to overcome problems they encountered during the last incarnation. The determination to do most of the assignment you commit yourself to, before you were born, is the answer to the progress of the soul through different spheres.

Question: In the book they say there are animal caretakers called trakers, is this so, and do animals have souls.

Answer: Do animals have souls is the question asked by millions of souls on your planet. God's creative powers are energy and this energy evolves in patterns that are related to each planet and its environment. According to the degree of evolution of each planet, the creation of animals, fishes or plants, have different form and purpose.

During the formation of your planet there was a protozoa, basically one of the most primitive expressions of life; with time and the evolution of weather patterns and new opportunities to grow in different environments on earth, this protozoa began to evolve. Under different climatic changes the multiplication of these protozoa took a new adaptation into more complicated forms. The evolution of each planet is different, as are the creative powers of God's expression.

There is a co-ordination of expression between the presence of animals and the environment. Each animal needs a special food, climate and purpose of existence.

Some animals that are called pets have learned how to please their owners in exchange for food and care. Their intelligent energy is part of the process of adaptation and instinct of survival. The soul is considered that part of a physical body, which is capable of expressing different emotions as love, hate, and empathy. When a pet reaches the vibration to feel these emotions, they become a soul. Yes, the most intelligent animals on your planet are the chimpanzee, and the dolphins (even in the wild). The degree of expression of the gift of positive deeds by a soul is what people feel as love. As you see, not all the animals, birds, and fishes have a soul. The process of perfecting several skills of the soul is necessary to express their intelligent energy.

Question: Why are animal caretakers call Trakers?

Answer: The caretakers are the souls of specialized persons, who work in between lives on a planet, and specialize in knowing the animal energy and form of the animal bird or fish that represent the fauna of the planet. Their purpose is to track the energy of a specific animal that was part of the life of a soul, who ask about their pet or pets during his last incarnation. This relationship between humans and animals called pets is a mutual healing and expression of empathy by the soul of each party.

Question: Are there caretakers who work for different planets, according to their special fauna and flora.

Answer: Yes, as you know, the evolutions of planets are different in each solar system.

Creation

JESUS AND BUDDHA BY MARCUS J. BORG

Gilda, the book you are reading is based on the premise that Jesus and Buddha are two prophets, who came to this planet to enlighten the minds and souls of the people. The writer explains the similarities and different points of view from their own experience and understanding. The message that Buddha gave to his people was, they will find God through meditation and discipline. The message that Jesus left to his followers is that according to their actions, they will be saved. The way to God is not through believing in Jesus or his accomplishments. The demonstrations and teachings of Jesus were necessary to change a society that was decadent and trying to justify their actions through offerings to pagan gods and goddesses. Jesus never assumed that He was God. He said: I and my Father are one. In that statement, He let us know that we are part of the essence of God's creation. To find God through Christian teachings, a soul will want to reach that innermost part of his soul, and acknowledge that Jesus is the way-shower or teacher, who will help him to find that place. The idea that these two different, and at the same time, similar teachings of Christianity and Buddhism, are the only way to live life, is an incomplete statement. The great social and economic impacts, which these two teachings brought to this planet, are the real substance. Each teaching is different according to the people, the time frame, and the necessity to convey these new ideas. Jesus and Buddha are representatives of a historic revolution in the minds and souls of their followers.

THE MESSAGE OF JESUS

The recognition that God is Love, Light, Life and Law, is the knowledge that Jesus the Christ was teaching and demonstrating more than 2000 years ago. His words were very simple, so the people would understand them at that time. The meanings of the parables are still being interpreted, according to the state of evolution of people today. Like Jesus, many other spiritual Masters have come at different times, to teach about God and His creative powers.

This is not the first time that a cataclysm has happened on Earth. Following the cataclysm, the reshaping of the continents, seas, and the weather patterns, will offer a new beginning to the survivors. We are ready to experience a new millennium. This planet will be allowed to enter into a more evolved sphere of vibration and understanding, as the position of our planet in relation to our solar system and the cosmos expands.

The reading of the Bible is a source of confusion and debate today because of all the different interpretations available. The source of truth is the voice of God through the Masters, and the guidance that they have provided to this planet since Jesus left this earth. The differences in the messages are not to be interpreted, as a rule, but as human error. Many of the writings of these verses in the Bible were written by monks or dedicated souls, who did their best with the material that they were provided.

The different journeys of the Apostles to different parts of the world, was a plan to distribute this knowledge to the different people and races. Yes, they were guided. The beginning of the concept of Christianity is a message of love, and explanations of the life of Jesus, and his crucifixion. The resurrection and ascension is an interpretation of visions and real witnesses of that moment, in the history of mankind.

Jesus is a Master and a Son of God. He offered his life and his service, as a demonstration that we are spiritual beings, and we are one with God. The ascension of Jesus was a demonstration; that the soul is that part of each individual that will return to the plane of light where it gravitates, at the time of death. When Jesus appeared to some of his disciples, he was in his ethereal body. He was able to assemble the molecules that were his former human self, and to provide an image for them. His demonstration symbolized the process of reincarnation. The concept of reincarnation was not a new concept in ancient times. Several other religious Masters had taught this concept in India, Tibet, and Egypt.

Jesus was born in Judea, and under Jewish law he was forbidden to teach reincarnation. Jesus wanted to demonstrate this concept, and because of that He ascended and returned in his ethereal body. To this day, the churches are reluctant to accept the concept of reincarnation. The reason is that they cannot explain the process of the afterlife. The idea of returning and being in another body is inconceivable to millions of Christians. The time has come to understand this concept, and be able to explain that life's acts and deeds have consequences, that have to be resolved, if not in the present life, in the next life. Life is eternal, which means, we are not limited by the concept of twenty-four hours, or months or years. The life of the soul or spirit lives in human form as an ethereal form.

The period of life on this planet is a demonstration of evolution that provides the soul with a plan to accomplish the several tasks necessary to repay karma, and to demonstrate free will, or choice of acts that will allow that soul to progress through the planes of consciousness in the Cosmos.

The period of life in the afterlife is a recollection of all the actions, both positive and negative of a person, to come to the understanding of why; he or she acted that way. Different souls will have different experiences, according to their religious belief. The etheric body, mind and the use of the emotional body, provides the soul with a vision of the place where he or she arrives, which is a reflection of beliefs in their mind. This mirage changes according to the questions the soul has about their surroundings, or about why they are there. These periods of recollections are long or short according to the desire to learn about how to lead a more positive and enlightened life. Some of these souls are approached by relatives or other souls, who have been in that dimension for a long period, and because of that, can serve as guides. After the process of recollection, the soul is able to realize that it is capable of continuing the process of learning. Then the soul can decide, to return to this planet or in the case of more advanced souls, be sent to other planets where there are beings in more advanced civilizations.

These explanations are not provided by the major religions of your planet, and the explanations that are in the "sacred" books, are mostly distorted interpretations by different representatives of those religions. The different planes of ascension that are mentioned in different religious books are based on the truth. These are vibrational places, and they are like magnets that attract different souls according to their vibrations. The vibration of a soul results from the evolution of that soul, and is not formed according to religion, race, education, or age. Each soul vibrates at a different rate, according to the understanding of the concept of God, their relationship with the creator, and the positive deeds that the soul has accomplished during their many lives.

BIBLIOGRAPHY

Beeson, Nancy. *Lineage.*

Brown, Dan. *The Da Vinci Code.* New York, NY: Doubleday, 2003

Carrol, Lee. *The twelve Layers of DNA Kryon Book 12* Sedona, Arizona: Platinum Publishing House, 2010.

Cavallo, Mauricio. *Beyond the Heavens*

Dowling, Levi. *Aquarian Gospel of Jesus the Christ.* Los Angeles, CA: Published by ES Dowling, 1919.

Dyal, Paul. *Marcus.*

Fillmore, Charles. *The Atom Smashing Power of the Mind*

Gobbi, Stefano. *Messages from the Virgin Mary*

Hay, Louise. *You Can Heal Your Life.* Random House, 2003

Jenner, Greg. *Planet X and the Kolbrin Bible.* Silver Springs, Nevada: Your Own World Books Inc., 2008

Larkins, Lisette. *Listening to Extraterrestrials: Telepathic Coaching by Enlightened Beings*

Mailer, Norman. The Gospel According to the Son

Masaru, Emoto. The *Hidden Messages in Water*

Melchizedek, Drunvalo. *The Ancient Secret of the Flower of Life, Volumes I and 2.*

Flagstaff, AZ: Light Technology Publishing, 1990

DVD, Higher *Self Connection with Drunvalo Melchizedek* Sedona, Arizona: One Lotus LLC, 1992

Melchizedek, Drunvalo. DVD, *Ultimate Love Story*. Sedona, Arizona: One Lotus LLC, 1992.

DVD, The *Birth of a NEW HUMANITY*. Sedona, Arizona: One Lotus LLC, 2010.

Myss, Caroline, PhD. *Anatomy of the Spirit: The Seven Stages of Power and Healing*

Newton, Michael, PhD. *Journey of Souls Case Studies of Life Between Lives* Woodbury, Minnesota: Llewellyn Publications, 1994.

Destiny of Souls, New case studies of Life between Lives. By Michael Newton Ph D. Woodbury, Minnesota: Llewellyn Publications, 2000.

Pagels, Elaine. *Beyond Belief: The Secret Gospel of Thomas.* New York: Random House, 2003.

Romanek, Stan. *Scrutiny* Sellier, Charles. *Miracles and Other Wonders*

TRUE DIRECTIONS

An affiliate of Tarcher Perigee

OUR MISSION

Tarcher Perigee's mission has always been to publish
books that contain great ideas. Why? Because:

GREAT LIVES BEGIN WITH GREAT IDEAS

At Tarcher Perigee, we recognize that many talented authors, speakers,
educators, and thought-leaders share this mission and deserve to be published –
many more than Tarcher Perigee can reasonably publish ourselves. True
Directions is ideal for authors and books that increase awareness, raise
consciousness, and inspire others to live their ideals and passions.

Like Tarcher Perigee, True Directions books are designed to do three things:
inspire, inform, and motivate.

Thus, True Directions is an ideal way for these important voices to
bring their messages of hope, healing, and help to the world.

Every book published by True Directions– whether it is non-fiction, memoir,
novel, poetry or children's book – continues Tarcher Perigee's mission to publish
works that bring positive change in the world. We invite you to join our mission.

For more information, see the True Directions website:

www.iUniverse.com/TrueDirections/SignUp

Be a part of Tarcher Perigee's community to bring positive change in this
world! See exclusive author videos, discover new and exciting books, learn
about upcoming events, connect with author blogs and websites, and more!
www.tarcherbooks.com

TRUE DIRECTIONS

AN AFFILIATE OF TARCHER PERIGEE

Printed in the United States
By Bookmasters